ICSELL

International Cooper Series in English Language and Literature
Volume 10

Series Editors

D. J. Allerton
Willy Elmer
Balz Engler
Hartwig Isernhagen

Schwabe Verlag Basel

Linguistics, Language Learning and Language Teaching

Edited by

D. J. Allerton, Cornelia Tschichold
and Judith Wieser

Schwabe Verlag Basel

Typeset by Karin Stettler assisted by Sixta Quaßdorf, Basel

© 2005 by Schwabe AG, Verlag, Basel
Printed in Switzerland by Schwabe AG, Druckerei, Muttenz/Basel
ISBN-13: 978-3-7965-2065-5
ISBN-10: 3-7965-2065-0

www.schwabe.ch

Table of contents

Abbreviations	vii
List of figures and tables	viii
Introduction	xi
Contrastive Analysis and the language learner: a new lease of life? *Carl James*	1
Recent advances in contrastive linguistics and language typology: the spin-off for language teachers *Christian Mair*	21
Teaching contrastive rhetoric(s): bridging the gap between English language competence and academic success in English for the non-native speaker *Tamsin Sanderson*	41
Cross-language homonymy and polysemy: a semantic view of "false friends" *D. J. Allerton and Judith Wieser*	57
Problems of adverbial placement in Learner English and the British National Corpus *Chris Gledhill*	85
Corpora and language teaching: what learner corpora have to offer *Nadja Nesselhauf*	105
Error Analysis with computer learner corpora: a corpus-based study of errors in the written German of British university students *Ursula Weinberger*	119
The comprehension and acquisition of metaphorical and idiomatic phrases in L2 English *Judith Wieser*	131
CALL and linguistics *Cornelia Tschichold*	147
Swiss English or simply non-native English? A discussion of two possible features *Yvonne Dröschel, Mercedes Durham and Lukas Rosenberger*	161

English teaching and learning in Hong Kong *R. Shui-Ching Ho*	177
Universal Grammar and Second Language Acquisition *Pius ten Hacken*	191

Index	205

Abbreviations

CA	Contrastive Analysis
CALL	Computer-assisted language learning
CEA	Computer-aided Error Analysis
CLI	Contrastive Linguistic Input
C-Rh	Contrastive Rhetoric
DaF	Deutsch als Fremdsprache
DLD	Dual-Lingual Discourse
EA	Error Analysis
ESP	English for special purposes
FL	Foreign Language
ICT	Information and Communications Technology
IL	Interlanguage
L1	first language, i.e. language learnt first and/or the predominant language for an individual speaker
L2	second language, i.e. language learnt after the first language and/or as a first foreign language
L3	third language, i.e. language learnt as a second (or further) foreign language
MLD	monolingual discourse
MT	Mother Tongue
NSE	Native Speaker of English
NSJ	Native Speaker of Japanese
POS	part(s) of speech
SLA	Second Language Acquisition
TELL	technology-enhanced language learning
TL	Target Language

List of figures and tables

Table 1.1	Contrasts between Hebrew and English	14
Table 2.1	English as a loose-fit language / German as a tight-fit language	23
Table 2.2	Dimensions of cross-cultural difference (German – English)	32
Table 3.1	Language of natural science publications as a percentage of total publications 1980–1996	44
Table 3.2	Language of social science and humanities publications as a percentage of total publications 1974–1995	44
Table 4.1	False friends amongst adjectives and adverbials indicating shortness of time and size	67
Figure 4.1	Overview of German-English false friends, categorized according to semantic relation and formal resemblance	68
Table 4.2	Example of the two false friend categories (T, P)	70
Table 4.3	False friend pairs involving cross-linguistic homonymy	72
Table 4.4	False friend pairs involving cross-linguistic polysemy	74
Table 4.5	The actions of temporarily giving and receiving something, as expressed in English, German and Swiss German	76
Table 5.1	The ten most frequent adverbs in Verb + Adjunct + Object position	89
Figure 6.1	*Economical* in the French subcorpus of ICLE	115
Figure 6.2	*Reason for/of* in the Spanish subcorpus of ICLE	116
Table 7.1	Details of the Pilot Corpus	124
Figure 7.1	Distribution of errors in the main categories across the four subcorpora	126
Figure 7.2	Decrease Rates in error frequencies in main categories from Aex to Bex and Aun to Bun	127
Table 7.2	Category "Lexical Errors" with subcategories	127
Figure 7.3	Subcategories of lexical error: Choice vs. Non-existent	128

Figure 7.4	Breakdown of lexical errors of Choice into parts of speech	128
Table 7.3	Percentage of wrong prefixes on verbs in relation to lexical errors on verbs and lexical errors in total	129
Figure 8.1	Metaphor as cognitive mapping process	133
Figure 8.2	Continuum of metaphoricity	134
Table 8.1	Metaphors denoting anger	144
Table 10.1	Distribution of standard and pluralized forms of *information* across native languages	167
Table 10.2	Distribution of standard and pluralized forms of *information* depending on the determiner	167
Table 10.3	Distribution of *since* and *for* across native languages	169
Table 10.4	A typological approach to the morphosyntactic structures of *information*	170
Table 10.5	Equivalents of *since* in German, French and Italian	172
Table 10.6	Equivalents of *for* in German, French and Italian	173

Introduction

The editors

Linguistics aims to be the scientific study of language and languages. A potential application of the discipline must be the way languages are learnt, and indeed in its early use the term "applied linguistics" referred almost exclusively to the application of linguistics to problems of language learning, particularly to the learning of a non-native language. Nowadays applied linguistics is understood as a multi-discliplinary field covering many areas including first language acquisition, discourse analysis and language planning. But the learning of languages other than the mother tongue remains a central aspect.

We are all familiar with the phenomenon of someone "speaking with an accent", for instance when a speaker has an unusual kind of *r*-sound or pronounces *thank* so as to be identical to *tank* or *sank*; regardless of whether they are native speakers, their pronunciation deviates from some sort of standard form of the language. In addition to unusual sounds, speakers can also produce unusual uses of words, as regards their meaning (e.g. *concept* with the meaning 'plan'), or their grammatical use (e.g. *informations* used as a plural noun), or their fixed expressions like idioms and collocations (e.g. *take (up) contact* instead of *make contact*). This can give speakers a lexico-semantic, grammatical or phraseological accent, so to speak. It even happens that outsiders depart from native speaker norms at the level of texts, as when they send in a job application or write a scholarly article that would be more appropriate to the linguistic community they were born in rather than the one they now aspire to. Whether or how such phenomena arise depends crucially, of course, on how non-native languages are learnt and taught.

It was such issues that the organizers of the 2003 meeting of the Joint Advanced Studies Group in Linguistics (JASGIL) had in mind when they entitled their colloquium "Linguistics, Language Learning and Language Teaching". On this occasion the English Department of the University of Basle (Englisches Seminar, Universität Basel) entertained the English Departments of the University of Strasbourg (Département d'études anglo-américaines, Université Marc Bloch, Strasbourg II) and the University of Freiburg (Englisches Seminar, Albert-Ludwigs-Universität, Freiburg) on 9th and 10th May. The teaching staff and students at this Helveto-Franco-German event were delighted to have Carl James, emeritus professor at the University of Wales Bangor to give the opening lecture. Most of the papers from that conference are published here, along with further invited contributions.

The first paper in the volume is devoted to Contrastive Analysis and its role in language learning and teaching. Carl James provides a critical overview of Contrastive Analysis and shows how has been enriched by new approaches. He also counters the criticism that Contrastive Analysis supports the monolingual bias in foreign language teaching, and demonstrates how learners can benefit from their L1 resources in noticing differences between their L1 and L2.

The next two papers are devoted to current research in contrastive linguistics and its usefulness for language teaching. Christian Mair shows how recent theoretical research in typological differences between languages can be helpful to both teachers and learners of English. He considers the contrastive grammar of English and German, discussing Hawkins's distinction between "loose-fit" (English) and "tight-fit" (German) languages. Mair then indicates in what ways communication between English and German speakers can be problematic, and how contrastive linguistics can alert learners and teachers to the different organization of text-types like CVs in the second language.

Tamsin Sanderson continues with the theme of contrastive rhetoric by examining intercultural and interlingual differences in the textual organization of academic discourse. She illustrates the importance of conforming to textual norms of academic publication, especially for non-native speaker researchers publishing in English, and the misunderstandings that may otherwise result. She suggests how contrastive research into academic discourse could be improved with respect to the features to be studied, selection of texts, corpus size and methodology.

In a joint paper, David Allerton and Judith Wieser take a semantic view of false friends presenting a classification into the two broad categories of cross-language homonymy and polysemy. Possible subtypes are illustrated with examples of German-English false friends, revealing the complexity involved in the lexico-semantic relations between many interlingual word pairs. Results from a pilot study by Wieser with German-speaking learners of English are then presented and discussed in this light.

The next three papers make use of learner corpora to examine problems experienced by learners of a second language. Chris Gledhill discusses the difficulties of adverbial placement for French learners of English, challenging the generative assumption that adjuncts are mere modifiers that cannot enter into lexical or phraseological patterns. He shows that adjuncts can occur in post-verbal position depending on semantic scope or thematic structure, but also depending on the relationship between the verb and its complements and on collocational restrictions. On that basis, he then explains why some adjunct uses by Francophone learners of English sound awkward.

Nadja Nesselhauf explores how learner corpora consisting of language produced by second language learners can be fruitfully used in language teaching. She provides an overview of other types of corpora that may have an impact on language teaching and examines the potential and limitations of learner corpora. She then illustrates how the findings gained from learner corpus analyses can be incorporated into ELT teaching materials, and how learner corpora can be used in the classroom for data-driven learning.

The strand of contributions focussing on learner language continues with a paper by Ursula Weinberger, who presents interesting findings from a study of German learner language, confirming and elaborating on earlier results from studies of English learner language that the vocabulary is the most persistent area of difficulty.

In a further paper, Wieser looks at the difficulty of understanding metaphorical expressions and the role lexicalization plays in this process for L1 and L2 speakers. The comprehension and especially the production of lexicalized phraseologisms seem to be a major obstacle for learners in their progress towards native-like fluency. The author argues in favour of making learners aware of multi-word units and their metaphorical origin where this helps acquisition.

In a paper on computer-assisted language learning, Cornelia Tschichold examines the contributions of linguistics in general, and computational and applied linguistics in particular, towards the development of this field. The author argues that, given the history of the field, only better collaboration will lead to significant improvements of such programs.

The last group of papers are descriptive rather than applied. The contribution by Yvonne Dröschel, Mercedes Durham and Lukas Rosenberger investigates two features typical of the English spoken in Switzerland in order to shed light on the question whether Swiss English is an emerging (endonormative) national variety of English or simply a conglomerate of non-native varieties. In this study, the authors look at instances of the word *information(s)* and at the temporal prepositions *since* and *for*.

In the next paper, we learn about another geographically limited variety of English. R. Shui-Ching Ho describes English in Hong Kong in its historical, social and linguistic dimensions, focussing on the school system and on the phonological characteristics of Hong Kong English as spoken by school leavers.

Finally, in the last paper of the volume, Pius ten Hacken takes a look at the relation between Chomskyan Universal Grammar and Second Language Acquisition. He explores the various hypotheses within Universal Grammar that have been proposed to explain the theoretical questions in first and second language acquisition and the possible links between these two processes.

These varied papers in the field of language learning and teaching give an impression of the range of multi-faceted linguistic issues involved. While the essays remain individual contributions, the natural links between them should be evident enough, and the editors believe they have managed to shape them into a coherent volume. In this task they have greatly benefited from the able assistance of their subeditor, Karin Stettler. The editors would finally like to express their gratitude for the financial support for this volume received from the European Confederation of Upper Rhine Universities (EUCOR) (with special thanks to Dr. Beat Münch) and from the James-Fenimore-Cooper-Fonds.

Contrastive Analysis and the language learner: a new lease of life?

Carl James

1. Current vitality of Contrastive Analysis

Contrastive analysis (CA for short) is understood as a procedure and the associated analytic theory for predicting those difficulties a learner of an L2 will encounter that emanate from the differences ("contrasts") that exist between forms and structures of that L2 and those of the learner's L1. Where L1 and L2 forms and structures are similar, CA predicts that the learning of the latter will be relatively unproblematic, and occasionally even facilitated. In the first paper I ever published on contrastive analysis (James 1971) I claimed that CA was "in the doldrums" and proceeded to answer much of the then current and misplaced criticism of CA, which I shall not repeat today. The question I shall ask, in what will probably be my last ever publication on CA, is: has CA returned to the doldrums?

To get some preliminary indication of its vitality, I went to the Internet and ran searches for publications on CA: "Global Books in Print" yielded 39 titles since 1973; "Linguistics & Language Behaviour Abstracts" (inclusive of articles and reviews) yielded 35 so-called hits since 1992; "Web of Science" yielded 17 since 1992. After Krzeszowski's *Contrasting Languages* (1990) and Mair and Markus's *New Departures in Contrastive Linguistics* (1992), there followed Ulla Connor's *Contrastive Rhetoric* (1996). Wierzbicka's *Cross-Cultural Pragmatics* (1992) has just had a paperback edition (2003). Fisiak's journal *Papers and Studies in Contrastive Linguistics* has sustained the discipline for over thirty years, but that alas has also been discontinued, or rather conveniently retitled *Papers and Studies in Contemporary Linguistics* (thus retaining the abbreviation *PSiCL*).

Even while CA was enjoying a limited come-back, as early as 1983 we saw the publication of *Language Transfer in Language Learning* (edited by S. Gass and L. Selinker 1983) and six years later of Terence Odlin's *Language Transfer: cross-linguistic influence in language learning* (1989). Notice the studied avoidance of notions with behaviourist associations, such as "interference" and even "error" in the titles. Notice also the confident focus on "transfer". Is this a case of new wine in old bottles?

Something else was being avoided too: the predictive pretensions of classical CA, the claim that it would be possible, on the basis of a careful comparison of the structures of a language learner's L1 with associated structures in the language being learnt, to predict what difficulties the learner would experience. In 1970 Ronald Wardhaugh had questioned the feasibility of such prediction, and suggested that CA should be viewed as coming in two versions: a strong (predictive) and a weak version, which more modestly claimed to be able to explain (or diagnose) errors once they had occurred and been recorded in the output of learners with a particular L1 learning a particular L2.

2. New directions in Contrastive Analysis

It was perhaps regrettably defeatist of applied linguists to abandon their high-hoped predictive aspirations when they did, since it was at a time (the 1980s and 1990s) when linguistics was stronger and more confident than it had ever been. Yes, the Chomskian paradigm had made ground and held out all kinds of promises for grammars which had cognitive (if not "psychological") reality, and was able to distinguish linguistic universals from language-specifics. This was exactly what contrastivists had been waiting for: the specifics were the interlingual differences while the universals provided the sameness. Since difference against a background of sameness is no other than contrast, we held the philosopher's stone!

CA was tremendously enriched by a set of interrelated concepts in the formal grammar of the 1980s and 1990s: language typology, parameters, markedness theory, contrastive rhetoric, implicational scales and accessibility hierarchies. Let me offer a brief reminder of some of these.

2.1 Language typology

Typology shows that human languages differ and conform in systematic ways. Contrasts between languages do not affect single, isolated features but affect whole bundles of related features at the same time. For instance, on the parameter of head-first vs head-last, half the world's languages fall into the pattern Pr^1/VO/NG (head-first), while half are Po/OV/GN (head-last). Moreover, the correlation between the three realizations of headedness is around 0.8. This means that there is an 80% chance of a language that prefers one of the three features listed here also preferring the other two. For instance, imagine a Martian linguist dropping in on London and hearing someone say *the Queen of England* (an NG structure): he can be 80% sure that these English humans will also say *on guard* (Pr) and *take care* (VN = Verb Noun). This is of course useful information for the learner and the contrastive analyst to have, for, once you find out which any one of these three properties your Target Language manifests, you can predict (by implication) the nature of the other two with a high degree of confidence. You can go from here to contrasting mother tongue and foreign language parameter settings: if they are different, some negative mother tongue parameter transfer is likely.

---

1 The following abbreviations are taken over from Greenberg (1990)
  Pr-N Languages with prepositions   Po-N Languages with postpositions
  VO   Verb Object   OV   Object Verb
  NG   Noun-Genitive   GN   Genitive-Noun

Another well-studied parameter is the PRO-drop parameter, which determines whether a language uses a set of subject pronouns (like English) or dispenses with them and relies for person identification on a paradigm of verb suffixes (like Latin: *amo, amas, amat,* etc.). Now, there are a number of features associated with PRO-drop. Portuguese is a PRO-drop language, so we say

> Conheço bem esta cidade.
> Know-1st sg. well this city.
> 'I know this city well.'

One also says in Portuguese

> Chegou meu pai.
> Arrived-3rd sg. my father.
> 'My father arrived.'

with VS order, or inversion of V and Subject noun.

> Não posso comer ostras.
> Not can-1st sg. eat oysters.
> 'I cannot eat oysters.'

displays an inflected modal while

> Parece que ...
> Seems-3rd sg. that ...
> 'It seems that ...'

> Está chovendo/a chover.
> Is raining.
> 'It is raining.'

lacking expletive *it* or *that* is the norm. Once again, this is very valuable information for the contrastive analyst to possess, since the predictions about ease of learning can now be extended beyond a single feature to embrace a cluster of related ones.

Of course, all CA predictions have to be empirically validated, and this is no simple matter. CA is synchronic in nature, but diachronic studies can help with predictions. Duarte (2000) has shown that Brazilian Portuguese (BP – a PRO-drop language) is beginning to use more subject pronouns than a generation ago. This is the way the language is managing the impoverishment of its inflectional system: whereas there were six verb inflections and 20% of subjects were overt pronouns in BP around 1845, there are today but three inflections in use and 74% overt pronoun subjects. Duarte concludes that:

> [...] in BP today there does not seem to be a single context in which referential pronominal subjects are obligatory null. (2000: 22)

You can use them freely, at will.

Duarte's is a diachronic CA, with reference points 1845 and 1992. Her work invites a synchronic comparison of Brazilian and European Portuguese. PRO-drop is more rigorously observed in the latter. It also suggests a pedagogic (or learner-oriented) CA, where some predictions (or diagnoses) of learner transfers would figure. We would want to see first whether say English, German, or French (all non-PRO-drop languages) learners of BP are finding BP more learnable as pronouns are more widely used. We would also like to see, both diachronically and synchronically, whether those features associated with PRO-drop fall away as overt pronouns prevail. If they do, in what order are they lost and what is the set of non-PRO-drop features that comes in to replace them?

2.2 Markedness

Markedness is unusualness, atypicality. If you have a feature in your L1 which is unusual, you will probably not transfer it to the foreign language you are learning, or, if you do transfer it, the outcome will tend to be wrong; so you will probably stop transferring it. The preverbal position of the object pronoun in French *Le chien LES a mangés* is rare among languages, so French learners tend not to transfer it to English, and *The dog THEM has eaten* is a rare error. On the other hand, English learners of French have no qualms about transferring their order to L2 French and do try *Le chien a mangé LES*. Kellerman (1983) worked on the psychology of markedness and pointed out that unlike the behaviourist's rats in a maze, humans learning FLs do not just transfer mechanically. They have intuitions about the relative transferability of L1 forms and look before they leap: he called such intuition learner PSYCHOTYPOLOGY. The value of Kellerman's work was not solely in releasing CA from behaviourism, and rebranding it as a strategy that learners chose to apply. It also explained why some CA predictions either were not borne out by learners at all, or were realized in one directionality of learning but not the other: in other words, the German learner's negative transfers or L1-induced learning difficulties when learning English are not mirror images of the English speaker's attempts at German. The fact that the mother tongue German speaker has difficulty voicing English final obstruents, producing *He let me by the hant* or *What a bik dok!* does not mean that the English have difficulty with German devoiced final obstruents.

So much for the impact that the Principles and Parameters approach to Language Typology and Markedness Theory had on the study of structural-typological constraints on mother tongue transfer. I would consider endeavours I referred to above as "standard" CA. This is because there is renewed interest today in other – let's call them "extended" – forms of CA. Those most worthy of mention are contrastive rhetoric, Neo-Whorfian "framing" contrasts, two-plus contrastive analyses and retroactive contrastive analyses.

2.3 Contrastive Rhetoric

Kaplan's (1966) yet seminal work, what he calls his "doodles paper" on cultural thought-patterns in written text (see also Sanderson, this volume) has provided one high-point in CA, culminating in the excellent survey by Ulla Connor (1996). Her definition of Contrastive Rhetoric (= C-Rh) places it unmistakably in the diagnostic category:

C-Rh is an area of research in second language acquisition that identifies problems in composition encountered by second language writers and by referring them to the rhetorical strategies of the first language, attempts to explain them. (1996: 5)

The sort of C-Rh that has proved the most illuminating is GENRE ANALYSIS. The reasons for this are complex, but factors that have promoted this sort of C-Rh include the availability of systematic, detailed descriptions of English realizations of genres, notably of academic writing. Descriptions of the English language version of the genre in Swales (1990) and Dudley-Evans (1986) are available as a model for the description of the other-language realization. The intractable problem of the criterion for comparison, the yardstick or *tertium comparationis*, which obsessed grammar contrastivists for decades, should not arise in C-Rh.

The recent C-Rh study of the generic structures of English and Japanese research articles in Applied Linguistics by Kaoru Kobayashi (2003) is proof of the nonproblematicity of comparison at the rhetorical level. She established that both English and Japanese texts of the genre have the same 6-section structure. Of these, four are obligatory: Abstract, Background & Method, Results and Discussion, while two sections – Introduction and Conclusion – are optional, but more often realized in English papers than in Japanese.

Each of the six Sections is now analysed into its constituent Moves, and their structure, sequence, and incidence of use. The same procedure is repeated for Steps (the constituents of Moves) and of sub-Steps. At this point comparisons are made of the lexical signals, and of the frequency and types of Metatext (similar to advance organizers; i.e. signposts to guide the reader) used in each move. These analytic procedures are reiterated, almost automatically, six times in the study, once for each Section of the article.

Michael Clyne's (1987) study "Cultural differences in the organization of academic texts" is a good example of C-Rh. In fact the study combines CA with error analysis, in that scientific articles written in their respective mother tongues by German and English scientists were contrasted, and these were compared to English L2 articles written by Germans. Clyne shows that the German and the Anglo-Saxon "essay rules" are different. The ones authored by German speakers were more frequently "digressive" (occasionally even containing a substantial *Exkurs*), while the ones written by English speakers were usually "linear". This observation accords with Kaplan's claim that the structure of the English paragraph is "direct" and conforms to Aristotelian logic, a claim that has exposed him to the charge of Anglocentricity.

Clyne also found German texts to be "asymmetrical", that is, there was considerable variation in the sizes of the essential sections comprising the essay. Third, the German writers tended to locate examples, statistics and diagrams less in-text than in appendices or footnotes. Fourth, the English speakers used more advance organizers than the German speakers, suggesting a higher considerateness in the English speakers. Finally, "English texts by German scholars tend to contain the same cultural discourse patterns as German texts" (Clyne 1987: 233). Interestingly, there was a magnification effect, which means that the distinctively German rhetorical features were more pronounced in L2 English texts written by German speakers than in their L1 German writing. Possibly the attention required when having to use and monitor L2 English lexis and syntax opens the floodgates to L1 rhetorical influences.

Note, apart from its diagnostic turn, first, that C-Rh is a type of SLA research that is very different from the earlier 1970s/1980s SLA research that worked so hard to undermine CA. The subjects of C-Rh research are advanced learners, while the focus of most early SLA research is early beginners trying to sort out their morphology. Note secondly that C-Rh involves the advanced, learnt skill of writing (in the sense of composition), whereas standard SLA research has focussed on naturalistic acquisition. What happened, notably in the work of Dulay, Burt, and Krashen (1982) is that the outcomes of adult (post-pubertal) school-based FL learning – the Audiolingual context in which CA was elaborated by Fries (1945) and Lado (1957) – were compared with the outcomes of untutored naturalistic L2 acquisition by children. Moreover, adding a further complicating factor, the mother tongue is inevitably a naturally acquired system, and this is juxtaposed to the foreign language, which is a system that is taught and formally learnt. It is hardly surprising that the predictions of the former failed to find confirmation by the latter. It may be the case that if mother tongues (L1s) were learnt as foreign languages are, then CA predictions of ease and difficulty would be validated. Perhaps the predicted transfers between L2s and L3s (see below) work better than those predicted from L1s to L2s quite simply because L2s and L3s share the feature of having been learnt rather than acquired. Moreover, this explains the liking for and efficacy of raising L1 awareness during FL instruction: LA work of this kind is an attempt to compensate for the non-intellectual (some would say "natural") nature of L1 acquisition. Language acquisition raising intellectualizes L1 acquisition, so that it more closely resembles L2 learning. Finally, it is legitimate to enquire whether those who do not believe in errors and challenge the need to adhere to native speaker norms (the anti-native-speakerists) in grammar or phonology would be as confident about releasing the learner from native speaker norms of rhetoric.

2.4 Neo-Whorfian "framing" contrasts

C-Rh is concerned with how writers organize their ideas, which are bundled together in genre-specific ways to produce discourse. Thus there are different "styles" in which for instance persuasion can be textualized in different language-cultures. The Whorfian Hypotheses of language relativity and determinism are a different way to conceptualize the relationship of language to thought. By "relativity" we mean the claim that all languages are different and therefore each should be described *sui generis*. Linguistic determinism is the doctrine that we see and categorize phenomena in the world around us through the cognitive prism of the language we speak (or, more precisely, of the language we are speaking at the time). Linguistically uncoded concepts are unattainable, so if you do not speak Welsh (as a native!) the concept of *hiraeth* ('longing') is out of your reach, even though you have a near-equivalent in German *Sehnsucht*, Russian *toska*, or even Portuguese *saudad(es)*. Hanks (1996: 234) highlights the "relationships between language form, routine patterns of use and habitual modes of thinking". This is all contrary to Pinker's (1994: 57) view that we all think in the universal language that he calls mentalese. He views the idea that thought is determined by language as "a conventional absurdity".

The work done by Berman and Slobin and discussed in several publications in recent years is based on Boas's (1911) idea that each language allows its speakers to think privately what – and however – they wish, but at the same time how that thought is expressed is constrained by the patterns and preferences of their language. This is known as "thinking for speaking". Slobin (1996) reports on the expression of verbal aspect and the lexicalization of verbs of motion by children speaking English, German, Spanish and Hebrew, each group telling the well-known Frog Story from a cartoon. The main contrast identified concerns how complex meanings are put together in motion verbs. English and German are satellite-framed languages, in which the verb conveys only the fact of motion *(gehen, go)*[2], sometimes also the manner of the motion, as in, *rush, crawl, travel* etc. It is the satellites (particles or prepositions) that convey the direction of the motion: *rush across the street, fall out of the tree.*

Romance languages are different: they are verb-framed, which means that the verb itself expresses direction e.g. Spanish *llegar, salir, descer, subir*. Manner is expressed by satellites such as participles. So we get contrasting expressions like:

El   buhio salió   volando del   árbol.
The   owl   came-out flying from-the tree.
'The owl flew out of the tree.'

Slobin concludes that

> Much of value could be learned from a systematic study of those systems of particular second languages that speakers of particular first languages find especially difficult to master. (1996: 23)

One wonders whether Slobin has ever read Lado (1957), the founding father of CA, who wrote forty years before that:

> [t]he plan of the book rests upon the assumption that we can predict and describe the patterns that will cause difficulty in learning, and those that will not cause difficulty, by comparing systematically the language and the culture to be learned with the native language and culture of the learner. (1957: vii)

2.5 Two-Plus Contrastive Analyses

There is a new direction in CA that I call the Two-Plus CA, since it involves identifying the interlingual transfers involved in third or fourth language learning. Standard CA was about incipient bilingualism. This newer sort is about multilingualism. Two-Plus CA has some intriguing questions to address. Are bilinguals better foreign language learners than monolinguals? Do foreign languages get easier to learn the more of them one knows? Do people learning an L3 transfer more from the L1 or from the

---

2   This was confirmed by the lift in a Swiss hotel: when I pressed the button to call it, a sign lit up *Aufzug fährt* ('lift moving') – totally minimal information, without mention of manner or direction of motion.

L2? These and other fascinating issues are taken on board in Cenoz and Jessner (2000) and in Cenoz, Hufeisen and Jessner (2001).

Important research findings reported in these volumes include the following:

- In L3 lexis learning about twice as much transfer goes on as in L2 learning: around 30% vs. 15%.
- Where L1 is Dutch, L2 is English and L3 is French, there is over twice as much L2-to-L3 transfer (22%) as L1-to-L3 transfer (9%). Here are Dewaele's (2001: 71) data:

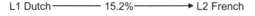

This confirms the view of Gibson et al.

> that the identity of the L1 has less of an impact on the ability to manipulate the L3 than [...] the identity of the intervening L2. (2001: 146)

In other words, it helps more for your L2 to be similar to the L3 than for your L1 to be. Learners of an L3 use their psychotypology: Cenoz (2001) showed that both L1 Basques with L2 Spanish and L1 Spanish with L2 Basque learners of L3 English transferred much more from Spanish than from Basque, irrespective of the L1/L2 status of Basque and Spanish. This confirms Ringbom (1987), who showed that L1 Finnish Finns transferred their Swedish L2 to L3 English more than their L1, whereas L1 Swedish speakers transferred little of their Finnish L2. The strongest predictor of language transfer is interlingual distance, which confirms Mackey's (1972) contention.

2.6 Retroactive Contrastive Analyses

Another "extended" form of CA that is enjoying some attention at the moment is the study of L2 transfer to L1, or retroactive CA, reported in Cook (2003). Cook justifies this enterprise by a reference to Uriel Weinreich who defined interference as

> those instances of deviation *from the norms of either language* which occur in the speech of bilinguals as a result of their familiarity with more than one language. (1953: 1; my emphasis)

Osgood (1949) had termed L1-to-L2 transfer "proaction" and L2-to-L1 transfer "retroaction" and his famous Laws of Interlist Similarity declared them to be symmetrical. It used to be objected by its critics that CA was based on the false assumption that proaction obeys the same laws as retroaction.

Baddeley (1972) pointed out that retroactive inhibition would be a useful predictor of "oblivescence" or the unlearning of the L1 by L2 learners. The studies reported in Cook are indeed mainly concerned with L1 attrition. Pavlenko shows how Russian narratives elicited from L1 Russian speakers long resident in the USA are permeated by anglicized forms on the lexical, syntactic, and discourse levels. In fact the Russians make much the same errors as English L1 Americans make when learning Russian as a FL. Their confusion of perfective and imperfective aspect verb forms is endemic. They also fail to differentiate determinate from indeterminate variants of motion verbs. For example, these immigrants misselected the indeterminate form of the verb "walk" *xodit'* in

Женщина *ходит по улице.
*Zhenshina *xodit po ulitse.*

instead of the determinate form *idjot* (идёт), to express the meaning 'The woman is walking along the street'. This is wrong because the woman is moving forward in a specific direction, requiring use of the determinate verb. Only if she had been walking back and forth would the use of the indeterminate form be justified.

Pavlenko also finds examples of L2-influenced framing among her subjects. Russian, since it makes use of verbs rather than of adjectives as in English, expresses emotions as if they were inner durative activities in which one engages voluntarily. So we have *veselit'sia* сердиться (literally 'to happy oneself' as in German *sich freuen*) corresponding to English *to be happy* (with an adjective). A further example is *stydit'sia* стыдиться (to be ashamed). These Russians adopted the English framing convention, using the verb *stat'* ('become') with an emotion adjective:

Она стала ещё более расстроенна
Ona stala eshjo bolee rasstroenna.
'She got even more upset.'

Jarvis identifies a high incidence of what she calls "unconventional Finnish" in the repertoires of one Finn eleven years resident in the USA. Jarvis shrinks from use of the term "L1 attrition", on the grounds that her subject's Finnish appears not to have been adversely affected by her L2 English. On the contrary, it appears to have been "enriched" by the incorporation of English forms occurring nonredundantly alongside Finnish forms, so allowing the subject to make finer semantic discriminations than the monoglot could.

Porte (2003) writes about English native speaker expatriate EFL teachers in Spain, who seem to be losing their English, or at least developing a Spanish-tainted patois mainly on the lexical plane. Much of the code-mixing attested by Porte was consciously crafted, often meant to fulfil an accommodative urge to group solidarity among the expatriates: *my friend in the *secretaria, when they reach the age of *selectivity*. Burrough-Boenisch (1999) showed how mother tongue English proofreaders of professional English texts in Holland can drop their guard and allow features of Dutch to encroach on their English versions: what she amusingly calls "English going Dutch".

3. New critique: CA supports monolingual bias in FL teaching

CA has recently faced a new wave of criticism, in the form of what I call a "veto on comparison". Before examining this veto, let's first agree that Applied Linguistics is all about comparisons, and CA especially so. The interlanguage continuum is a statement of the paired relationships between three languages, the learner's mother tongue (= MT), the target language (= TL) and the Interlanguage (= IL):

Mother Tongue (L1) IL_n IL_{n+1} Target Language (L2)

This allows us to define branches of Applied Linguistics as follows:

- CA as involving MT:TL comparisons,
- Error analysis as involving IL:TL comparisons, and
- Transfer analysis as involving MT:IL comparisons

Note here first the relationship between standard contrastive analysis (comparing mother tongue and target language) and transfer analysis (mother tongue and interlanguage): insofar as interlanguage is a *fait accompli*, something that is observable and describable, the purpose of making this mother tongue vs interlanguage comparison is to verify observations that the IL bears some specific resemblances to the mother tongue.

De Angelis and Selinker (2001: 43), in their contribution to thinking on L3 acquisition, speak of "the influence of a non-native language on another non-native language". They label this "interlanguage transfer", which I think is a misnomer. One definition of IL is a sequence of states of knowledge that is gradually approximating the TL norms. Learners do not totally revise their knowledge as they progress from one stage to the next. It is likely that they will in fact transfer linguistic knowledge across ILs, from one *état de langue* to the next. An attempt to predict or to diagnose these transfers within the IL continuum will constitute another form of CA, one based on the comparison of IL_n with IL_{n+1}.

It seems then that applied linguistics involves the pairwise comparisons of learners' languages, first, inter, second, erewhile and subsequent. Yet many applied linguists are not happy about comparisons and the veto on comparison has been voiced by a number of them. Bley-Vroman (1983: 15) calls it "the mistake of studying the systematic character of one language by comparing it to another". Instead each language should be described in its own terms – or *sui generis*. There seems to be no objection to describing ILs *sui generis* and then comparing different learners' ILs or different stages of one learner's IL. But as soon as the native speaker, the speaker of the TL, is introduced into the equation, there is trouble. This comes in the form of an accusation of native-speakerism, defined by Byram (1988: 11) as "the unattainable and insidious ideal of imitating and evaluating communicative performance by comparison with the native speaker". Chomsky (1986: 16) has his own way of expressing the same idea. He suggest that when we describe a child or a foreigner learning English we ought to say that "the person has a perfect knowledge of some language L, similar to English but still different from it". We don't say that however: instead we say the learner is making do with a corrupt version of the FL. Cook (2002: 4) even suggests it is demeaning to call anyone a "language learner" and prefers "language user". This new terminology will, Cook (2003: 4) insists, convince us of the wisdom of "seeing the L2 user as a person in his or her own right, not as an approximation to a monolingual native speaker", since after all it is not the aim of FL teaching "to manufacture *ersatz* native speakers" (Cook 1991: 114). Of the three sub-disciplines on the IL continuum, it is CA that attracts most odium for its native-speaker-centredness, for the simple reason that not one, but two native speakers are involved, each imposing his/her own set of norms.

It has been my experience that foreign language learners do not object to being turned into *ersatz* native speakers of the target language, provided that this determines only how they express themselves, rather than the content of what they say. I do not think learners feel embarrassed about using exotic sounds or sentence structures of the FL, but they do about having to imitate the cultural mores of the native speakers, such as shaking hands at breakfast, or men kissing. But let's see whether CA really does show monolingual bias. I hope to show the contrary.

4. Escaping the charge of monolingual bias

4.1 Building bridges from L1 to the foreign language: Interlinguas

I argued many years ago (James 1980: 160) that it would be wise to view positive L1 transfer as cumulatively creating an Interlingua (not to be confused with Interlanguage) between mother tongue and foreign language. So, for example, the Russian using the form *sputnik* in 1957 (just after this word had been borrowed by English) was a passable but not ideal way to compensate for his ignorance of the true English target *satellite*. I suggested that the Pole who transferred his mother tongue interrogative structure with the initial interrogative marker *Czy pan go zna?* could get by in German with the rarer but fully functional *Ob er ihn kennt?* In teaching pronunciation one can similarly make use of a rare mother tongue allophone to pave the way toward mastery of a central FL phoneme: the L1 English student of German struggling with the voiceless palatal fricative [ç] in *sich, mich* can be helped along the way by exaggerating and isolating his pronunciation of the first sound in a dramatic *hhhuge*!! I have helped English learners to gain an insight into German negation by reminding them of the biblical protest *I know NOT a man*. Eddy Roulet (1980: 110*ff*) once suggested how the German *sondern/aber* couplet can be associated with English *but*[1] and *but*[2] in sentences like the following:

She's not Polish, but[1] Czech.
She's not Polish, but[2] she speaks the lingo.

These are cases where it is enough to get by. We might call them halfway houses.

This is one way to approach the FL via the mother tongue. It is interesting to enquire what "via" means here. It carries the meaning of half-way, not yet perfect, but passable. It involves also to some extent viewing the mother tongue in terms of the FL. The teacher guides the learner towards a facilitated (nativized) perspective on the FL. It is an act of refocussing. A phrase commonly used in bilingual parts of Wales is "through the medium of", and some schools offer French classes through the medium of English alongside "Ffrangeg" (the Welsh word for 'French') classes through the medium of Welsh, according to the learners' L1. Unfortunately there is no research on the implementation of this policy, but it would be interesting to know exactly how much Welsh metalanguage teachers know and use to present and explain "Ffrangeg". It would be interesting to know whether the Welsh materials are really Welsh, or merely translations of English originals. The whole enterprise might even be unfounded: the research on L3 learning I reviewed above suggests that the policy is ill-advised, for the simple reason that mother tongue Welsh learners of French will transfer more from their English L2 than from their Welsh L1.

There is a new series of grammars published by Edward Arnold for English-speaking students of German, French, Spanish, Italian and Russian. Paradoxically, these are not grammars OF French, German, etc., but grammars FOR French, etc. As the publishers claim in their promotional literature:

> They offer a step-by-step explanation of a concept as it applies to English and a presentation of the same concept as it applies to the target language. The similarities and differences between the two languages are highlighted, especially the common pitfalls for English speakers. (publicity for Morton 1999)

This really is applied CA. Morton first tells us about say possessive adjectives in English, then proceeds to a parallel description of possessive adjectives in French. Then comes the CA:

> Like English, a French possessive adjective changes according to the possessor, but unlike English [note the contrast: CJ], it also agrees, like all French adjectives, in gender and number with the noun possessed. (Morton 1999: 88)

There follows an algorithm for generating correct possessive adjectives in French. It involves first raising Awareness[3] of the relevant part ('his') of the L1 English sentence *Paul is looking at his mother*. Next the learner decides that Possessor 'his' is coded as 3rd person singular possessor, marked in French by [s–] and then, that since the possessed noun *mère* is feminine singular, the adjacent vowel will be [–a]. Combining the initial *s–* and the following *–a–* yields *sa*, the correct form. The alternative, *his father*, would have yielded *son* by a combination of *s–* and *–on*.

These L1 grammars for L2 reflect a conviction that L1 Awareness is a prerequisite for learning a FL in the classroom. They represent an alternative way to deal with the mother tongue (facing it head-on) from the option of burying your head in the sand and hoping that effortless acquisition will take place in time.

---

3 For a perceptive and up-to-date account of Language Awareness, see Murray H. (2003). Tracing the development of language awareness. *Arbeitspapiere* 40. Universität Bern, Institut für Sprachwissenschaft.

A third pointer for pedagogy concerns the complementary roles of local and native speaker teachers, as discussed by Peter Medyges in *The Non-Native Teacher* (1994). In the light of what Porte (2003) discovered about expatriate teachers' L1 attrition, it would perhaps be counterproductive to insist that expatriate teachers should learn their pupils' mother tongue, since in so doing they might lose their own. In that case one of the native teacher's prime functions should be to identify and cater for mother tongue influences in FL teaching. Alternatively, one could argue that the expatriate teacher ought to know a great deal about her pupils' mother tongue, without necessarily speaking it: her own consciousness of the contrasts might help raise the pupils' awareness of the transfer possibilities.

What emerges from these developments is that CA can now come out of the closet, and cross-language Awareness can be practised in classrooms as a legitimate activity; for it will at the very least sensitize learners to the decisions to be made in their FL production, advising them when they can and cannot resort with profit to the mother tongue.

4.2 Noticing and Contrastive Linguistic Input

Noticing is essential to acquisition, since intake is by definition that part of the input that the learner notices (Schmidt 1990: 139). Obviously features that are in some respect salient stand a better chance of being noticed – and therefore learnt – than low-profile features. French clitic pronouns as in *[Mon père] me l'y [a envoyé]* and English 3rd person *-s* are low-salience features, and are consequently late-acquired. Some features are intrinsically noticeable, while others less salient can be put into contexts that either compensate for their low salience or invest some salience in them, by association. A third source of salience is contrastive salience: the salience of a FL feature is highlighted or enhanced by its contrastive association with the corresponding mother tongue item, very much in the same way as two colours clash. Our fascination by the exotic would explain this effect to some extent.

Odlin (1996) demonstrates how proficient bilinguals are able to identify certain errors in the attempted FL performance of learners as resulting from mother tongue interference in cases where there is a high degree of L1:L2 contrastivity. Successful learners, having struggled to escape these same interference traps, retain vivid memories of their source.

For example, successful mother tongue Spanish learners of FL English (hence "bilinguals") found it easy to identify the following typical [head noun + modifier] order errors in the attempted English of mother tongue Spanish students:

The *[girl pretty] ...   The car is the*[transport most popular].

Comparisons were possible of the respective bilinguals' ability to attribute different mother tongue transfer error types. Thus, 14 out of 16 Koreans correctly saw the following as resulting from Korean influence, while only one out of 9 Spanish speakers was willing to attribute it to mother tongue Spanish influence:

*a different country man ('a man from a different country')

Symmetrically, while 8 out of 9 Spanish speakers correctly saw *Many discoveries have been *possibles* as coming from Spanish, a mere two out of 16 Korean speakers were inclined to. What is important is that these perceptions correspond to the facts.

Kupferberg and Olshtain (1996) went a step further than Odlin, in demonstrating experimentally that in FL learning there is an optimal noticing point (when the FL form enters short-term memory) where L1:L2 comparisons (contrasts) can most advantageously be executed. Facilitating the discovery of these interlingual contrasts and ensuring that the contrasts learners identify are valid and productive is the job of teachers and materials. Such engineered input qualifies as Contrastive Linguistic Input (= CLI). Whereas the role of old classical CA was to predict or diagnose errors, in the CLI framework, CA is used for the definition of salient FL input which may assist L2 learners. Kupferberg and Olshtain gave an experimental group of 67 Israeli learners of English some CLI about compound nouns and relative clauses in English and Hebrew, while a matched control group received comprehensible TL-only input. In other words, the experimental group received direct contrastive evidence which told them "Look how your mother tongue and English contrast here", while the control group received only indirect positive evidence, on the basis of which incidental learning could take place. Compound nouns in these students' mother tongue Hebrew contrast with English compound nouns in two features: Hebrew has [head + modifier] order, English [modifier + head] order; and Hebrew has number differentiation in the modifier while in English the modifier noun is invariably singular, even when implicitly plural as in *pencil* (m) *case* (h), which means of course a 'case for pencils'. We even have singular trouser pockets! Reduced restrictive relative clauses (RRRCs) such as that bracketed inside *The student (reading the book) is clever* are nonexistent in Hebrew. A further contrast is the occurrence of resumptive pronouns in Hebrew relative clauses versus their absence in English.

These contrasts, the focus for the CLI, can be summarized as in Table 1.1:

Table 1.1 Contrasts between Hebrew and English

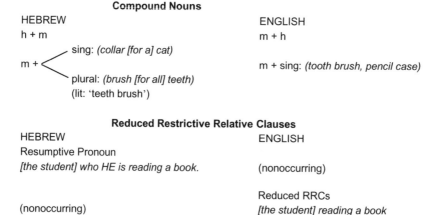

The experimental group's recognition and production scores on these two contrasting patterns were significantly higher than those of the control group's, suggesting that FL learners in formal settings do benefit from receiving explicit CLI. In other words, even somewhat artificial contrastive input can obtain better learning results than mere exposure to comprehensible input alone. This is something teachers have always known, and have been inclined to provide, often in defiance of a veto not only on mother tongue use but also on mother tongue mention. There are welcome signs that a process of reappraisal is under way.

4.3 Dual-lingual discourse

I would like to suggest a new way of overcoming monolingual bias: by practising Dual-Lingual Discourse (= DLD). I feel it is especially relevant in this context, since DLD is living CA.

DLD is dyadic discourse (spoken or written) in which each speaker produces only their own first language and thus hears or reads only messages in their interlocutor's mother tongue. As a concrete example we can imagine a native speaker of Japanese (NSJ) coming face-to-face with a native speaker of English (NSE). Each is a learner of the other's native language. Under the DLD convention each speaks (S) only his native language (SE or SJ), and hears (H) only the language he is learning (HE or HJ). This kind of interaction can be configured thus:

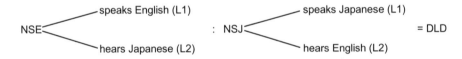

In fact DLD is well established. Here is an example of what Stern and Swain (1973: 179) wrongly call Canadian "bilingual immersion" between a teacher T and a child C. In fact this is not immersion but DLD. Immersion is marked by mid-utterance code-switching, which is absent here.

> C: Madame, can I paint?
> T: Est-ce que tu veux peindre? Oui. Vas-y.
> C: I want to show you something.
> T: Tu veux me montrer quelque chose? Qu'est-ce que c'est?

DLD is a linguistically symmetrical form of discourse in which language switches occur only at turn ends and not inside turns. So bilingual code-switching is not to be equated with DLD. In DLD the switch to the current speaker's L1 is made by convention and its purpose is didactic. DLD holds considerable potential as a format for FL learning which is likely both to promote FL proficiency and favour the multilingual option. Let me list the potential benefits of getting learners to do DLD.

(i) DLD avoids pidginization and semilingualism. Critics of bilingual immersion (Hammerly 1991) have pointed out its undesirable tendency to encourage an off-target learner pidgin. By exposing learners to fully-developed forms of the TL rather than to degenerate code-mixed and similar models such as foreigner talk, DLD removes the probable cause of semilingualism, or inadequate competence in both languages.

(ii) DLD reduces L1 interference by removing the need to produce the TL prematurely. This relaxation also lowers the Affective Filter, since, for most learners, having to speak in the FL is the most stressful activity.

(iii) DLD capitalizes on two facts: that the 'ideal speaker-hearer' is truly ideal, since receptive competence is in excess of productive, and that this advantage can bring about overall gains, as Ringbom's (1987) comparative study of the learning of English by Swedish-speaking and Finnish-speaking Finns has shown. DLD also supports the observation that speaking is a result of learning (not a cause) and is harmonious with the ethos of the receptive learning movement as in Total Physical Response (see Asher 1986).

(iv) DLD accords with coordination theory (Clark 1982), which claims that the learner learns by coordinating production with reception, i.e. closing the gap/mismatch between the two. The only limiting factor is that in DLD the learner's opportunity to match his/her own production with heard input is postponed to the next time he/she is involved in production practice. This is not necessarily undesirable, since it gives the learner a chance to reflect on new input and integrate it into current knowledge.

(v) DLD offers a further alternative to the several modes of L-equalization in teaching, current variants of which are: using one language in the morning and the other in the afternoon; timetabling L1-medium subjects vs. L2-medium subjects; tandem programmes such as those developed by Henri Holec (1988) and more recently at Trinity College Dublin through pupils' e-mail interactions (Appel 1999); and Reciprocal Teaching.

(vi) DLD solves the problem of over-accommodation in cross-language encounters, when the well-meaning but misguided bilingual switches to the NL of the newcomer. Such apparent convergence prompts quite the opposite reaction to the one intended. Robbing the learner of a practice opportunity (or more precisely of a chance to hear some of the FL) in this way usually creates resentment and conflict. Getting used to DLD helps us to rise above the impression of non-compliance that it gives.

(vii) Involving as it does the simultaneous activation of two languages, DLD escapes objections (Grosjean 1985; Cook 1992) that EFL teaching is permeated by an English-only monolingual bias and a fractional view of bilingualism. DLD recognizes (and exploits) the fact that the other language is never totally de-activated (Grosjean 1985: 472). The best way for L2 learners and even proficient L2 users to avoid this drift towards monolingualism through the kinds of language attrition discussed earlier is to keep producing their mother tongue, while encouraging the interlocutor to use his/hers.

(viii) It has been shown by Paivo and Lambert (1981) that repetition of a concept in two languages gives better retention than repetition in the same language. DLD allows learners to make on the spot comparisons of the different ways used by the L1 and the FL to express the same concept, for the simple reason that the conversational contributions cover notional common ground. In fact DLD is a natural way for the learners to be provided with Contrastive Linguistic Input (CLI) (Kupferberg and Olshtain 1996), that is, instances of structures that are formally contrastive in L1 and the FL whilst being matched for meanings and therefore potential causes of interference and resultant slow-down or fossilization in SLA.

(ix) DLD, by limiting FL processing to reception, releases attention needed for NOTICING some of the forms in the input. Noticing is postulated to take place when the TL item enters short term memory (STM), or immediately after hearing/seeing it – at a time when one should not have to be preparing one's response in the TL and crowding the recent TL image out of STM, which is what happens when monolingual discourse is forced from learners. In other words, it solves the phenomenon of DIVIDED ATTENTION in FL performance, which results from having to attend to what the interlocutor is saying in the TL, while at the same time preparing one's response in the same TL. This problem of divided attention is similar to that of restricted capacity. Thus you cannot easily monitor your output for fluency and for accuracy at the same time: one of the two has to be neglected. Likewise you cannot process for acquisition and for meaning simultaneously. DLD removes the need to divide attention between mother tongue and FL, and enhanced noticing is the outcome.

A small informal study was undertaken by the author to uncover some of the mysteries of DLD. The subjects were ten German students at a British university, non-linguists by specialism, with an upper intermediate proficiency in English. They were divided into two matched sets, though each subject was treated and tested individually. The five control subjects were interviewed separately in a monolingual discourse (MLD) mode: only English was spoken by the interviewer and the subject. The members of the experimental set operated in DLD. The conversations covered academic and domestic matters of interest to a foreign student.

After each 15 minute interaction (which was sound-recorded) each German student was presented with ten sets of four paraphrases of a notion that occurred in the interview. The occurrence of each of these expressions was predicted and engineered by the researcher before the interview, based on a pilot study. Since they were virtually synonymous, any one of the four paraphrases could have been used, but only one was. Each subject was asked to wait for thirty minutes and then to select the paraphrase which they thought had been used by the interviewer, a native speaker of English. Here is a typical paraphrase set. The option marked √ is the one actually used.

> Your courses here A) complemented your courses in Germany
> B) added what you had not studied at home
> C) were a supplement to those you had taken in Göttingen
> D) √ made up for what you had not studied in Göttingen

Preliminary results are encouraging. Under the DLD condition, 80% of used forms were noticed, whereas under the MLD condition the figure falls to 53%. We can interpret learners' ability to pick out the item used in the interaction as a measure of the degree to which they noticed the FORM of the expression: since all items meant the same, they could not have relied on the meaning of the expression for retrieval from memory.

The next logical step in this enquiry will be to see to what extent MT-to-FL contrastivity contributes, by heightened salience, to the noticeability and therefore the learnability of the FL expression.

5. Conclusions

I have attempted here to show that Contrastive Analysis, while no seen as longer the panacea for all FL learning problems, has nevertheless maintained a level of activity that would justify any claim to be one of the major branches of Applied Linguistics. Having abandoned its predictive aspirations and accommodated to a more cognition-based learning psychology, CA has benefitted greatly from its association with some major trends in theoretical linguistics, notably language typology and the associated domains of parameter setting and markedness theory. Some reactivation has also followed from renewed interest in the Sapir-Whorf hypothesis, with special relevance being indicated in the "framing" conventions in different languages.

There have also been some significant new initiatives: Contrastive Rhetoric, Two-Plus CA with its focus on L3 learning and the transfer effects at force in the process, and Retro-CA marking a return full-circle to the origins of CA in native language loss among immigrant communities to the New World.

Some new criticism of CA has come from those who react strongly to the "monolingual bias" they see in some traditional branches of Applied Linguistics. I hope to have shown here that there has also been a long tradition of attempts to link mother tongue and FL in the pedagogic process.

Ways have been devised to help the learner conceive of the FL in terms of his/her mother tongue by means of an Interlingua (see section 4a) acting as bridge between the two. More recently, interlingual contrast has been used as a means to make input more salient. The paper concludes with a suggestion that the monolingual bias could be avoided by ceding some teaching time to the practice of Dual-Lingual Discourse. Contrastive Analysis is still steering clear of the doldrums!

Bibliography

Appel, M. C. 1999. Tandem language teaching by email: some basic principles and a case study. *CLCS Occasional Paper* 54. Dublin: Trinity College.
Asher, J. 1986. *Learning another Language through Actions: the complete teacher's guidebook.* Los Gatos, CA: Sky Oaks Publications.
Baddeley, A. D. 1972. Human memory. In: Dodwell, P. C. (ed.), *New Horizons in Psychology.* Vol. 2. Harmondsworth: Penguin Books. 34–63.
Berman, R. A. and Slobin, D. 1994. *Relating Events in Narrative: a crosslinguistic developmental study.* Hillsdale, NJ: Lawrence Erlbaum.
Bley-Vroman, R. 1983. The comparative fallacy in interlanguage studies: the case of systematicity. *Language Learning* 27/1. 1–12.
Boas, F. 1911. Handbook of American Indian Languages. *Bulletin* 40, Part 1, Bureau of American Ethnology. Washington, DC: Government Printing Office. [Reprinted in: Boas, F. 1966. *Introduction to Handbook of American Indian Languages.* Holder P. (ed.) Lincoln: University of Nebraska Press.]
Burrough-Boenisch, J. 1999. *Righting English that's Gone Dutch.* The Hague: Sdu Uitgevers.
Byram, M. 1988. *Cultural Studies in Foreign Language Education.* Clevedon: Multilingual Matters.
Cenoz, J. B. and Jessner, U. (eds.). 2000. *English in Europe: the acquisition of a third language.* Clevedon: Multilingual Matters.
Cenoz, J. B., Hufeisen, B. and Jessner, U. (eds.) 2001. *Cross-Linguistic Influence in Third Language Acquisition: psycholinguistic perspectives.* Clevedon: Multilingual Matters.
Chomsky, N. 1986. *Knowledge of Language: its nature, origins and use.* Praeger: New York.
Clark, E. 1982. Language change during language acquisition. In: Lamb, M. and Brown, A. (eds.). *Advances in Developmental Psychology* 2. New Jersey: Lawrence Erlbaum Publications.
Clyne, M. 1987. Cultural differences in the organisation of academic texts – English and German. *Journal of Pragmatics* 11. 211–247.
Connor, U. 1996. *Contrastive Rhetoric: cross-cultural aspects of second-language writing.* Cambridge: Cambridge University Press.
Cook, V. J. 1991. *Second Language Learning and Language Teaching.* London: Edward Arnold.
Cook, V. J. 1992. Evidence for multicompetence. *Language Learning* 42/4. 557–591.
Cook, V. J. (ed.). 2002. *Portraits of the L2 User.* Clevedon: Multilingual Matters.
Cook, V. J. (ed.). 2003. *Effects of the Second Language on the First.* Clevedon: Multilingual Matters.
De Angelis, G. and Selinker, L. 2001. Interlanguage transfer and competing linguistic systems in the multilingual mind. In: Cenoz, Hufeisen, and Jessner 2001. 42–58.
Dewaele, J.-M. 2001. Activation or inhibition? The interaction of L1, L2 and L3 on the language mode continuum. In: Cenoz, Hufeisen, and Jessner 2001. 69–89.
Duarte, M. E. L. 2000. The loss of the "avoid pronoun" principle in Brazilian Portuguese. In: Kato, M. and Nagão, J. (eds.), *Brazilian Portuguese and the Null Subject Parameter.* Madrid und Frankfurt am Main: Iberoamericana Publishers / Vervuert. 17–36.
Dudley-Evans, T. 1986. Genre analysis: an investigation of the introduction and discussion sections of M. Sc. Dissertations. In: Coulthard, M. (ed.), *Talking about Text.* Birmingham: English Language Research, University of Birmingham. 129–145.
Dulay, H., Burt, M. and Krashen, S. D. 1982. *Language Two.* Oxford: Oxford University Press.
Fries, C. C. 1945. *Teaching and Learning English as a Second Language.* Ann Arbor: University of Michigan Press.
Gass, S. and Selinker, L. (eds.). 1983. *Language Transfer in Language Learning.* Rowley, MA: Newbury House.
Gibson, M., Hufeisen, B. and Libben, G. 2001. Learners of German as an L3 and their production of German prepositional verbs. In: Cenoz, Hufeisen, and Jessner 2001. 138–148.
Greenberg, J. H. 1990. *On Language.* Denning K. and Kemmer S. (eds.) Stanford, CA: Stanford University Press.
Grosjean, F. 1985. *Life with Two Languages.* Cambridge, MA: Harvard University Press.
Gumperz, J. J. and Levinson, S. C. (eds.). 1996. *Rethinking Linguistic Relativity.* Cambridge: Cambridge University Press.
Hammerly, H. 1991. *Fluency and Accuracy: towards balance in language teaching and learning.* Clevedon: Multilingual Matters.
Hanks, W. F. 1996. Language form and communicative practices In: Gumperz and Levinson 1996. 232–271.

Holec, H. 1988. *Autonomy and Self-Directed Learning*. Project No. 12. Strasbourg: Council for Cultural Cooperation.
James, C. 1971. The exculpation of contrastive linguistics. In: Nickel, G. (ed.), *Papers in Contrastive Linguistics*. Cambridge: Cambridge University Press. 53–68.
James, C. 1980. *Contrastive Analysis*. London: Longman.
Jarvis, S. 2003. Probing the effects of the L2 on the L1: a case study. In: Cook 2003. 81–103.
Kaplan, R. B. 1966. Cultural thought-patterns in intercultural education. *Language Learning* 16. 1–20.
Kellerman, E. 1983. Now you see it, now you don't. In: Gass, S. and Selinker, L. (eds.), *Language Transfer in Language Learning*. Rowley, MA: Newbury House. 112–134.
Kobayashi, K. 2003. *A Genre Analysis of English and Japanese Research Articles in the Field of Applied Linguistics: a contrastive study*. Unpublished PhD Thesis, Fakulti Bahasa dan Linguistik. Malaysia: University of Malaya.
Krzeszowski, T. 1990. *Contrasting Languages: the scope of contrastive linguistics*. Berlin: Mouton de Gruyter.
Kupferberg, I. and Olshtain, E. 1996. Explicit contrastive instruction facilitates the acquisition of difficult L2 forms. *Language Awareness* 5/3 & 4. 149–165.
Lado, R. 1957. *Linguistics Across Cultures*. Ann Arbor: University of Michigan Press.
Mair, C. and Markus, M. (eds.). 1992. *New Departures in Contrastive Linguistics*. Innsbruck: University of Innsbruck Press.
Mackey, W. F. 1972. *La distance interlinguistique*. Quebec: Laval University Press.
Morton, J. 1999. *English Grammar for Students of French: the study guide for those learning French*. London: Edward Arnold.
Murray H. 2003. Tracing the development of language awareness. *Arbeitspapiere* 40.
Odlin, T. 1989. *Language Transfer: cross-linguistic influence in language learning*. Cambridge: Cambridge University Press.
Odlin, T. 1996. On the recognition of transfer errors. *Language Awareness* 5/3 & 4. 166–179.
Osgood, C. E. 1949. The similarity paradox in human learning: a resolution. *Psychological Review* 56. 132–143.
Paivo, A. and Lambert, W. 1981. Dual coding and bilingual memory. *Journal of Verbal Learning and Verbal Behavior* 20. 532–539.
Pavlenko, A. 2003. "I feel clumsy speaking Russian": L2 influence on L1 in narratives of L2 users of English. In: Cook 2003. 32–61.
Pinker, S. 1994. *The Language Instinct*. Harmondsworth: Penguin Books.
Porte, G. 2003. English from a distance: code mixing and blending in the output of long-term resident overseas EFL teachers. In: Cook 2003. 103–120.
Ringbom, H. 1987. *The Role of the First Language in Foreign Language Learning*. Clevedon: Multilingual Matters.
Roulet, E. 1980. *Langue maternelle et langues secondes: vers une pédagogie integrée*. Paris: Hatier-Crédif.
Schmidt, R. W. 1990. The role of consciousness in second language learning. *Applied Linguistics* 11/2. 129–158.
Slobin, D. I. 1996. From "thought and language" to "thinking for speaking". In: Gumperz and Levinson 1996. 97–114.
Stern, H. H. and Swain, M. 1973. Notes on language learning in bilingual kindergarten classes. In: Rondeau, G. (ed.), *Contributions canadiennes à la linguistique appliquée*. Montreal: Centre Educatif et Culturel. 177–188.
Swales, J. M. 1990. *Genre Analysis: English in academic and research settings*. Cambridge: Cambridge University Press.
Wardhaugh, R. 1970. The contrastive analysis hypothesis. *TESOL Quarterly* 4/2. 123–130.
Weinreich, U. 1953. *Languages in Contact*. The Hague: Mouton.
Wierzbicka, A. 1992. *Cross-Cultural Pragmatics: the semantics of human interaction*. Berlin: Walter de Gruyter.

Recent advances in contrastive linguistics and language typology: the spin-off for language teachers

Christian Mair

Let's begin by taking a brief look back on the history of contrastive linguistics. The early boom of contrastive linguistics – from the late 1940s to the late 1960s – was founded on a firm belief that the systematic comparison of pairs of languages was the best way to put language teaching on a scientifically informed foundation and increase its efficiency.[1] As noted by James (this volume), contrastivists were forced into rapid retrenchment soon afterwards. The contrastive hypothesis in its strong or predictive form was becoming untenable in the face of mounting empirical counter-evidence, while in its weak or "diagnostic" form it did not retain a lot of explanatory power. Consequently, many scholars abandoned the contrastive enterprise altogether, while those who continued working in this framework re-grouped.

As far as I am aware, it was Fisiak (1971) who first proposed a division between "theoretical" and "applied" contrastive linguistics, which he promoted energetically throughout the following decade, cf. his own summary of his activities in Fisiak (1990: 5–6) with further references. The immediate benefit of such a distinction was obvious. Work in contrastive linguistics no longer needed to justify itself merely in terms of results in the classroom, and some confusion both in the field and among its critics was thus resolved. As Sajavaara put it:

> Purely theoretical research has often been assessed against applied objectives, or theoretical contrastive analysis has been performed for the purposes of language teaching. (1983: 177)

In the long run, however, the division meant that the two branches of contrastive linguistics started drifting apart rather rapidly – with the applied stream merging with activities in the fields of error analysis, empirical interlanguage studies and, most recently, the study of digitized corpora of learner language (as in Granger 1998), while on the theoretical level the comparison of language pairs was redefined as the minimal case of linguistic typology (cf., for instance, König 1992). Given that by the early 1990s theoretical and applied contrastive linguists were working within completely different

---

[1] See also the two classic statements of the position by Charles C. Fries and Robert Lado:

> The most efficient materials are those that are based upon a scientific description of the language to be learned, carefully compared with a parallel description of the native language of the learner. (Fries 1945: 9)

> [...] we can predict and describe the patterns that will cause difficulty in learning, and those that will not cause difficulty, by comparing systematically the language and culture to be learned with the native language and culture of the student. In our view, the preparation of up-to-date pedagogical and experimental materials must be based on this kind of comparison. (Lado 1957: preface, n.p.)

methodological frames of references, dialogue between the two camps ceased almost completely.

This is an unfortunate situation, and the aim of the present paper is to demonstrate that, perhaps surprisingly, recent theoretical research in typologically informed contrastive linguistics has quite a lot to offer to teachers and learners if its results are approached in an appropriate way. The first area for deomonstrating this point is recent theoretical work on the comparative grammar of English and German; the second is contrastive work in textlinguistics and pragmatics.

1. English and German grammar: historically close, typologically distant

The slogan-style headline of the present section summarizes the development of the grammars of the two languages over the past 1500 years. As members of the West Germanic branch of the Germanic group, English and German are among the most closely related extant languages of the Indo-European group, and the similarities between Old English and Old High German are obvious to any reader of, say, a translation of a biblical text into these languages. In its subsequent development, the grammar of Old High German has moved a very small way away from the synthetic towards an analytical type, although Modern Standard German is still a basically inflectional language with rather free order of constituents in the clause. The grammar of Modern English, by contrast, has been turned inside out typologically, with almost every basic Old English morphological and grammatical preference being reversed – inflection in the noun phrase making way for a fixed constituent order and analytical function words, prefix+ stem verbs making way for phrasal verbs (the type *upset* → the type *set up*), finite subordinate clauses receding against nonfinite ones, and so on.

Not surprisingly, therefore, it is easy to find English grammatical constructions whose literal rendering into German sounds bizarre (1), or the other way round (2):

(1a)   That's got to be put an end to.
       * Das muß ein Ende bereitet werden.

(1b)   a type of military tent that sleeps up to eight people
       * eine Art Militärzelt, das bis zu acht Leute schläft

(2a)   Hier liegt sich's gut.
       * Here it lies itself well.

(2b)   Er tat / gab seiner Frau Oliven in den Martini.
       * He put / gave his wife olives in the Martini.[2]

---

2   The idea is obviously easy to render: *he put olives into his wife's Martini*. The argument here is concerned with structural parallels only.

On the other hand, there are surprising and unexpected parallels. If, for example, talk is about something that is unfair, we can expand the idea and say that the action in question is unfair "to somebody" ("jemandem gegenüber" or "für jemanden"), or that it is unfair "of somebody" ("von jemandem") to perform it. Logically, it should be possible to combine the two into one and the same clause but this seems as impossible in English (3a) as in German (3b):[3]

(3a) It is unfair of you to do this.
      It is unfair to him to do this.
      * It is unfair of you to him to do this.

(3b) Es ist unfair von dir, das zu tun.
      Es ist ihm gegenüber unfair, das zu tun.
      * Es ist von dir ihm gegenüber unfair, das zu tun.

A criticism often raised against older studies in German-English contrastive syntax was that they tended to confine themselves to finding and listing many such comparisons without arriving at a systematic description, let alone an explanation. Inspired by research in functional typology, Hawkins published a landmark study in 1986 whose title is programmatic: *The comparative syntax of English and German – unifying the contrasts*. The book is an attempt to derive all the major grammatical contrasts between English and German from one fundamental difference in the typological orientation of the two languages. English is said to be a "loose-fit" language, in which the mapping between syntactic form and propositional-semantic function in the clause is not dependent on explicit morphological marking and therefore rather flexible, while German is a "tight-fit" language, which maps function onto form in a morphologically explicit and hence more rigid way. This is illustrated in Table 2.1:

Table 2.1 English as a loose-fit language / German as a tight-fit language (Hawkins 1986)

	English	**German**
subject	position before the verb	morphologically marked nominative case
direct object	position following the verb	morphologically marked accusative case
mapping of morphosyntax onto semantics	loose fit	tight fit
speaker's encoding effort	lesser	greater
listener's decoding effort	greater	lesser

3 Again, the argument is a structural one. There are other, perfectly acceptable ways of rendering the idea in the two languages: *it is unfair to him for you to do this* (with *for you* functioning as the notional subject of the infinitival clause) or *es ist ihm gegenüber unfair, wenn du das tust*, where the excessive prepositional complement is similarly shunted into a subordinate clause.

Here are some examples illustrating the concrete consequences of this contrasting typological orientation.

1.1 Passives

In German, what is explicitly marked as an accusative object can become the subject of a passive sentence; dative objects, prepositional objects and adverbials cannot.[4] In English, every post-verbal noun phrase that can be seen as being in a transitive relationship to the preceding verb can become a subject in a corresponding passive clause. The limits of passivization can thus be pushed to include apparently adverbial constituents such as *in this bed* in (10) below – on the assumption that sleeping in a bed (SVA) means ruining it (SVO) for use by someone else in the present context. In (11) the issue seems to be whether the noun phrase following the verb *run* can be construed as an institutionalized racing distance, in which case passivization is allowed because "run a race" is apparently more transitive than "run the 250 yards from my door to the corner" or "run two miles every morning," where the noun phrase is seen as more like an adverbial.

(4) Sie unterstützten ihn.
Er wurde unterstützt.

(5) Sie halfen ihm.
*Er wurde geholfen.[5]

(6) He was helped / supported.

(7) She was given / awarded the prize.
The prize was given / awarded to her.

(8) She was read the usual bedtime story.
The usual bedtime story was read to her.

(9) The topic was much talked about.
Such behaviour was looked down on.

(10) This bed must have been slept in. [i.e. ... must have been used.]

(11) A mile can't be run in under three minutes.
* Two miles were run by us every morning.

---

4 Dative objects can be fronted in impersonal passives: *ihm wurde geholfen* (cf. *es wurde ihm geholfen*), but obviously even then they are not nominative subjects.
5 The notorious Telegate commercial featuring actress Verona Feldbusch promising "Hier werden Sie geholfen," which spawned numerous similar uses in other domains is, of course, not a counter-example because in addition to the television star's looks it is the slogan's purposeful ungrammaticality which serves as an attention-getting device.

1.2 The semantics of subjects

While there are some exceptions, the normal semantic role of a German subject is to function as an agent. English, by contrast, is full of secondary subjects (Rohdenburg 1974), in which underlying (manner, locative, temporal) adverbials or other prepositional phrases (mostly of the 'experiencer' type) can function as subjects. They are called secondary subjects because the clauses containing them can be derived from bases which preserve a more direct form-function correspondence. In (12a, b) below, German and English are alike in allowing the construction with a primary subject:

(12a) You could have bought a Caribbean holiday with / on 250 pounds ten years ago
Man hätte sich vor zehn Jahren mit 250 Pfund einen Urlaub in der Karibik leisten können.

It is only in English, however, that fronting is combined with turning the fronted element into a grammatical subject through such "secondary" subjectivization:

(12b) 250 pounds would have bought you a Caribbean holiday ten years ago
Mit 250 Pfund hätte man sich vor zehn Jahren einen Urlaub in der Karibik leisten können.

(13) This hotel does not allow / forbids sandals.
In diesem Hotel sind Sandalen nicht erlaubt / verboten.

(14) Her violin broke a string during the concert.
An ihrer Geige riss während des Konzerts eine Saite.

(15) The star's memoirs sold a million copies during the first year.
Von den Memoiren des Stars wurden im ersten Jahr eine Million Exemplare verkauft.

(16) Tonight will be fine in the Dallas-Fort Worth metropolitan area.
Heute abend wird es in der Gegend von Dallas-Fort Worth schön sein.

(17) Dallas-Fort Worth will be very humid tonight.
In Dallas Fort-Worth wird es heute abend sehr schwül sein.

(18) The tank was leaking / oozing kerosene.
Aus dem Tank tropfte Flugbenzin.

(19) His weird sense of humour lost him many a friend.
Durch seinen komischen Humor verlor er so manchen Freund.

(20) I burst my pants.
Mir ist die Hose geplatzt.

1.3 Fused constructions

Fused constructions, i.e. complex sentences (usually involving nonfinite clauses) in which there is a mismatch between the surface syntactic form of a constituent and its underlying function, have become a central feature of Modern English grammar, while their use is extremely restricted in German. They are the most obvious instance of a loose fit between form and function/meaning, because form can go directly against function in typical "garden-path" fashion. In *I believe this rumour to be utterly false* or *they expected many students to skip this particular class*, online processing in real time[6] suggests two provisional readings *(I believe this rumour* and *they expected many students)*, in which the noun phrases following the verbs *believe* and *expect* are analysed as direct objects in the main clause, which then have to be cancelled because the following parts make it clear that, functionally, these noun phrases are the notional subjects of the embedded nonfinite clauses. The most common types of constructional fusion in contemporary English are illustrated in the following examples. Very few of them have German equivalents:

"subject-to-subject raising":

(21a) It seems that the students aren't interested in this topic.
Es scheint, daß die Studenten an dem Thema nicht interessiert sind.

(21b) The students don't seem to be interested in this topic.
Die Studenten scheinen an diesem Thema nicht interessiert zu sein.

(21c) He turned out to be a complete idiot.

(21d) We happened to find the book only after we no longer needed it.

(21e) United looked to be the winning team during most of the first half.

(21f) This remark is likely/certain/sure to cause offence.

"subject-to-object raising":

(22) * I want that you come with me.[7]
I want you to come with me.

"object-to-subject raising":

(23a) It is difficult to cultivate such a rich-lady image.
Such a rich-lady image is difficult to cultivate.

(23b) Some people find it dangerous to live with her.
Some people find her dangerous to live with.

---

6 Outside psycholinguistics, this activity is also known as "listening".
7 That the supposed underlying form is ungrammatical used to be a problem in older versions of Generative-Transformational grammar but should not affect the argument here.

(23c) It is difficult to get a rapid answer out of such students.
Such students are difficult to get a rapid answer out of.

To save space, I have refrained from giving ungrammatical German structural parallels for these perfectly ordinary English fused constructions. A common type that has not even been considered is the following variants of (23), in which the adjectival matrix predicates have come to superficially serve as premodifiers of nouns, and the infinitival clauses postmodify the nouns:

(24a) That is a difficult image to cultivate.

(24b) Some people find her a dangerous person to live with.

(24c) These are the difficult students to get rapid answers out of.

1.4 Wh-movement

Another area of the grammar in which the loose-fit orientation acquired by English in the course of its history manifests itself is extraction across clause boundaries in questions and relatives. This is possible only within severe limits in German but operates almost unrestrictedly from English nonfinite clauses. It could be argued that this freedom to move elements across clause-boundaries, which is also apparent in many of the fused constructions discussed in the preceding passage, is a compensation for the loss of word-order flexibility within the clause:

(25) Who did you tell the news (to)?
Who did they want you to tell the news (to)?
Who did they want to encourage you to tell the news (to)?
Who were they most likely to want to encourage you to tell the news (to)?

And so on, to the degree of complexity allowed by the powers of the speaker's or listener's short-term memory.

1.5 Typology in texts: the classroom perspective

Fascinating as these typological insights may be from a theoretical-linguistic perspective, we should not expect the average foreign-language teacher (or our students in teacher-training) to get too excited about them. This, I would argue, is a great pity, as all that it takes to make them directly relevant to the classroom is a small change of perspective. Hawkins's generalization was proposed to account for contrasts between the systems of English and German grammar, but it is very easy to apply it also to language-in-text, and then it holds a key to some stylistic contrasts between the languages which every advanced learner or beginning translator should know about.

In fact, manuals for German-English translation (e.g. Friederich 1969) feature several isolated hints about the linking function of English nonfinite clauses, and in an old-style comparison of the major languages taught in German-speaking schools Hans Glinz made the following observation on English sentence structure back in 1965:

> It is the very essence of the English sentence that its constituents and dependent infinitival, participial and gerundial constructions, and even entire subordinate clauses are not separated and delimited from each other rigidly; rather, the reader / listener easily moves from one to the other – led by the meaning without paying particular regard to formal boundaries.[8] [...]
>
> *He did not move, seeking the root of an ecstasy he had not dreamed was part of his nature.*
> (Arthur Miller)
>
> Er rührte sich nicht, er suchte die Wurzel eines Hochgefühls, von dem er nicht im Traum gedacht hätte, daß es ein Teil seines eigenen Wesens sein könnte. (Glinz 1994: 95, 96)

Looking at authentic language samples in this light shows us not only that the fused constructions, "funny" subjects and extractions that Hawkins sees as the results of the typological reorientation that the English language has undergone are indeed common, but also makes us aware of their functional and stylistic potential. Consider this passage from a news magazine as a first illustration:

> One reason, as a series of studies has shown, is that [the] Miranda [procedure for arresting suspects], precisely because it is so intrusive, specific, and detailed – in short, so resolutely 'activist' – **is easily enforceable, and easy to train officers to obey.** Whatever its jurisprudential deficiencies, it is at least easy to follow. (*New Republic*, 19 Dec. 1988, p. 22)

Out of context, the sentence *the procedure is easy to train police officers to obey* sounds like exactly the type of contrived example formalist linguists have long used to make arcane points about some grammatical models, i.e. a feature of the type of academic linguistics which has got a bad name in teaching circles. Seen in context, however, it becomes instantly obvious that the structure fits: it helps co-ordination with a preceding adjective, and the full or underlying form of the sentence would be much more complex *(it is easily enforceable – and it is easy to train officers to obey it)*. In terms of English-German translation, such examples help raise awareness of the fact that – given the fundamentally different typological orientations of English and German – translating grammatical constructions is not a good idea. In the following example, it is uncontroversial that the translated version which departs from the structure of the original and re-casts the content is the better one.

> Given its need to instill confidence in the markets the bank **is likely to want to be perceived as ready and able to operate effectively** in the dollar market, for which substantial dollar reserves may be required. (*Financial Times*, 18 Nov. 1997)
>
> – ?? *wahrscheinlich, daß die Bank als bereit und fähig betrachtet werden will, wirkungsvoll im Dollarmarkt zu operieren ...*
>
> – *... wird die Bank wahrscheinlich den Eindruck erwecken wollen, daß sie bereit und fähig ist, wirkungsvoll im Dollarmarkt zu operieren ...*

The same is true for the following sample:

---

8 "Der englische Satz lebt davon, daß Satzglieder, satzwertige Infinitive und Partizipien (oder Gerundien) und ganze Gliedsätze nicht scharf voneinander abgehoben und abgegrenzt werden, sondern daß man von einem zum andern gleitet, geführt von den Inhalten, und sich gar nicht um Formalgrenzen kümmert." [translation by CM]

Another kind of book Harris needs would be something like "Logic for Beginners". Such a **book would help him avoid trying to claim both that** Derrida didn't understand Austin and that he didn't like Austin because he understood only too well that he was merely repeating what Austin had already said. (*TLS,* 18 April 1997: 15)

- ?? würde ihm helfen, zu vermeiden, zu behaupten zu versuchen, daß ...
- würde ihn vor der Behauptung bewahren, daß ...

If in the above examples it was at least possible to find a structural equivalent in German of the English patterns, this is doubtful in the following case – an extract from a novel by Kingsley Amis:

Let into the wall below this she noticed a commemorative plaque, perhaps the **one Alun had been so fed up at not being asked to unveil the previous year.** (Amis, *Old Devils*, p. 43)

What I have aimed to show in the preceding argument is that theoretical work in contrastive syntax and language typology has consequences beyond its stated aim, the description of abstract and decontextualized linguistic systems. Among other things, it helps to explain differences between the ways the two languages concerned are used in texts. The theoretically driven comparison of languages thus enables us to develop a deeper understanding of the writing and speaking styles characteristically associated with the two languages, or with particular genres within them, and this is of instant and obvious practical benefit to the advanced learner, the language teacher, and the translator.

2. English-German communication: generally unproblematical, with minor exceptions

2.1 English-German communication problems: the folk perspective

It definitely means stretching the concept of cross-cultural or inter-cultural communication somewhat to deal with misunderstandings between English and German speakers under this heading. After all, centuries of co-existence in close geographical proximity and deep and continuous currents of cultural exchange have ensured that speakers of English and German generally communicate in a shared context whose unspoken assumptions are those of "modern", "Western", "industrial", "democratic-pluralist" societies. If anything, considering the internal heterogeneity of the two groups, one could argue that communication between certain groupings of English speakers, or between certain groupings of German speakers, is fraught with more problems in spite of their sharing the same language than communication across a language divide involving internationally mobile and open-minded groups such as students or business executives.

Nevertheless, the folk-tradition of writing on English-German miscommunication is so rich that, even after due allowance has been made for the effects of humorous exaggeration and national stereotyping, enough remains to warrant a serious inquiry. Below, there is – in ascending order of seriousness – advice from three sources to speakers of English on the proper way of "meeting and greeting" their German interlocutors. The first extract is from Stefan Zeidenitz and Ben Barkow's *The Xenophobe's Guide to the Germans* (Horsham, 1993):

> The Germans will shake hands at the drop of a hat. Hand-shaking is an unavoidable fact of life, and you will do well to reconcile yourself to pumping the flesh on all occasions. You must shake hands on meeting, on parting, on arriving, on leaving, on agreeing something, and on agreeing to disagree. The Germans believe in the firm handshake which, done properly, should dislocate at least half a dozen of the smaller bones. (p. 25*f*)

Susan Stern's *These Strange German Ways* was first brought out in 1994 by "Atlantik-Brücke", a civic association whose board of directors at the time including Walther Leisler Kiep or Dr. Arend Oetker suggests anything but flippant humour. And indeed, in keeping with the association's name, the overall tone is one of benign support for efforts to bridge the Atlantic Divide on the interpersonal level. On the question of shaking hands, the reader is instructed as follows:

> Meeting Germans for the first time is as easy as meeting anyone else; first and foremost, it requires a smile (big or small, depending on the formality of the meeting). Most Germans still tend to shake hands, although students on campus, for example, usually don't among themselves. Some men may incline or nod their head (particularly to a woman) as they firmly pump your hand. [...] Throughout the handshaking ceremony, the left hand must be visible – that is, not tucked into a pocket. (p. 39)

There is no doubt in the seriousness of the advice extended in the *Culturgram* series edited by the David M. Kennedy Center for International Studies of Brigham Young University in Provo, Utah. The series comprises almost 200 four-page folders which aim to provide Americans with the essential cultural background required for successful communication abroad. They are all designed on the same template, the country name in English being followed by maps and the text opening with a brief passage on "Customs and Courtesies". The latest version of the *Culturgram* for Germany reads:

> A handshake is the most common form of greeting and should be extended to women before men. If a person's hand is dirty, they may offer an elbow or forearm to be shaken. In groups, several people do not shake hands at once, because crossing someone else's handshake is inappropriate.

It is surprising what details the ethnographic gaze will turn up even if it is directed at a broadly familiar social environment.

Occasional trouble seems to lie ahead also for those who have negotiated the difficult first steps with due smiling and hand-shaking and have managed to establish emotional rapport with a German partner. The following extract is from a female American student's diary who has trouble with a German-speaking boyfriend who is unresponsive to indirect speech-acts.

> When I said something (in English) to my (German) boyfriend like 'Would you like to go to the cinema tonight?', which means to me 'I want to go to the cinema tonight and you're taking me' – and it's got much more force than it sounds as though it has – he would just say 'No, not really'. (quoted in House 1996: 351)

As I hope to show below, current research on cross-cultural pragmatics can help us to develop such anecdotal observations into a systematic picture which will benefit advanced learners.

2.2 English-German communication problems: the research perspective

In spite of the very different subject matter dealt with, the principle required to bring some order to the vast and complex field of cross-cultural communication resembles the one successfully employed in typologically based contrastive grammar. Variation may be confusing and complex at first sight, but it is not arbitrary and unlimited, because it follows a number of universal principles. This claim is supported, for example, by a human-ethological study of communication among and with the Eipo, a small tribal community in the highlands of Papua-New Guinea, which was largely untouched by contact with the outside world when the research was undertaken and which therefore represents an uncontroversial case of truly cross-cultural communication. The investigators write that:

> How to de-escalate in the face of aggressive behaviour, how to go about getting what one wants, how to attract attention, etc. – these are strategies which in principle are based on identical sequences of actions. As human beings, we apparently have only a limited number of options to achieve these goals – certainly several different ones for each goal, but not an unlimited number.
> (Eibl-Eibesfeldt, Schiefenhövel, Heeschen 1989: 15)[9]

This is an idea familiar to linguists working on cross-cultural pragmatics. In fact, the title of Brown and Levinson 1987, (*Politeness: Some Universals of Language Usage*), a classic in the study of politeness, is programmatic. Politeness is a linguistic universal in the sense that its principles can be shown to operate in any community; the observable differences in politeness codes are due to the fact that not all principles have the same priority in different communities. Leech, for example, has pointed out that while it would be vacuous to claim that some languages or communities of speakers are more polite than others in absolute terms, the degree of "relative politeness" (Leech 1983: 84) is a genuine indicator when two people communicate across a linguistic boundary. As an example, he suggests the following generalization, which, incidentally, holds the key to a solution of the German-speaking boy-friend's problems reported by House's informant: "the English language, in particular the British variant of it, is rich in indirect impositives" (Leech 1983: 84).

House herself proposes the following five dimensions as relevant to a systematic description of German speakers' and English speakers' differing communicative orientations. These are given in Table 2.2.

---

9 "Wie man eine Aggression abblockt, wie man es anstellt, um etwas von jemandem zu bekommen, wie man sich ins Zentrum der Aufmerksamkeit rückt und dergleichen mehr wird im Prinzip überall mit der gleichen Folge von Handlungsschritten versucht. Um diese Handlungsziele zu erreichen, stehen uns Menschen offenbar nur beschränkte Möglichkeiten zur Verfügung, für jedes Ziel sicher mehrere, aber nicht unbeschränkt viele." [translation by CM]

Table 2.2 Dimensions of cross-cultural difference (German – English) [adapted from: House 1996: 347]

directness	←→	indirectness
orientation towards self	←→	orientation towards other
orientation towards content	←→	orientation towards addressees
explicitness	←→	implicitness
ad-hoc formulation	←→	verbal routines

This table not only contributes to a theory of English-German contrastive pragmatics, but can easily serve as a useful grid for language teachers or materials writers who want to improve their students' communicative competence.

Even easier to teach are differences between English and German written textual genres because codification here tends to be more rigid. Let me demonstrate this point with the following exercise in computer-aided contrastive text-type typology for advanced learners of English with German as their mother tongue. The task is writing a "Lebenslauf" or "curriculum vitae", which is a realistic challenge faced by many of them. Pragmatically naïve learners may pay a lot of attention to matters of orthographic and grammatical correctness, but follow a textual design broadly in line with the model in appendix 1. For practical purposes it would, of course, be enough to alert German-speaking students to the fact that the curriculum vitae is a text-type which is organized differently in English-speaking countries and send them to one of many manuals giving advice on the matter (e.g. Neuhaus and Neuhaus 1997, or Neuhaus and Neuhaus 1998). A strategy more productive in the long term, however, would be to take the task as a starting point for an exercise in data-driven learning.

As a first step, students could be encouraged to consult advice on the writing of CVs which is given on the web pages of almost every academic institution in the English-speaking world. In this way, they would be able to learn about the broad similarity of the relevant conventions, but also about interesting minor regional differences in different parts of the English-speaking world. These concern, for example, the rigour with which the code of political correctness is enforced. Here it seems to be American institutions which are in the lead, as is shown by the recommendations given by the University of California at Riverside (UCR), which represent the right-on spirit of political correctness in its purest form (see Appendix 2).

The insights a German-speaking student can gain from these recommendations are that the text-type "Lebenslauf" in English is internally heterogeneous, and that a CV is not necessarily the same as a resumé, that knowledge of Latin grammar is not presupposed in academic contexts in the United States, but most of all that information which it is customary to give in German curricula without hesitation is considered "tasteless to illegal", as illustrated in the last paragraph of the first text in appendix 2, reprinted here:

> On the other hand, <u>DO NOT</u> include on your curriculum vitae the kinds of personal information that have nothing to do with your qualifications for the position. Here are some items that range from taste-

less to illegal if included. Do not list your height, weight, or any other physical characteristic. Do not give your age, marital status, sexual preferences, racial or ethnic identity, political or religious affiliations, place of birth, or other information of this kind. Do not attach a photograph.

To the student who happens to begin with an analysis of UCR's advice, it will come as a relief that elsewhere in the English-speaking world matters are regarded in a more relaxed way, as is illustrated by the corresponding pages of the University of Waikato, New Zealand (see Appendix 2).

What the student is being reminded about is that standard English now is a pluricentric language, and that what is a rule in the United States need not apply in New Zealand: compare, for example, the easy dismissal of the distinction between a CV and a resumé.

The most fruitful opportunity for self-directed learning, however, is that the World-Wide Web will enable students to compare institutional recommendations with speakers' own practice. After all, tens of thousands of authentic CVs are available on the Web for inspection.

Taking the cue from an apparently trivial comment in the Waikato webpage ("A statement that your health is excellent just takes up valuable space."), we might, for example, undertake a search for the phrases "excellent health" combined with "curriculum vitae", and this search will take us from the practical concerns of language teaching and learning into the domain of cultural studies.

An applicant's state of health is, of course, relevant to his/her ability to do a job, and hence relevant information even on the very narrow criteria applied, for example, by the University of California at Riverside. On the other hand, a person's medical record is confidential, personal information, and bringing it into the open subverts the general recommendation that anything personal should be left out of a CV.

The Waikato webpage dismisses this problem as a mere triviality. Scanning hundreds of CV's that contain mentions of applicants' "excellent health", however, the picture that emerges is more sinister. Thus, it is probably not an accident that such mentions are particularly common in web material from South Africa (domain restriction .za); it seems that in view of the country's AIDS/HIV problem, the phrase is developing into a polite code for drawing readers' attention to one's negative HIV status.

3. Conclusion

"Applied" contrastive linguistics as it was taught in the 1950s and 1960s cannot, and indeed should not, be revived today. To this extent the future of contrastive linguistics is as a theoretical-linguistic approach which is grounded in linguistic typology.

However, this does not mean that the insights gained are irrelevant to the language classroom. As I have shown in a discussion of two major learning problems facing the student of English – one grammatical, and one pragmatic – theoretically driven work will often help teachers to describe their experience more systematically and more comprehensively. I would go even further and argue that, in line with a current revival of cognitive-reflective approaches in foreign-language teaching (cf. the discussion of "[critical] language awareness", see Fairclough, 1992), not only the teacher, but also the advanced learner, especially the student in a university foreign-language department, will profit from integrating the linguistics and language teaching components of his or her course more closely in the way described.

The domain of application I envisage for contrastive linguistics today is probably best described by Béjoint, who – as a lexicographer – also works in a field which is frequently torn between conflicting theoretical and practical-commercial concerns. Like lexicography, modern-style applied contrastive linguistics must situate itself in "a domain that extends half-way between inapplicable theory and unfounded practice" (Béjoint 1994: 209).

Bibliography

Béjoint, H. 1994. *Tradition and Innovation in Modern English Dictionaries*. Oxford: Clarendon Press.
Brown, P. and Levinson, S. C. 1987. *Politeness: Some Universals in Language Usage*. Cambridge: Cambridge University Press.
Eibl-Eibesfeldt, I., Schievenhöfel, W. and Heeschen, V. 1989. *Kommunikation bei den Eipo: eine humanethologische Bestandsaufnahme*. Berlin: Reimer.
Fairclough, N. (ed.) 1992. *Critical Language Awareness*. London: Longman.
Fisiak, J. 1971. The Poznań Polish-English contrastive project. In: Filipović, R. (ed.), *Zagreb Conference on English Contrastive Projects*. Zagreb: Zagreb University. 87–96.
Fisiak, J. 1990. On the present status of some metatheoretical and theoretical issues in contrastive linguistics. In: Fisiak, J. (ed.), *Further Insights into Contrastive Analysis*. Amsteram: Benjamins. 3–22.
Friederich, W. 1969. *Technik des Übersetzens: englisch und deutsch; eine systematische Anleitung für das Übersetzen ins Englische und ins Deutsche für Unterricht und Selbststudium*. München: Hueber.
Fries, C. C. 1945. *Teaching and Learning English as a Foreign Language*. Ann Arbor MI: University of Michigan Press.
Glinz, H. 1994. *Grammatiken im Vergleich: Deutsch – Französisch – Englisch – Latein ; Formen – Bedeutungen – Verstehen*. Tübingen: Niemeyer, 2nd edition. [1st edition: 1965]
Granger, S. (ed.). 1998. *Learner English on Computer*. London: Longman.
Hawkins, J. A. 1986. *The Comparative Typology of English and German: unifying the contrasts*. London: Croom Helm.
House, J. 1996. Contrastive discourse analysis and misunderstanding: the case of German and English. In: Hellinger, M. and Ammon, U. (eds.), *Contrastive Sociolinguistics*. Berlin, New York: Mouton de Gruyter. 345–361.
König, E. 1992. Contrastive linguistics and language typology. In: Mair, C. and Markus, M. (eds.), *New Departures in Contrastive Linguistics*. Vol 1. Innsbruck: Institut für Anglistik. 137–154.
Leech, G. 1983. *Pragmatics*. Harmondsworth: Penguin Books.
Lado, R. 1957. *Linguistics Across Ccultures: Applied Linguistics for Language Teachers*. Ann Arbor MI: University of Michigan Press.
Neuhaus, D. and Neuhaus, K. 1997. *Das Bewerbungshandbuch für Europa*, 3rd edition. Bochum: ILT-Europa-Verlag.
Neuhaus, D. and Neuhaus, K. 1998. *Das Bewerbungshandbuch für die USA*. Bochum: ILT-Europa-Verlag.
Rohdenburg, G. 1974. *Sekundäre Subjektivierungen im Englischen und Deutschen: vergleichende Untersuchungen zur Verb- und Adjektivsyntax*. Bielefeld: Cornelsen-Velhagen und Klasing.
Sajavaara, K. 1983. Cross-language analysis and second language acquisition: preface. *Applied Linguistics* 4: 177–178.
Stern, S. 1994. *These Strange German Ways: The New Book*. Frankfurt: Atlantik-Brücke.
Zeidenitz, S. and Barkow, B. 1993. *The Xenophobe's Guide to the Germans*. Horsham, Sussex: Ravette Books.

Appendix 1: Sample German "Lebenslauf"
(source: http://www.elektro-ing.de/Bewerbung/Muster_1.html)

Lebenslauf   (Foto)

Name:	Lucas Kruppa
Geburtstag, Ort:	26. April 1971 in Wuppertal
Staatsangehörigkeit:	deutsch
Konfession:	evangelisch
Familienstand:	verheiratet, 1 Kind
Schulbildung, Ausbildung:	4 Jahre Grundschule, 2 Jahre Gymnasium, 4 Jahre Realschule, 3 Jahre Fachoberschule, Fachrichtung Elektrotechnik, 18 Monate Grundwehrdienst, 10 Semester Fachhochschule, Abschluß Juni 1997: Dipl.-Ing. Elektrotechnik (FH) Gesamtnote "gut"
Berufsausbildung:	Während des Studiums (März 1994 – September 1997) absolvierte ich ein 18monatiges Praktikum in der Entwicklungsabteilung Nachrichtentechnik bei der Firma Fern-Hören in Paderborn, davon 1 Jahr in der Niederlassung Utah, USA.
Berufstätigkeit:	Seit Oktober 1995 bin ich nebenberuflich als Verkaufsberater bei der Firma Fern-Hören tätig.
Sprachkenntnisse:	Englisch verhandlungssicher, gutes Technik-Englisch; Französisch ausbaufähig.

Paderborn, den 25. Juni 1997

(Unterschrift: Vor- und Zuname)

Appendix 2: Advice on writing CVs and letters of application
University of California at Riverside (USA)
(source: http://www.careers.ucr.edu)

Who should use a curriculum vitae?

The curriculum vitae (or CV) is an essential document in applications for academic employment. Persons applying for teaching, research, and some administrative positions are expected to submit a CV along with a rather detailed letter of application and other supporting materials. The CV is also used by professional educators who are seeking positions in school administration and other education-related careers.

Generally, academic institutions are the only employers who want to see a CV. Most other employers in private business and government strongly prefer a short, one-page resume; sending these employers a CV can, in fact, be counterproductive. When in doubt, check with your advisor or career counselor as to whether to send a CV or a resume.

What is a curriculum vitae, and what is it used for?

A curriculum vitae is much like a resume, only much longer and more detailed. The CV generally ranges from two to dozens of pages in length, depending upon such factors as the extent of one's research record or the stage of one's career. Entry level CV's in higher education tend to be only a few pages in length.

[…]

What is the proper use of the terms "vitae" and "vita" and "CV"?

The minutiae of this controversial question remain the topic of vigorous debate. However, a recent issue of the *Chronicle of Higher Education* served to standardize the usage somewhat by passing along the following information:

The term "curriculum vitae" translates as something close to "course of life." The term "vita" translates as simply "life." The correct label for one's (single) document can be either "curriculum vitae" or simply "vita." In other words, one does not use the term "vitae" by itself, nor does one write "curriculum vita".

In informal conversation we often hear academicians call this document a "CV," thus avoiding the Latin forms altogether. This practice is widely accepted, but we do not recommend your putting "CV" at the top of your curriculum vitae for employment applications. It is better to use one of the two acceptable forms shown above.

What information should I include on my vita?

In general, DO include any and all information that is pertinent to your qualifications for the job. The following is a list of possible categories of information to include:
Name, Address(es), Phone Number(s), E-mail Address
Objective: What exactly are you applying for?
Academic Preparation: College degrees with details

Relevant Work Experience
Specific Skills: Computer programs, Lab techniques, etc.
Publications/Exhibitions/Performances
Papers etc. submitted for publication
Current research interests
Paper/Posters presented at conferences
Grants received
Travel
Languages
Professional organization memberships
Professional services
Honors and awards
References

On the other hand, <u>DO NOT</u> include on your curriculum vitae the kinds of personal information that have nothing to do with your qualifications for the position. Here are some items that range from tasteless to illegal if included. Do not list your height, weight, or any other physical characteristic. Do not give your age, marital status, sexual preferences, racial or ethnic identity, political or religious affiliations, place of birth, or other information of this kind. Do not attach a photograph.

The University of Waikato (NZ)
(http://www.waikato.ac.nz)

Preparing a CV (Curriculum Vitae)
The purpose of a Curriculum Vitae is to summarise your skills, abilities and work history. Ideally your CV will convince the employer that they should meet you.

[…]

In New Zealand, Curriculum Vitae and Resume mean the same thing.

[…]

There is no ideal format for a "winning" CV as each application needs to reflect the particular interests of the employer you are applying to. You never get a second chance to make a first impression. The following information is intended to help you to start thinking about the sorts of information that you might like to include.

How Should I Prepare my CV?
Your CV must be succinct and concise. Two to four pages is the current 'standard' length.
It must be clear and well-organised. If your CV is muddled and disorganised, the employer will assume that you are too.
As already mentioned, it is no longer acceptable to have a general CV. Each application you make should be targeted to the job you are applying for. The more you know about the employer the easier it will be to write your CV. The job description is a great place to start and may in fact be all you need. From the job description you should be able to match your skills to the person specification. If you haven't been able to get a job description, then you will need to do a little bit more work. You can find out about the company from annual reports and sometimes the yellow pages will have some information about what the company does.

There are resources in the Careers Office that can help you work out the sorts of skills required for specific job types, and of course the Internet will be a great source of information.

What to include

Photos

It is unnecessary to include a photo – the way you look does not reflect your ability to do the job. However, if you want to include a photo, then go ahead. If you do, make sure it is a professional photo and one that photocopies well. You may want to consider a digital photo that you can include in the body of your CV.

[…]

Date of Birth

You do not have to include your date of birth – it is not relevant to your ability to do the job.

Health

A statement that your health is excellent just takes up valuable space.

Nationality

Not really necessary.

Education

Secondary education is somewhat superseded by your university qualifications. If you have little work experience, then a brief summary of your secondary schooling can help to paint a picture of your abilities.

University – It is highly unlikely the employer will know exactly the content of the papers you have taken even if she/he has graduated from the University of Waikato. Instead of listing all the courses, it is better to outline what is special about your degree and how it relates to the job you are applying for. One paragraph would be enough.

[…]

Work experience

Think carefully about the responsibilities you have had and the skills that you have gained from all the work experience you have had. Try and think in terms of transferable skills if you have not had direct experience with the skills and abilities required by the job you are applying for. Remember employers may have little idea what your position(s) involved, or worse, a stereotypic view of what you have been involved with. They may not appreciate your achievements, skills and abilities, so you will need to make sure you tell them. Your experience will often be more relevant than you first think. Come in and see use if you are having problems.

Personal Statement

This is no place to be coy or vague about yourself. Examine your experience and interpret it in terms that an employer will see as relevant to their needs. Build up a vocabulary of words and phrases to describe yourself. They must be positive statements which can be supported by reference to your experience.

Interests

Your interests will help the employer imagine you as a real person. It is important that your CV shows you as a person, not just a series of facts on paper. Because employers will attribute all sorts of personal qualities to you on the basis of your interests, those few words can work very hard on your behalf.

Personal Skills and Abilities
When you are outlining these qualities, be sure to back up what you are saying with examples. When you say you have excellent communication skills, make sure you also say how you have demonstrated this skill. For example, the "A" you got for your group assignment, or the fact that you are capable of delivering written material to university standards.

Referees
Two are usually sufficient. Ask people whom you know reasonably well and whom you trust to speak well of you. Referees need to know what is expected of them. Give them a copy of your CV and a job description if you are applying for a specific position. Go over these documents with them emphasising the parts where you think their knowledge of you will be positive, helpful, and most relevant to the position. Keep your referees up to date with what's happening.

Teaching contrastive rhetoric(s): bridging the gap between English language competence and academic success in English for the non-native speaker

Tamsin Sanderson

While I was working on this paper, I happened to notice a short piece in a newspaper reporting the initial failure of peace talks between the Nepalese government and Maoists in Nepal (*Badische Zeitung*, 22.4.03, 4). According to the article, the talks had failed due to an argument about the agenda: by way of explanation, Maoist spokesperson Krishna Bahadur was quoted as saying that the government did not want to talk about the main problems immediately. I was suddenly struck by this situation: here were two groups of people who apparently agreed on the fundamental need for discussion, on the language in which to speak with each other, and even on the topics for discussion. Yet when it came to the ostensibly minor issue of the *order* in which these particular issues were to be addressed, they disagreed so vehemently that it was enough to lead to total communication breakdown. This seemed to connect nicely with the central point of my paper: that it is not just what you say, but how and when you say it. Few people would argue with this statement in regard to general communication, but it can be shown that it also holds true for communication between researchers. Successful academic exchange, that is, is as much about form as it is about content.

1. The importance of form for (mal)functioning academic exchange

A statement like this contrasts with the orthodox view of academic exchange as content-focussed, so that the form which communication takes is not of great importance. After all, research has to do with facts and these are supposed to be independent of the form in which they are presented. Yet research is a human activity, which takes place within a particular social and cultural framework, and researchers, too, are members of a particular society and culture.[1] Or as the cultural theorist Robert Young puts it:

> [...] the progress of science is not a rational, deductive affair, confined to the realm of idea, but a human, institutionalised process. (1996: 198)

It would be extremely unusual if this were to have no effect on the form which research usually takes, which is language.

---

1 I distinguish here between "society" and "culture". By "society" I mean a particular grouping of people. "Culture" I take to be the accepted ways in which people behave within a group. There may therefore be many cultures within a given society.

The way we use language in its academic function is shaped by the position of research and of researchers in our particular society and culture, and by the way researchers see themselves within this society and culture. For example, if research as a pursuit and its findings are perceived as something inappropriate to the mass of the population, and if research is regarded as an elite activity and researchers revered as 'gods in white coats' *(Götter in weiß)*, then it is likely that this will be reflected in the kind of language used. In such a society, there might be comparatively little effort made to present research findings in a way that they are comprehensible to the general population. By writing in a manner that the vast majority of citizens cannot understand their material, researchers are able support and confirm their power (in the sense that superior knowledge is power) over others. They can do this either by writing in another language, as most scholars in Europe did up to the 18th century, or by conceiving and applying a form of the same language which differs so much from everyday language that comprehension becomes difficult. Research, therefore, is not just about content, but also about form.

2. Problems with content within cultures

If research were really solely concerned with content, and were indeed largely independent of form, then academic fakes would not exist, since a fake consists of nonsensical, even farcical, content packaged in such a convincing form that readers are wooed into accepting even nonsense as serious research. There are however countless cases of academic fakes in all branches of academic activity. One famous recent example concerned the publication of an article entitled 'Transgressing the Boundaries: Toward a Transformative Hermeneutics of Quantum Gravity' in the Spring/Summer 1996 issue of the noted journal of cultural and political analysis *Social Text*. The author was Alan D. Sokal, a professor of Physics at New York University. A few years ago, Sokal became annoyed at what he described as an "apparent decline in the standards of intellectual rigor in certain precincts of the American academic humanities" (Sokal 1996), and so decided to try what he called an experiment. Sokal faked an essay in cultural studies, writing a deliberate parody of how he perceived recent articles in the field; he summed up his article as "nonsense which sounded good". Nowhere in the paper, he wrote later, was there "anything resembling a logical sequence of thought; one finds only citations of authority, plays on words, strained analogies, and bald assertions" (Sokal 1996). Sokal could not believe his eyes when his calculated send-up was published in a highly-regarded journal.

Academic fakes demonstrate that in some fields academic publishing is a game in which the rules of academic communication count for more than content. Once would-be pranksters have mastered the lingo, the jargon and the text structure of a particular discipline and text type, it is possible for them to convince even insiders of their membership of the exclusive in-group of 'experts', even though their contribution has little worthwhile content. Keeping to the rules is enough to beguile people. Such embarrassing episodes as the Sokal hoax are the triumph of language over facts, and show us that in some cases, research is defined far more by form than by content.

3. Problems with form across cultures

The opposite situation from academic fakes also occurs: texts with valuable content are rejected because they do not conform to formal textual norms. The problem is that ideas about what constitutes the 'proper' form for scientific facts to take differ much across languages and cultures. This is where the real challenge for empirical linguistic research and pedagogy based on its findings lies, because there are a great many more non-native speakers unconsciously writing formally atypical, anomalous or non-standard English-language texts than there are smart-alec English native speakers attempting to fool the establishment.

The difficulties faced by professional researchers publishing in a foreign tongue have, however, not always been recognized, particularly those difficulties which persist after generally adequate command of the target language has been achieved. In 1979, Widdowson propounded his theory of the universality of academic discourse, according to which all researchers have a common culture, regardless of how dissimilar their individual origin. The appropriate passage reads thus:

> I assume that the concepts and procedures of scientific inquiry constitute a secondary cultural system which is independent of primary cultural systems associated with different societies. So although for example, a Japanese, and a Frenchman, have very different ways of life, beliefs, preconceptions, and so on deriving from the primary cultures of the societies they are members of, as scientists they have a common culture. In the same way, I take it that the discourse conventions which are used to communicate this common culture are independent of the particular linguistic means which are used to realize them. (Widdowson 1979: 51)

It was nearly ten years before studies of actual texts proved Widdowson's theory untenable. Research undertaken for example by the Australian linguist Clyne (1984, 1987) indicated that academic texts produced by speakers of even such comparatively similar languages as English and German display important differences at the macro- and microstructural levels. Importantly, these differences influence the way these texts, and the ideas contained within them, are received by readers. Clyne's groundbreaking work was based on a study in which he examined 26 English- and 26 German-language academic articles from the fields of sociology and linguistics. Subsequent work undertaken on different language combinations, and examining texts from different disciplines (see for example the summary in Connor 1996: 28–55) has supported Clyne's finding that the cultural origin of each researcher leaves a distinct mark on the work he or she produces.

4. Dilemmas and problems faced by non-native speaker researchers

Studies of academic discourse across cultures have been carried out against the background of dramatic changes in the linguistic situation of the international academic community. Longitudinal studies such as that by Tsunoda (1983) of the languages employed in academic publications show us that, at the beginning of last century, French and German were used just as frequently as English as a language of research. The situation is now radically different, as a statistical analysis of the largest discipline-specific bibliographic databases in both the natural sciences and the humanities, undertaken by Ammon, confirms:

Table 3.1 Language of natural science publications as a percentage of total publications 1980–1996 (data from Ammon 1998: 152)

	1980	1984	1988	1992	1996
English	74.6	77.1	80.5	87.2	90.7
French	3.1	2.4	2.4	1.6	1.3
German	3.5	3.3	2.9	1.6	1.2
Russian	10.8	9.2	6.9	3.9	2.1
Japanese	2.3	2.5	2.1	2.3	1.7

Table 3.2 Language of social science and humanities publications as a percentage of total publications 1974–1995 (data from Ammon 1998: 167)

	1974	1978	1982	1986	1990	1995
English	66.6	69.1	69.9	70.6	71.7	82.5
French	6.8	6.6	5.9	5.9	5.9	5.9
German	8.0	5.2	6.0	5.4	5.7	4.1
Spanish	3.8	3.6	3.6	4.0	3.8	2.2

This means that researchers of non-English speaking backgrounds are currently under a great deal of pressure to publish in English rather than in their mother tongue. As an English-speaker linguist summarizes:

> For a researcher to publish in a language other than English therefore is increasingly to cut herself off from the worldwide community of researchers who publish in English. The work may then be ignored simply because it is published in a language unknown to the rest of the world. (Wood 1997)

This sentiment is shared by non-native speaker researchers: Ammon (1993: 21) commented that researchers with other mother tongues have "basically no other choice"[2] but

---

2 "letztlich kaum eine andere Wahl" [all translations by TS]

to compose their publications in English if they want to be internationally noticed. The general sentiment among much of the non-native-speaking academic community seems to be that, if you wish to be heard, you have to say things in English. In a detailed survey of the working habits and attitudes of 2000 German researchers undertaken by Stickel in 1999, 81.1% of respondents were of the opinion that, in their particular discipline, publications written in German were seldom or definitely not regarded internationally (Stickel 2000: 135). Since no researcher likes being ignored, the trend towards ever more publications in English reinforces itself: the more researchers publish in English, the more they are forced to publish in English, for fear of being disregarded by the English-publishing majority (of which they are now a member). The drawback, as expressed by a Polish linguist, is clear:

> In an international discourse community founded on English, a non-native speaker of that language is disadvantaged from the very beginning. (Duszak 1997: 21)

5. Misunderstanding each other in the same language

We therefore have the unhappily undemocratic situation of researchers being effectively forced to write in English, which is difficult enough, not to mention time-consuming and often expensive (for a personal account, see Ammon 1989). To make matters worse, it is unfortunately not enough to speak the same language. Clyne observed twenty years ago that (although)

> German researchers are nowadays often competent in English at the phonological, lexical and morphosyntactic levels (Clyne 1984: 92)[3]

and the same could meanwhile be said of researchers from many other European and non-European nations, there remain dramatic problems with understanding.

This initially seems an outlandish proposition: how can it be possible for two people to misunderstand each other quite dramatically if they both speak excellent English? The problem lies at least partially in our lack of awareness of the problem. The majority of non-native speaker researchers would believe that once they have learnt the English language, they have no need to worry any more, yet the relationship between good English and a successful academic presentation is not necessarily so simple. Just as many native-speakers of English would have no idea how to construct a satisfactory academic paper, there are innumerable non-native speakers who, though their English language skills may be excellent, are writing papers which are unlikely to be accepted as adequate presentations.

Professional academics and researchers, and also many non-professional researchers or students, may well have an idea of what an academic text in their mother tongue should be like (in their own discipline). These ideas are usually unsystematic or vague,

---

3 "Deutschsprachige Wissenschaftler sind heutzutage auf phonologischer, lexikalischer und morphosyntaktischer Ebene häufig des Englischen mächtig."

and are based on many things, such as tuition received at school or university, or on years of familiarity with similar texts. It seems that these standards are generally applied to all the academic texts we read, whether in our mother tongue or in foreign languages. This means that, when we read texts which do not behave as we expect, misunderstandings can occur. Sometimes people feel that the argument of an article or book they are reading is somehow not 'logical', but ideas of what is logical and what is not differ from culture to culture. As Kaplan commented:

> Logic (in the popular, rather than the logician's sense of the word), which is the basis of rhetoric, is evolved out of a culture; it is not universal. (1966: 2)

The cultural relativity of academic discourse, however, appears to be forgotten, or disregarded, by researchers when reading material written by colleagues from a different cultural background:

> Some recent publications by important German researchers have been savagely criticised by English-speaking reviewers based on particular criteria of reader-friendliness, without the argument or theory being in any way deficient. "Laboured", "muddled", "long-winded" and "chaotic" are expressions which often appear. On the other hand, Germans often accuse English-speakers of producing texts that are superficial, essayistic and unscientific. (Clyne 1991: 376)[4]

Differences in preferred styles of academic communication can lead to harsh judgements being formed, and sometimes publicly expressed, not just about the form of the text – which is after all what is causing the annoyance – but also about the content, and sometimes even about the author's ability and character. Somewhat disturbing evidence for this can be found in reviews of academic publications. Here is an extract from an American historian's review of a folklore-studies monograph, which was written by a German researcher and translated into English by an American colleague:

> While the topic is extremely important, the book is a translation and its readability suffers from awkward sentence construction and the overly-frequent naming of German bureaucratic organizations. It is unfortunate that the monograph is rather poorly written and difficult to follow. The author jumps from describing individuals and outlining their careers in folklore to discussing political infighting among various contending folkloric groups. Had the monograph been more clearly written, it would serve well as yet another reminder of the Third Reich's subversion of scholarship. It would also be more accessible to a wider readership than the academic audience for whom it is obviously intended. (Deshmukh 1996)

The criticisms levelled after the initial qualification that "the book is a translation" are clearly not due to the fact that the book is a translation at all; the American researcher takes issue with features of the text structure and style, which are unlikely to have been changed by a translator. The American reviewer also criticizes the monograph for not being written more 'clearly' (whatever this may mean), which would have had the

---

[4] "Manche Neuerscheinungen bedeutender Deutscher sind von englischsprachigen Rezensenten aufgrund bestimmter Kriterien der Lesbarkeit vernichtend kritisiert worden, ohne dass die Theorie oder das Argument mangelhaft war. 'Schwerfällig', 'konfus', 'weitschweifig' und 'chaotisch' sind Ausdrücke, die häufig vorkommen. Andererseits wird Englischsprachigen von Deutschen oft vorgeworfen, dass sich ihre Texte oberflächlich, essayistisch und unwissenschaftlich lesen."

desirable side-effect of rendering the monograph more accessible to a wider readership. It is possible, however, that such accessibility was neither wished nor aimed at by the German author. The ability to write for a wider or general audience, which is unthinkingly praised by this American researcher, is generally regarded as a shortcoming in German academic texts, indicative of a deficiency in the written style or an inability to adopt the correct academic tone. While popular research publications constitute a valued, and even admired, academic pursuit in many English-speaking countries, the appropriate adjective in German, *populärwissenschaftlich*, is nearly always derogatory.[5] It is therefore possible that the German researcher is here being criticized for failing to achieve something he/she would never even wish to aim at. The criticism that the monograph is "difficult to follow" – if we accept this subjective judgement at face value – may also be due to a cultural misunderstanding. A recent contrastive study suggests that German and English-speaking authors use text-commenting devices in different ways and for different purposes, a situation which the authors state

> can have far-reaching consequences for the perception and assessment of an academic text which is sometimes hard to separate from the research it is reporting on. (Fandrych and Graefen 2002: 36)

It is likely that this American reviewer, accustomed to a particular type and use of text-commenting devices, may indeed find texts written by German researchers difficult to follow. However, the reviewer automatically interprets what is probably a cultural difference in preferred ways of easing text comprehension as a fault on the part of the German author.

A rather more extreme example can be found in an Austrian researcher's review of a collection of German-language political science essays, to which non-native speakers also contributed:

> One contribution has not yet been mentioned by me: that of X [a Hungarian political scientist]. This is the contribution I referred to previously as the regrettably negative exception [to the generally high quality of the collection]. Written in a simply indescribably superficial, prattling tone, either badly written or incredibly poorly translated, in bad style and with irritating grammatical errors, this contribution is simply out of place. Was it accepted only because a participant from a non-EU country meant extra funding was brought in? An embarrassing case, especially since the author is both a professor and a research director, and refers to "numerous German, English and French publications". (Handl 2003)[6]

---

5 There is a long tradition in English-speaking countries of famous researchers publishing popular science books and articles alongside their 'serious' academic contributions: one thinks of academics such as Bertrand Russell, Douglas R. Hofstadter or Stephen Jay Gould, as well as countless other examples. Such publications are often praised by other academics for their skill in condensing, simplifying and explaining complex content for the interested layperson, and many have become best-sellers.

6 "Ein Beitrag ist von mir noch nicht erwähnt worden: der von X. Es ist jener, den ich eingangs die bedauerliche negative Ausnahme nannte. In einem schier unsäglichen, oberflächlichen, geschwätzigen Ton, entweder schlecht geschrieben oder höchst mangelhaft übersetzt, in schlechtem Stil und irritierend fehlerhafter Grammatik, ist dieser Beitrag fehl am Platz. Hat man ihn nur aufgenommen, weil ein Teilnehmer aus einem Nicht-EU-Land zusätzliche Fördermittel einbrachte? Eine Peinlichkeit, auch oder gerade, weil der Autor Professor sowie wissenschaftlicher Direktor ist und er auf 'zahlreiche deutsch-, englisch- und französischsprachige Publikationen' verweist."

The same review continues, in a footnote:

> The style resembles that of an Eastern-bloc bureaucrat such as those familiar from the 60s, with inappropriate pathos. The stereotypical repetition of clichés such as "this is self-explanatory", the rhetorical questions, which artificially name points of view or problems, for which there is no proof, in order to then contrast them with arguments, tires and alienates the reader. (Handl 2003)[7]

The insinuation that X – whose name I have deliberately excised – was included in the volume only as a token foreigner in order to pull in extra funding, is demeaning. The reviewer does not make clear what is meant by an "indescribably superficial, prattling tone", but, since the author is a professor at a respectable Hungarian university, one can assume that the article is written in a tone acceptable in the academic discourse of his culture. As for the "stereotypical repetition of clichés" and apparently annoying rhetorical questions, the issue appears to be whether such rhetorical figures and devices belong in an academic text. The German reviewer strongly believes they do not; the Hungarian author appears to believe they do.[8] As in the review above, features which could well be due to cultural differences are automatically defined as a fault on the part of the foreign author. And in all this, there is not a single comment relating to the CONTENT of the piece, not even the vaguest indication of its topic.

Until we know roughly what each culture defines as an adequate academic presentation, we are left alone with our vague inklings and suspicions. This means that non-native speakers are essentially at the mercy of such ungracious – and ultimately inappropriate – native-speaker judgements. In the absence of empirically sound studies of differences in academic discourse norms across cultures, the help that foreign language teachers can offer in such situations is also limited.

6. Moving away from "vague inklings" to linguistic research: two famous hypotheses

Since linguists are not satisfied with vague inklings, they have tried to pin down and represent the differences between cultures in academic traditions and styles. The more or less systematic study of structural differences in academic texts produced by members of different cultures is based upon a now famous 1966 article by Kaplan entitled "Cultural thought patterns in inter-cultural education". He examined nearly 600 student papers, and noted that authors from different cultural and linguistic backgrounds organized paragraphs differently. He therefore postulated that they also organize their thoughts

---

[7] "Der Stil ähnelt dem Ostbürokratenton, wie man ihn aus den Sechzigerjahren kennt, mit unangebrachtem Pathos. Die stereotype Wiederholung von Floskeln wie 'das verseht sich von selbst', die rhetorischen Fragen, die artifiziell Positionen oder Probleme nennen, für die es keinen Beleg gibt, um dann daran Argumentationen zu kontrastieren, ermüdet und befremdet."

[8] Of course, whether this one German researcher and one Hungarian author are representative of their respective culture's preferences as regards academic texts is an entirely different matter on which, in the absence of any research on this subject, I cannot offer an opinion. The point is that, in cases of doubt, a reviewer should exercise caution in condemning the work of a foreign colleague on the basis of presentation alone.

and arguments differently. The article was accompanied by a memorable graphic representation of different national types of discourse simeture, in which "Semitic" refers to Arabic and Hebrew-speaking authors, "Oriental" to Chinese and Korean but not Japanese and "Romance" to Spanish, Portuguese and French authors.

Kaplan later freely acknowledged that there were "serious flaws" in his "initial articulation of the notion of CR [contrastive rhetoric]"; he summarized them thus:

> The 1966 article contrasted professional writing by native speakers with student writing by second-language learners; it did not control for topic, for genre, or for length. It was ethnocentric because it looked at the writing of speakers of languages other than English from the perspective of English; it did not look at the perception of English or other languages by speakers of languages other than English (although it recommended such research). It was, in fact, based on an admittedly relatively poor research design. (Kaplan 2000: 83)

To this catalogue one could add the observation that the representation of English paragraph structure as a straight line is a value judgement, and a culturally relative one at that. When contrasted with the faintly ridiculous Oriental circle (an English speaker is reminded of an argument "going round in circles") and dotty Russian detours, the English straight line is unfortunately reminiscent of claims by members of many different cultures that their language is the most logical, clear and beautiful. I am thinking here of countless examples through the ages, from the Ancient Greeks to Antoine de Rivarol:

> French, by unique privilege, has remained faithful to direct ordering, as if it were pure reason, and the ordering can be concealed through the most varied movements and all sorts of stylistic devices, but it must always be present. (Rivarol 1783/1998: 72)[9]

to the modern-day linguistic nationalism found for example in the Balkans, Turkey and Sri Lanka.

The second famous contribution in this area, by the Norwegian self-titled 'peace researcher' Galtung[10], is entitled "Structure, culture, and intellectual style: An essay comparing saxonic, teutonic, gallic and nipponic approaches" (Galtung 1981). Galtung's article, in contrast to Kaplan's, has no empirical basis. The author describes his contribution as being based on "intuitions and experience during many years of travels and stays in various intellectual climates around the world" (Galtung 1981: 817). The essay makes for entertaining reading, and is in no way inferior to Kaplan's in creative representation (see Galtung 1981: 839).

It is extremely difficult to take Galtung's essay seriously, a possibility the author himself appears to have recognized, for Galtung warns readers that

> the figures should not be taken too seriously [...] but they do contrast the very small saxonic pyramids, built on solid empirical ground, the gigantic teutonic pyramidal constructions covering so much, the dialectical tension in the gallic form of presentation and the vague attempts at chaining data together in what might become an emerging nipponic style based on the Bhuddist wheel. (Galtung 1981: 839)

This extract speaks for itself.

---

9 "Le français, par un privilège unique, est seul resté fidèle à l'ordre direct, comme s'il était tout raison, et on a beau par les mouvements les plus variés et toutes les ressources du style, déguiser cet ordre, il faut toujours qu'il existe."
10 Johan Galtung now lectures at the 'Transcend Peace University', which is part of the 'Transcend Peace University Global Centre' in Cluj, Romania.

Kaplan's article, however, remains still much quoted, and constitutes the founding contribution to the discipline of contrastive rhetoric. It is relatively easy to find texts which conform to Kaplan's expectations – for example, Arabic-language texts which contain elaborate parallelisms – because Kaplan's theses contain little specific detail. It is in fact similarly easy to find English texts which contain parallelisms, though difficult to conclude what influence such a stylistic device has on a macro-structural feature such as linear thematic progression. In any case, since there is no explanation of how linearity could be measured and compared in actual texts produced by members of different cultures, it is most difficult to test Kaplan's hypotheses. It is also impossible to teach them.

7. Recent contrastive studies of academic discourse

Since Kaplan's 1966 article, there has been ever more interest in variation in academic discourse across cultures and therefore an ever greater number of studies examining the phenomenon in languages from Arabic to Czech and Finnish. For the purposes of this article, however, the discussion is restricted to studies concerned with English and German. Recent contrastive work on academic discourse in these two languages is unfortunately marred by four main difficulties, which concern analytic scope, data selection, sample size and methodology.

First, most work already undertaken examines only very small or isolated features of academic discourse, such as Busch-Lauer's work on the length of selected *Teiltextsegmente* (parts of texts), Kreutz and Harres's study on hedging, Fandrych and Graefen's project on speech act verbs or Clyne's research into propositional networks. While this is understandable, given that any one researcher has only limited resources, it makes it virtually impossible to gain an overview of the characteristics of any particular text type as a whole. This is however precisely what is required before teaching implications can be drawn.

Second, many studies are marred by eccentric text-selection processes. One researcher admits to having chosen the disciplines that interest him personally, while a recent study relies upon an unmatched corpus of 19 German and 17 English-language research articles drawn from roughly 17 different disciplines (Fandrych and Graefen 2002). This calls the conclusions posited in such studies into question. If such important variables as discipline are not controlled for in the data basis, one cannot distinguish between differences due to the variable culture as opposed to the variable discipline. Even studies which are restricted to two or three disciplines rarely indicate why these disciplines were selected. Any implications formulated for foreign language teaching (though the market for the latter in the academic arena is limited) based upon such work must therefore be treated with great caution.

The third problem which recurs in newer studies concerns corpus size. Some recent studies make broad generalizations about academic discourse in English and German, despite the fact that they are based on corpora of only four (Buhl 1999) or six texts each (Baumann 1998), and these from unrelated disciplines. As we have seen above, one of the most famous contributions in this area, the 1981 essay by Galtung, dispenses with any empirical basis altogether, though it comes to wild conclusions all the same. Again, as for the third difficulty, it is appropriate to exercise caution here as regards possible teaching recommendations.

The fourth and final difficulty characteristic of recent studies concerns the methodology. Two researchers politely refer to this as a "certain amount of disarray in the methodology of studies mounted to test [Kaplan's] claim" (Taylor and Chen 1991: 319). The important point is that the current lack of any reliable or conclusive methodological framework for contrastive studies of academic discourse makes comparison of the myriad conclusions nearly impossible. Where studies produce contradictory results – a likely scenario given the diversity of text types, disciplines and methodological approaches – the foreign language teacher has no criteria for choosing between them.

Research on English and German academic discourse, which is what we are concerned with here, has focussed on academic texts – usually research articles – taken from a dizzying array of disciplines, from sociology, linguistics and economics (Clyne 1984, 1987) to mechanical engineering, economics and linguistics (Oldenburg 1992), psychoanalysis (Gerzymisch-Arbogast 1997), physics and popular science (Buhl 1999), ancient and modern history, communication science and management (Baumann 1998) and sociology and nutritional science (Hutz 2001). The trouble here, as indicated in the second point above, is that preferred use of language and text structure can differ widely across disciplines and even sub-disciplines. Taylor and Chen suggested that

> the discourse structures in social science of some Anglo-American Marxists writing in English might be much closer to those of a German Marxist writing in German than to those of an Anglo-American liberal empiricist in either language (Taylor and Chen 1991: 321)

an assumption then confirmed by their data (introductions to 31 academic papers in four related disciplines). "Overall", the authors conclude, "there appears to be a strong disciplinary effect on discourse structure", and later:

> an important aspect of our findings is that there is considerable difference between papers, not on national lines but rather with respect to disciplinary differences. (Taylor and Chen 1991: 329, 332)

Busch-Lauer's analysis of German and English medical and linguistics articles also found significant differences between disciplines, which were independent of the origin of the author (Busch-Lauer 2001). The studies listed above, which compare academic texts from such eclectic combinations of disciplines, therefore emerge to be highly problematic. Many of the differences posited as being due to putative cultural differences may in fact be due to discipline-specific conventions.

8. Future contrastive studies and teaching implications

The primary concern for future contrastive studies of academic discourse, if they are to be considered for teaching purposes, must be a solid empirical basis. This means that future corpora must strive to compare texts which are as similar as possible across the cultures being examined. This is of course a caveat which applies to all studies, not just those examining English and German language texts.

First, unmatched collections of different text types should not be compared with each other. In practice, this probably means that studies should be restricted to one text type. Research articles, abstracts, book reviews, grant proposals and forwards in monographs are some examples of academic text types that could be examined with a view to differences across cultures, whereas full scholarly monographs are generally too long to allow a close analysis. Second, particularly in the case of research articles, studies would be most useful either if restricted to a single discipline, or containing matched subcorpora of such. Third, if at all possible, attention should also be paid to sub-discipline; an article by a generative linguist and an eco-linguist are both counted as belonging to the same discipline, yet it is obvious even to a non-linguist that the representation of academic facts within them is of a different nature. This will influence the results of studies that do not control for this variable.

Other variables which might usefully be considered are gender and age: it is likely that a female graduate student will write in a different style from an elderly male professor acknowledged as a leader in a particular field. Within languages, it may also be helpful to distinguish between major varieties: Duszak (1997) for example groups all English-speakers together as representatives of an "Anglo-American" style, as do Taylor and Chen (1991), but there may in fact be significant differences in the preferred academic style and text structure of British and American (not to mention Australian, Canadian, South African, etc.) researchers, as Clyne warned (1987: 215–216):

> we cannot take it for granted that discourse structures are the same for Americans, British and Australians or for East and West Germans, Austrians and Swiss.

Future studies should ideally take this into account.

The number of texts selected will depend on the resources available to each particular study. As in all branches of empirical research, it is uncommonly difficult to dictate what sample size will be sufficient. For such a sensitive area of research as the characterization of cultures and cultural preferences, the more texts examined the better. Whether any text selection can be truly representative is a complex question not to be examined here (for a meticulous discussion, which concludes that the question is ultimately unanswerable, see Adamzik, 1998). Certainly, four texts controlled for none of the above factors can have less claim to represent a culture than a balanced collection of 100 or more texts.

While studies of student papers may continue to be of interest for general language teaching, future studies would be of most use for specialist language pedagogy if they were based on texts written by professional language users, the reason being that this is what most people using a foreign language (overwhelmingly English) for academic communication are. The language use, aims and requirements of non-native speaker professional researchers employing English (or in some cases perhaps German) as an academic lingua franca are not comparable to those of non-professional learners or students. For teaching purposes, it would be useful to have contrastive analyses of both texts written in different languages by native-speakers and of text production in the same language by both native and non-native speakers. Another factor too often ignored in recent studies is that it is likely that academic discourse norms change over time: it is therefore advisable for studies to restrict their analyses to texts written at approximately the same time, certainly not over a span of over 50 years, as is the case in one recent study (Hutz 2001).

The last point to be made regarding ways of optimizing the pedagogical usefulness of future studies concerns the nature of the analysis conducted. Most phenomena encountered in intercultural research into academic discourse cannot be adequately represented by purely quantitative analysis. Tables of figures cannot do justice to these texts as discourse wholes, which are not just collections of passive or active sentences or any other quantifiable grammatical feature. The important questions, as Adamzik (1998: 114) points out, are much more when and why specific features – grammatical as well as textual – occur, and how these are employed by different authors for different purposes in different types of texts.

My own work seeks to address these concerns. It is based on a corpus of 100 English and German language research articles, 25 by British, 25 by American and 50 by German authors, all of whom are native speakers of the language/variety they are writing. The corpus contains ten articles each from the following five disciplines: folklore, history, philosophy, literary studies and English/German linguistics. The articles are taken from high-prestige journals, and the majority was published in 2002 and 2003, though there are a few from 1997 and 1999, where technical constraints dictated this. The corpus is balanced for author gender and subdiscipline.

The analysis concentrates on phenomena such as meta-communication and hedging, both of which cover a large variety of discourse strategies and features, while also examining a range of other features such as intertextuality, introduction and variation of technical terms, use of comparisons, metaphors and examples, concretizations and redundancy. In contrast to earlier work undertaken by Clyne (1984, 1987), which examined overarching discourse features such as propositional networks in English and German academic texts, the study concerns itself with many micro-structural features of discourse not previously examined with regard to cultural differences. The expectation is that it is not only at the level of macro-structure that English and German academic texts display significant differences, which are of import for the reception and production of texts written by German researchers in English for an international audience.

9. Bridging the gap between English-language competence and academic success in English

It is possible that future studies, with a more solid data basis and perhaps more standardized or accepted methodology, will be able to offer practicable suggestions for non-native speakers of English and their teachers. It is however not clear whether these suggestions should be implemented.

Given that the situation is that researchers from all over the world are now communicating in English, and that we are now aware that these researchers have differing, sometimes even mutually exclusive, conceptions and definitions of 'good, logical' structure and style in academic texts, questions about the ownership of academic English arise, which parallel those in the general debate on ownership of English as an international (i.e. post-national) language. This means that Kaplan's initial assertion that "each language and each culture has a paragraph order unique to itself, and part of the learning of a particular language is the mastering of its logical system" (Kaplan 1966: 14) cannot be left unchallenged. The opposite position is represented by Clyne, who maintains that "such pragmatic features are so closely connected with the own culture and individual personality that it would not be appropriate to expect people to adjust to foreign norms" (Clyne 1993: 4). The central question, however, is not whether it is reasonable to expect non-native speakers to adjust to native-speaker norms (once we know what these are, that is), but whether native-speakers can surrender their expectation for non-native speakers to do so. At present, there is little evidence of tolerance on the part of native-speakers for texts which do not meet their expectations. One native-speaker linguist asserts that

> international users of scientific English should have the right to determine the type of English deemed acceptable or standard in that community. Scientists should determine that regardless of their native language. [...] The owners of international scientific English should be international scientists not Englishmen or Americans. (Wood 1997)

yet this proclaimed right is of little actual use it if is constantly flouted by native-speaker journal editors and reviewers.

For this reason, many non-native speaker researchers adopt a more prosaic, cautious tone. One German linguist, made aware by personal experience of the harshness with which native-speakers often enforce native textual norms, warns of the difficulties that face non-native researchers attempting to publish in an academic world dominated by native-speakers:

> Those who, after more or less extensive language training, try to cope by themselves and whose work is actually received by a publisher, can be sure of receiving from the Anglo-Saxon world, which has the say in science, similar reactions [to those I have experienced] [...] only these will most likely never reach their ears. The effect of a contribution on many readers is compromised by unavoidable deviations from native-speaker norms. (Ammon 1989: 268)[11]

It is doubtful whether non-native speakers, especially those such as Ammon who have already been publicly subject to unfavourable native-speaker judgements, would support

---

11 "Wer aufgrund mehr oder weniger ausgiebiger Sprachstudien ganz auf eigene Faust zurecht zu kommen sucht und dessen Beitrag dann auch tatsächlich gedruckt wird, kann sich in der wissenschaftlich tonangebenden angelsächsischen Welt auf ähnliche Reaktionen verlassen [...]; nur dürften sie ihm in aller Regel nicht zu Ohren kommen. Die Wirksamkeit seines Beitrags wird durch unvermeidliche Abweichungen von der muttersprachlichen Norm bei vielen Rezipienten gemindert."

Clyne and wish to retain the text structure of their mother tongue even when writing in English. That they often do so cannot be taken as evidence of any deliberate decision.

Ideally, the novel situation represented by the current international status of English for academic communication would be accompanied by a co-operative spirit in forging new, post-national norms according to discipline- and audience-specific needs. At the very least, one could hope for some cooperation in negotiating what Duszak calls "acceptability thresholds" (1997: 19) for English-language texts by speakers from different cultural backgrounds. Duszak warns that

> [...] negotiation of preferred levels of interactivity in academic texts is one of the most pressing needs facing the process of internationalization of scholarship (1997: 19)

yet leaves one unenlightened as to how and where such negotiation could take place. Eventually, the English native-speaker gatekeepers of academic discourse will have to adjust to the changed international reality of English as the worldwide language of research and start to relax their often intolerant attitudes to texts which differ from their expectations, if for no other reason than that the number of non-native speakers is continually increasing, and these people constitute a huge market for academic publications. It is doubtful whether non-native speakers would continue to purchase journals in which none of their colleagues is represented, and in which work by members of their culture is either ignored or made risible. One suspects however that this process of adjustment may take rather a long time.

Bibliography

Adamzik, K. 1998. Methodische Probleme kontrastiver Textsortenstudien. In: Dannenberg and Niederhauser 1998. 103–129.

Ammon, U. 1989. Die Schwierigkeiten der deutschen Sprachgemeinschaft aufgrund der Dominanz der englischen Sprache. *Zeitschrift für Sprachwissenschaft* 8 (2). 257–272.

Ammon, U. 1993. Wissenschaftssprache: Kein Grund zur Resignation ... aber die goldenen Zeiten der Wissenschafts-Sprache Deutsch sind vorbei. *Deutsche Universitätszeitung* 18 (17th September). 20–22.

Ammon, U. 1998. *Ist Deutsch noch internationale Wissenschaftssprache? Englisch auch für die Hochschullehre in den deutschsprachigen Ländern*. Berlin: de Gruyter.

Baumann, K.-D. 1998. Die sprachliche Realisierung von Wissensstrukturen in Fachtexten des Englischen und Deutschen. In: Dannenberg and Niederhauser 1998. 299–317.

Buhl, S. 1999. Gestaltungsprinzipien wissenschaftlicher Texte im Sprachenpaarvergleich Deutsch – Englisch am Beispiel von Texten Einsteins und Russells zur Relativitätstheorie. In: Gerzymisch-Arbogast, H. (ed.), *Wege der Übersetzungs- und Dolmetschforschung*. Tübingen: Gunter Narr, 117–141.

Busch-Lauer, A. I. 2001. Kulturspezifik in englischen und deutschen Originaltexten – Medizin und Linguistik im Vergleich. In: Fix, Habscheid and Klein 2001. 51–69.

Clyne, M. 1984. Wissenschaftliche Texte Englisch- und Deutschsprachiger: Textstrukturelle Vergleiche. *Studium Linguistik* 15. 92–97.

Clyne, M. 1987. Cultural Differences in the Organization of Academic Texts – English and German. *Journal of Pragmatics* 11. 211–247.

Clyne, M. 1991. Zu kulturellen Unterschieden in der Produktion und Wahrnehmung englischer und deutscher wissenschaftlicher Texte. *Info DaF* 18 (4). 376–383.

Clyne, M. 1993. Pragmatik, Textstruktur und kulturelle Werte – eine interkulturelle Perspektive. In: Schröder, H. (ed.), *Fachtextpragmatik*. Tübingen: Gunther Narr. 3–18.

Connor, U. 1996. *Contrastive Rhetoric: Cross-cultural aspects of second-language writing.* Cambridge: Cambridge University Press.

Dannenberg, L. and Niederhauser, J. (eds.). 1998. *Darstellungsformen der Wissenschaften im Kontrast. Aspekte der Methodik, Theorie und Empirie.* Tübingen: Gunter Narr.

Deshmukh, M. F. 1996. Review of: Hannjost Lixfeld, Folklore and Fascism: The Reich Institute for German Volkskunde, Bloomington: Indiana University Press, 1994. [Retrieved 10.7.03 from the World Wide Web: http://www.ess.uwe.ac.uk/genocide/reviewstr10.htm].

Duszak, A. (ed.) 1997. *Culture and Styles of Academic Discourse.* Berlin: Mouton de Gruyter.

Fandrych, C. and Graefen, G. 2002. Text commenting devices in German and English academic articles. *Multilingua* 21. 17–43.

Fix, U., Habscheid, S. and Klein, J. (eds.). 2001. *Zur Kulturspezifik von Textsorten.* Tübingen: Stauffenburg.

Friedensgespräche in Nepal vorerst gescheitert. *Badische Zeitung.* 22.4.03, 4.

Galtung, J. 1981. Structure, culture, and intellectual style: An essay comparing saxonic, teutonic, gallic and nipponic approaches. *Social Science Information* 20–6. 817–856.

Gerzymisch-Arbogast, H. 1997. Der Leserbezug in Sigmund Freuds psychoanalytischen Schriften im Spiegel der englischen Übersetzungen. In: Wotjak, G. and Schmidt, H. (eds.), *Modelle der Translation – Models of Translation.* Frankfurt am Main: Vervuert. 231–233.

Handl, H. L. 2003. Universitäten in der Zivilgesellschaft. Review of: Emil Brix, Jürgen Nautz (ed.), Universitäten in der Zivilgesellschaft, Wien: Passagen, 2002. Retrieved 20.6.04 from the World Wide Web: http://www.snag.at/zg_uni.htm

Hutz, M. 2001. Insgesamt muss ich leider zu einem ungünstigen Urteil kommen: zur Kulturspezifik wissenschaftlicher Rezensionen im Deutschen und Englischen. In: Fix, Habscheid and Klein 2001. 109–130.

Kaplan, R. P. 1966. Cultural Thought Patterns in Inter-Cultural Education. *Language Learning* 16. 1–20.

Kaplan, R. P. 2000. Contrastive rhetoric and discourse analysis: who writes what to whom? In what circumstances? In: Sarangi, S. and Coulthard, M. (eds.), *Discourse and Social Life.* London: Pearson. 82–102.

Kreutz, H. and Harres, A. 1997. Some observations on the distribution and function of hedging in German and English academic writing. In: Duszak, A. (ed.), *Culture and Styles of Academic Discourse.* Berlin: Mouton de Gruyter. 181–201.

Oldenburg, H. 1992. *Angewandte Fachtextlinguistik – 'Conclusions' und Zusammenfassungen.* Tübingen: Gunther Narr.

de Rivarol, A. 1783/1998. *L'universalité de la langue française.* Paris: Arléa.

Sokal, A. 1996. A physicist experiments with cultural studies. *Lingua Franca.* 62–64. [Retrieved 27.04.03 from the World Wide Web: http://physics.nyu.edu/faculty/sokal/lingua_franca_v4/lingua_franca_v4.html].

Stickel, G. 2000. Deutsch als Wissenschaftssprache an außeruniversitären Forschungsinstituten. In: Debus, F., Krollmann, F. and Pörksen, U. (eds.), *Deutsch als Wissenschaftssprache im 20. Jahrhundert. Vorträge des Internationalen Symposions vom 18./19. Januar 2000.* Mainz: Akademie der Wissenschaften und der Literatur. 125–142.

Taylor, G. and Chen T. 1991. Linguistic, cultural and subcultural issues in contrastive discourse analysis: Anglo-American and Chinese scientific texts. *Applied Linguistics* 12/3. 319–336.

Tsunoda, M. 1983. Les langues internationales dans les publications scientifiques et techniques. *Sophia Linguistica.* 144–155.

Widdowson, H. G. 1979. *Explorations in Applied Linguistics.* Oxford: Oxford University Press.

Wood, A. 1997. International scientific English: some thoughts on science, language and ownership. *Science Tribune.* [Retrieved 2.11.02 from the World Wide Web: http://www.tribunes.com/tribune/art97/wooda.htm].

Young, R. E. 1996. *Intercultural Communication: pragmatics, genealogy, deconstruction.* Clevedon: Multilingual Matters.

Cross-language homonymy and polysemy: a semantic view of "false friends"

D. J. Allerton and Judith Wieser

It seems reasonable to take it for granted that speakers who operate in more than one language or dialect may, under the influence of their other language(s), produce linguistic patterns not typically used by monolingual speakers. Although opinions differ on the importance of this phenomenon, its existence seems beyond doubt. In this contribution it will be referred to by the rather unfashionable but unambiguous term "interference". Linguistic interference, in this sense, can be found at a minimum of three distinct levels, i.e. phonological, lexical and grammatical (although the grammatical level will not concern us here). As regards the systematic kinds of interference, it is worth bearing in mind Weinreich's (1968: 18–19) categorization of non-correspondence types between items in a system into cases of ITEM SUBSTITUTION (i.e. treating rough equivalence as perfect equivalence), UNDERDIFFERENTIATION (i.e. failing to make a distinction made in the target language) and OVERDIFFERENTIATION (i.e. insisting on making a superfluous distinction because it is made in the first language). This distinction is particularly relevant at the phonological and lexical levels.

At the phonological level there can be interference between any aspects of a phonological system: within the consonant and vowel systems it may happen that phonemes are given a deviant phonetic value, or that a phonemic distinction is not made, or again that a superfluous phonetic distinction is made (as when German-speaking learners of English regularly pronounce English /ɪ/ with widely spread lips, to distinguish it (irrelevantly) from German /ʏ/ as in *Hütte*, although in lip-rounded contexts (e.g. *wish, witch*) English has a pronunciation much closer to /ʏ/). In a similar way there can be interference between the stress patterning of words, or in the area of the phonotactic patterns of words. Then in phrase phonology we find conflicting patterns of consonant assimilation, of vowel and consonant elision, of liaison phenomena, while in sentence phonology differing intonation patterns can influence each other.

At the lexical level both underdifferentiation and overdifferentiation are found: English has only one word *screen* corresponding to a number of German words, including *Leinwand* and *Bildschirm*, while German has only one word *einschlafen* corresponding to the three English complex lexemes *fall asleep, get to sleep* and *go to sleep*. In such cases native speakers of the language with just one lexical item may tend to underdifferentiate by using just one of the two or more words of the other language or by using two (or more) words indiscriminately. Speakers of the language with two or more lexical items may be tempted to overdifferentiate by seeking artificial ways of making a distinction that is superfluous in the other language (as when an English-speaking user of German insists on saying *meine Ehefrau* rather than *meine Frau* to make it clear that he means 'my wife' and not 'my woman'). Most common of all is item substitution, i.e. when words in different languages have a rough correspondence in meaning, and there is a temptation for the user of two languages to simplify and assume a perfect equivalence. The English word *acquaintance* and the German word *Bekannte(r)* correspond in the majority of cases, but the German word has a wider use than the English one and sometimes corresponds to English *friend*.

The lexical, phonological and grammatical levels of interference involve linguistic systems. But in addition every language has another vital aspect, i.e. the way its phonological and lexical systems are connected, in other words, the particular phonological sequences that are used to represent lexemes. We could call this the PHONOLEXICAL CONNECTION. Generally speaking, languages have an arbitrary link at this level, as de Saussure emphasized. But to any speaker the L1 connections always seem the most natural because they were learnt so early. Lexical items in the L2 often formally resemble items in the L1, even though they are not always semantically equivalent. Such resemblances may be phonological or graphemic or a combination of the two. This means that there can be a misleading formal resemblance, as between English *become* and German *bekommen* (roughly 'receive'): apparent "friends" are actually "false friends". On the other hand, there are many "true friends" (Helliwell 1989: 4) that not only look or sound similar, but also roughly correspond in their meaning (main senses), such as German *Milch* and English *milk*[1]. These true friends are often etymologically related (cognates). This is also the case for many false friends, and their common origin may partly explain their similar form. The criterion of etymological relatedness has to be kept in mind when examining interlingual relations between closely related languages, such as English and German. Yet we do not consider it a necessary condition for false friends because there are false friends that are not cognates, but merely happen to have a similar form.[2]

Following the traditional definition, lexico-semantic false friends are interlingual word pairs that exhibit a high degree of phonological or graphemic resemblance but do not correspond in their meaning. The phenomenon of false friends should be viewed in its relation to true friends. False friends that differ in one of their senses, but are otherwise partly equivalent (e.g. German *Mann* and English *man*) are said to be true friends at the same time. These partly equivalent terms are usually referred to as "partial" false friends. In contrast, there are "total" false friends, i.e. similar terms that have different

---

1 It goes without saying that it is a rarity to find a precise correspondence between all senses of two lexemes in different languages. But where there is an approximate cross-language correspondence between two lexemes, it is possible to think of the translation equivalents as "friends". What we have referred to as "true friends" might alternatively be called "evident friends". Where there are reasonable translation equivalents with totally different phonological or graphemic forms (as is usual between unrelated languages) we could speak of "concealed friends".
2 Lado (1957: 83) does not consider etymological relatedness to be a necessary condition for false friends, despite using the alternative term "deceptive cognates". Welna (1977:75) argues that "deceptive cognates" is a less appropriate term because it covers words "in which formal similarity is purely accidental", but the term itself suggests etymological relatedness. Such unrelated false friends still cause problems for learners, see Kroschewski (2000: 38).

meanings and would not be acceptable as translation equivalents, e.g. German *breit* and English *bright* (see Breitkreuz 1991: 12, Fanning 1992: 272; Gläser 1992: 282). However, some items traditionally referred to as total false friends, though not equivalent, are clearly semantically or even morphologically related. In addition, some terms classified as partial false friends are polysemous in one language, whereas others are homonymous and thus merely happen to have the same form. Consequently, this classification represents an oversimplification, because it conflates a number of criteria. In the discussion that follows we aim to present a more subtle classification on semantic grounds that keeps these criteria separate. For this purpose, we will only consider examples with phonetic and/or graphemic similarity.[3]

Looking at the overall set of correspondences between items in the two languages used by an individual speaker, it is possible to imagine the speaker operating with a compound (phono-)lexical system for the two languages, like Weinreich's "Type B" (1968: 9–10), rather than as operating with two totally independent linguistic systems, especially when dealing with cognates or interlexical homographs[4], as studies on bilingual access have shown (de Groot 2002: 53*f*). Viewing matters in this way, we might argue that the (partly) bilingual speaker is combining lexical items from two languages to produce a kind of cross-language lexical ambiguity, erroneously retrieving false friends in a non-selective way (like true friends) because of their similar form, at least in the initial stage of retrieval.

It might then be worth distinguishing two types of lexico-semantic false friends:

– cross-language homonymy, for cases when the two false friends are semantically unrelated and merely happen to have a similar form,
– cross-language polysemy, for cases when the two false friends are semantically related. This involves three main subtypes, which will be presented below.

In what follows, we will first examine these two possible relationships for false friends each in turn, giving examples of German-English false friend pairs (considering true friends and etymological relationship where necessary). In the second part, we will present preliminary findings from an empirical pilot study about the difficulties that German-speaking learners of English experience with different false friend types.

1. Cross-language homonymy

Let us imagine two lexemes, *p* and *q*, in the learner's first language (= language 1), which are semantically unrelated. Let us further assume that *p* and *q* correspond seman-

---

3 We will not consider examples of false friends due to "linguistic analogy", i.e. word pairs that make use of corresponding morphemes in a similar morphological structure, but are not necessarily phonetically very similar, e.g. *selbstbewusst – self-conscious, ausgesprochen – outspoken*. Cf. Breitkreuz (1991).
4 The term "interlexical homographs" refers to items from different languages that share the same orthographic form.

tically to *x* and *y* in a second language (= language 2), but that *q* also has a purely formal (i.e. phonetic-graphemic) resemblance to *x*. This potential interference situation could be regarded as a kind of "cross-language homonymy", which could be represented thus:

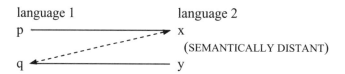

In this diagram (and in those following), lines represent equivalence in meaning, and arrows with a broken line stand for the choice of a word from the other language as a false friend, in the direction the arrow is pointing to. The German words are always given on the left (*p*, *q*), and their English translation equivalents on the right (*x*, *y*), but the diagrams can be read both ways. The classification code indicated in the left-hand corner of each diagram refers forward to the false friend types listed in Figure 4.1 on page 68 below in order to facilitate later identification.

An example of this situation, with German as the first language and English as the second, is the following:

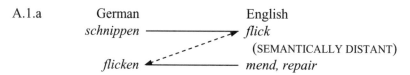

It is reasonable to call this situation "cross-language homonymy"[5] whenever the two wrongly connected items have a purely phonological or graphemic resemblance, with virtually no semantic connection, but they will probably not occur to us as candidates unless they are of the same basic word class. In situations like this the possibilities for interference are symmetrical: a foreign language learner coming from either direction might easily use the foreign word with the wrong meaning, that of its false friend in the L1. This is a frequently occurring false friend type.

If there is some semantic feature shared by the false friends, then we have moved one step in the direction of cross-language polysemy rather than cross-language homonymy. Consider a case like:

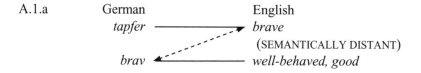

---

5 The term "interlingual homonym" has been used especially by Slavist lexicographers, see the website by Daniel Bunčić at <http://www.uni-bonn.de/~dbuncic/staatsarb/>, last visited on 23.6.2004.

Presumably English *brave* and German *brav* share at least the one semantic feature of what we might term 'approved quality'; that feature would not be quite enough for us to regard the two items as polysemically linked.[6] Again the likely consequences are symmetrical: the German-speaking learner of English might say *brave* in the sense of 'brav', while the English-speaking learner of German will do the converse.

A complication arises if there is a phonetic resemblance between the two items in one language that are linked by cross-language homonymy (*x* and *y*). Consider the next example, where the English false friend *(bright)* resembles the true friend *(broad)* because the German term *(breit)* has a formally similar English translation equivalent:

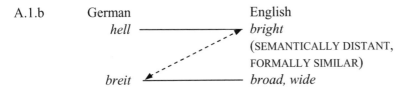

A.1.b   German   English
             hell ——————————▶ *bright*
                                    (SEMANTICALLY DISTANT,
                                    FORMALLY SIMILAR)
             breit ◀—————————— broad, wide

In such cases the true friend may, through the mere accident of similar phonological realization, become "contaminated" by the false friend link and avoided through fear of an error. In this example, for instance, a German-speaking learner of English might avoid the cognate *broad* as an equivalent of *breit* and prefer *wide*.

Similarly, if the English false friend has a German cognate as its translation equivalent *(p)*, the German words (*p* and *q*) can also closely resemble each other in form. An example of this situation would be:

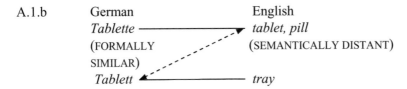

A.1.b   German   English
             Tablette ——————————▶ *tablet, pill*
             (FORMALLY   (SEMANTICALLY DISTANT)
             SIMILAR)
             Tablett ◀—————————— tray

Because of the correspondence between the German word *Tablette* with the phonetically similar English *tablet*, learners can be tempted to render *Tablett* with the same English word.

When one of the items is involved in homonymy or polysemy in its own language, things can be even more complex. If one of the semantically unrelated false friends (*q* or *x*) is homonymous in its own language, it may well correspond to two different lexemes in the language of its false friend. We could represent this situation diagrammatically as follows:

---

6 Both *brav* and *brave* were borrowed from French. The German word *brav* originally denoted military bravery and thus coincided with the English meaning. See the entry in Kluge (1963).

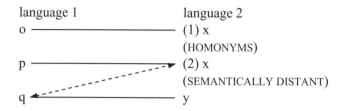

An example of this situation would be:

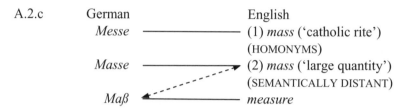

In this example the possibility of confusion is of course increased by the fact that all five lexical items are phonologically similar[7]. But through false friendship, German-speaking learners of English might wrongly use English *mass* in the sense of 'measure'. English-speaking learners of German, on the other hand, might wrongly use German *Maß* in the sense of 'mass'; but equally because of the homonymy of English *mass*, they might fall prey to underdifferentiation, confusing *Masse* and *Messe*.

Another type of cross-language homonymy involves internal homonymy in German (p and q), as in the false friend pair *Golf/golf*:

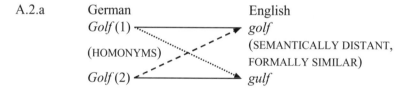

The German graphemic sequence *Golf* stands for two semantically unrelated lexemes, GOLF$_1$ and GOLF$_2$, that are represented by English *golf* and *gulf* respectively. The very similar form of the terms introduces an additional difficulty – they could both be used as false friends by German speakers. This false friend type is one-directional (asymmetrical), i.e. it is mainly problematic for speakers of the language with the homonymous words (cf. section 2 for internal polysemy, which also involves identical forms).

There are cases in which the "friendship" of two true friends is put at risk because both of them are homonymous. Consider the following example:

---

7 A further complication of this example is that some British Catholics distinguish phonologically between *mass$_1$* (pronounced /mɑːs/) and *mass$_2$* (pronounced /mæs/).

A.2.b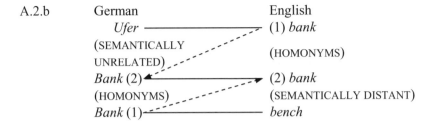

The English graphemic sequence *bank* or its underlying phonological form /bæŋk/ is ambiguous between the homonymous lexemes BANK₂ 'financial institution' and BANK₃ 'edge of river, etc.'. Equally the German graphemic sequence *Bank* or its underlying phonological form /baŋk/ is ambiguous between the homonymous BANK₂ 'financial institution' and BANK₁ 'bench'. The items here referred to as BANK₂ in the two languages are of course true friends and internationalisms. But their homonymous "clones" (or "Doppelgänger") have totally different values and each one can lead to the use of a (one-directional) false friend in the production of the other language as they may be confused with the formally identical word BANK₂.

If one of the semantically unrelated false friend terms (q or x) is polysemous in its own language, it may well correspond to two different lexemes in the language of its false friend. We could represent this situation diagrammatically as follows:

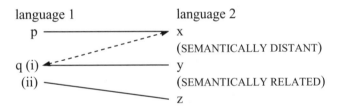

An example of this is the false friend pair *Rezept//receipt*:

A.3.a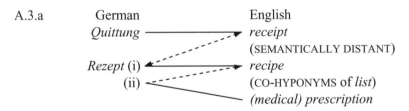

This example is perhaps less than perfect, because it could be argued that there is a weak semantic relationship between English *receipt* and *recipe*, because both are short documents of a kind (co-hyponymy). In addition, they are graphemically and phonetically similar and can easily be confused by German learners of English. It can nevertheless serve as an example of this kind of relationship, in which a polysemous lexeme in one language is involved in cross-language homonymy. Yet apart from *Rezept* and *receipt*, there is a second false friend pair in this example, *Rezept/recipe*, in which the polysemous (i.e. semantically related) senses of *Rezept* correspond to two English lexemes (cf. cross-linguistic polysemy below). As learners know that REZEPT (i) is rendered by *recipe* in English, they may not be aware of there being two different terms in English, and also erroneously translate REZEPT (ii) as *recipe* instead of *prescription*. We will examine this case of false friendship more closely in the next section.

A further example of internal polysemy of one false friend term that illustrates the complexity of the semantic and formal relations, is the following:

A.3.a

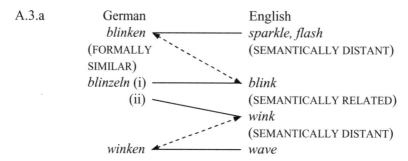

This example, like many other examples, is actually more complex than the diagram suggests, in that *flash* in one sense (a single flashing, rather than repeated flashing) corresponds to *blitzen* rather than to *blinken*. A further complication arises because in addition to polysemy, there is phonological resemblance not only between the two false friends (*blinken* and *blink*) but also between one of them and the translation equivalent of the other, i.e. the German words *blinken* and *blinzeln*. In addition, the semantically closely related English words *blink* and *wink* are phonetically very similar. If the additional false friend pair *winken/wink* is added, matters get even more complex, leading to an increase in formal similarity because the unrelated German lexemes *winken* and *blinken* only differ in their initial consonants.

2. Cross-language polysemy

The basic format for cross-language polysemy is the same as for cross-language homonymy, with the only difference that the two false friends (*q* in language 1, and *x* in language 2), while clearly different (i.e. non-synonymous) in meaning, are nevertheless semantically related. This situation can be represented as follows:

If *p* and *q* are semantically related as co-hyponyms, polysemous readings or members of the same word family, this situation can lead to cross-language polysemy. An example of cross-language polysemy with co-hyponymy is:

B.1.a
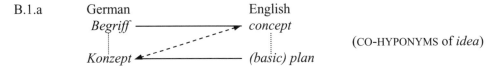
(CO-HYPONYMS of *idea*)

In some cases of co-hyponymy, there is the extra complication of phonetic resemblance between the two items linked by cross-language polysemy, i.e. between the false friend and its translation equivalent. An example of this is:

B.1.b
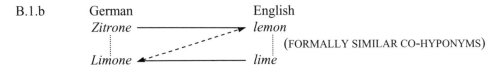
(FORMALLY SIMILAR CO-HYPONYMS)

This additional phonetic resemblance between the co-hyponyms in the one language can only increase the likelihood of confusion. For this particular example, the effect may well be for English learners of German that the German word *Limone* appears to be phonologically half-way between its English false friend *lemon* and its true friend *lime*. In addition, the German terms also resemble each other, sharing the first vowel [i] and the ending *–one*.

A second type of cross-linguistic polysemy involves a close morphological relation instead of co-hyponymy. The German words and the English words are not only phonologically, but also morphologically similar and belong to the same word family. An example of this is German *Mord* (= English *murder*) and *Mörder* (= English *murderer*), where the items in each language only differ in one morpheme:

B.2
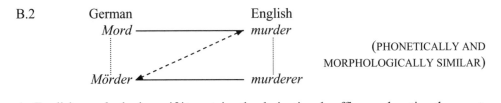
(PHONETICALLY AND MORPHOLOGICALLY SIMILAR)

As English *murder* looks as if it contains the derivational suffix *–er* denoting the agent, it can be erroneously used for *Mörder* by German speakers. Another example is the word family based on the English stem *photograph,* which involves two morphologically as well as semantically related false friends (see section 3).

In some cases there is "true friendship" between items in the two languages that are formally similar, but false friendship is caused by the semantic difference between the two languages. Although perhaps a core meaning is common to two languages, one of them may have a polysemous submeaning lacking in the other language. These false friends are often cognates or even internationalisms that are polysemous in one language and partly correspond in meaning, but also partly differ. This type largely corresponds to the "partial" false friend category. An example given by Breitkreuz (1991) is the differential use of English *swim* and German *schwimmen*: German has an extra meaning, roughly 'float', that is lacking for English *swim*. The situation of internal polysemy in German can be displayed thus:

B.3.a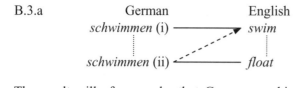

The result will of course be that German-speaking learners are in danger of using English *swim* in contexts where *float* would be more appropriate. Since only one polysemous lexeme is involved for German but two for English, such situations can also be described as cases of underdifferentiation. This is not the case where polysemy is found in both languages (as will become clear).

There are many more examples of German-English false friends with internal polysemy in German. Whereas *swim* is a (one-directional) false friend for German speakers, a case of polysemy in English may result in underdifferentiation by speakers of English, as the following example from Gläser (1992: 285) illustrates:

B.3.c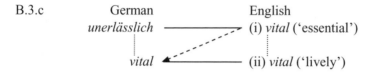

There can even be cases of polysemy in both languages. Consider the English word *cabin* and the German word *Kabine*. They correspond perfectly in one submeaning (designated as [ii] below), which can be roughly glossed as 'part of a ship or aircraft set aside for passengers'. But the other polysemous reading differs between the two languages: German *Kabine* can also refer to a very small room in a building used for a specific purpose, such as changing clothes, undressing, hairdressing; English *cabin*, on the other hand, has the alternative meaning 'hut or simple primitive habitation'. Bearing in mind that all these meanings in both languages fall within a semantic field that we could designate as 'small living space for people', we could represent this complex set of semantic correspondences schematically thus:

B.3.b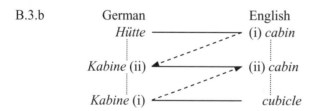

The potential for confusion between the two languages is clear: English *cabin* could be deviantly used to refer to a cubicle, while German *Kabine* could be deviantly used to refer to a mountain hut or something similar.

Polysemy in languages can be quite complicated, with half a dozen submeanings involved. Since the overlap of polysemous readings can be limited to one or two submeanings, quite complex situations can arise. If we add in a case of underdifferentiation for one language, and further include phraseological units, extreme complexity can result. An example of such complexity is portrayed in Table 4.1.

Table 4.1 False friends amongst adjectives and adverbials indicating shortness of time and size

The examples of Table 4.1 make it clear that, looking at things from the viewpoint of the German-speaking user of English, there are four potential false friend groupings in this set of correspondences:

(i) Assuming correctly that English *short* and *brief* are near-synonyms, but not realizing that *brief* has a purely temporal meaning, a speaker could wrongly use *brief* in a spatial sense, e.g. **a brief corridor*.
(ii) Again on the basis of the synonymy of *short* and *brief* German-speaking learners probably feel entitled to assume that *kurz* as a duration adverbial (meaning 'for a short time') must correspond to *shortly*, so that they might well produce sequences like **... met shortly over coffee*. But since the English word *shortly* can only mean 'in the near future', it is a false friend, and in the durations adverbial use needs to be replaced by the true friend *briefly*.
(iii) The German word *kürzlich* has an even stronger superficial resemblance (at least morphologically) to the English word *shortly*; but once again, these are false friends, because *kürzlich* corresponds semantically to *recently*.

(iv) The German phrase *in Kürze* superficially resembles the English phrases *in short* and *in brief*, and so (despite the fact that *Kürze* is a noun meaning 'shortness') speakers might be tempted to say something like *... *will be leaving in short*, when what is required is *shortly*.

Figure 4.1 Overview of German-English false friends, categorized according to semantic relation and formal resemblance. German is taken to be the L1 and English the L2, so that bold words represent English false friends for German-speaking learners. Grey boxes denote non-existing categories, and blank boxes mean that no example has been found.

SEMANTIC RELATION (p-q and x-y)	PHONETIC AND/OR GRAPHEMIC SIMILARITY (OR IDENTITY)			
	between false friends only	L1 (p-q) terms	L1 (p-q) & L2 (x-y) terms	L2 (x-y) terms
A. CROSS-LINGUISTIC HOMONYMY (semantically distant items)				
1. basic type **a** no similarity **b** similarity	schnippen = **flick** flicken = mend	Tablette = **tablet** Tablett = tray		hell = **bright** breit = broad
2. internal homonymy **a** in L1 (p-q)			$Golf_1$ = **golf** $Golf_2$ = gulf	
b in L1 and L2			Ufer = $bank_1$ $Bank_2$ = $\mathbf{bank_2}$ $Bank_1$ = bench	
c in L2 (x-y)			Messe = $mass_1$ Masse = $\mathbf{mass_2}$ Maß = measure	
3. intralingual polysemy of one term **a** L1 (p or q)		blinzeln (i) = wink blinzeln (ii) = **blink** blinken = sparkle	Quittung = **receipt** Rezept (i) = recipe Rezept (ii) = prescription	
b L2 (x or y)				
B. CROSS-LINGUISTIC POLYSEMY (semantically related items)				
1. co-hyponymy **a** no similarity **b** similarity	Begriff = **concept** Konzept = basic plan		Zitrone = **lemon** Limone = lime	
2. morpholog. relation (same word family)			Mord = **murder** Mörder = murderer	
3. intralingual polysemy (true & false friends) **a** in L1		schwimmen (i) = **swim** schwimmen (ii) = float	Brust (i) = **breast** Brust (ii) = chest	
b in L1 and L2			Hütte = (ii) cabin Kabine (i) = (i) **cabin** Kabine (ii) = cubicle	
c in L2			physikalisch = (i) physical physisch = (ii) physical	vital = (i) vital unerlässlich = (ii) vital

In this semantic area false friends seem to be lurking at every corner. The main types of false friends discussed above are summarized in Figure 4.1.

3. Empirical pilot study of false friend use

After considering the false friends scenarios presented in Figure 4.1, we may wonder which of these actually are stumbling blocks for German-speaking learners of English. To answer this question, we obviously need some experimental data. We now summarize the most important findings of an empirical pilot study conducted by J. Wieser in 1998. It tested 72 pupils from two Swiss-German schools on their knowledge of 34 false friends classified as "easy" by Breitkreuz (1991), using a German-English translation task. The informants were mostly aged between 17 and 19 (average age 18.5) and had received English tuition for four to six years.

The study originally aimed to examine whether there was a difference in difficulty between the two categories of "total" and "partial" false friends often distinguished in the research literature (for instance by Breitkreuz 1991: 12). Whereas the meaning of total false friends never corresponds to the meaning of the deceptively similar word in the other language, partial false friends partly correspond, but also partly differ in meaning. The hypothesis the study sought to verify predicted that there would be more errors with the partial false friends because the English false friend partly corresponds in meaning to the polysemous German word (e.g. *dick* = English *thick* or *fat*), and learners are tempted to underdifferentiate and also use the similar English word (e.g. *thick*) in contexts where a different word is necessary in English (e.g. *fat*). Breitkreuz (1991: 17) writes:

> Partial false friends are a group that is particularly error-prone. This false friend type is tricky because one false friend differs in meaning in one area and corresponds in meaning in another area.[8]

In contrast, total false friends look similar, but their meanings never coincide, so learners may be less likely to use them on semantic grounds. Yet total false friends can also present problems for learners, precisely because there is often not even a slight chance of an overlapping meaning between the L1 and the L2 word, and learners have to take care to avoid them.

The questionnaire used to test the pupils' knowledge of these false friend types contained 34 false friends (see Appendix and Table 4.2), half of which were total false friends mostly involving cross-linguistic homonymy, e.g. *Flur//floor* (divided by two slashes). The other 17 examples were partial false friends mostly involving cross-language polysemy with internal polysemy in German, e.g. *dick/thick* (divided by one slash). Our

---

8 "Halbwahre False Friends bilden eine besonders fehleranfällige Gruppe. Das Tückische an diesem False Friends-Typ besteht darin, dass es bei einem False Friend teils bedeutungsverschiedene, teils bedeutungsgleiche Bereiche gibt." [translation by JW]

classification does not completely overlap with the distinction between total vs partial false friends, and diverging cases will be discussed in detail below.

In the questionnaire, the German false friend terms were presented in German sentence contexts. For each of the false friend pairs, two sentences were provided. Sentence A contained a German word (e.g. *Flur, dick*) which should not be translated by the English false friend (e.g. *floor, thick*). Sentence B functioned mainly as a control sample, and presented the German translation equivalent of the English false friend (e.g. *Boden, dick*) to test pupils knowledge of the English words involved. The questionnaire thus consisted of 68 German sentences presented in random order (see Appendix).

Table 4.2 Example of the two false friend categories (T, P) with the corresponding sentences (A, B) used in the questionnaire. The questionnaire thus comprises the four categories TA, TB, PA, and PB.

False friend type	Example	Sentences
Total false friend = T (mostly cross-linguistic homonymy)	Flur//floor	**TA**: Sie traf ihren Nachbarn auf dem **Flur**. Flur = corridor, hall(way), landing **TB**: Sie liegt auf dem **Boden** und liest ein Buch. Boden = floor
Partial false friend = P (mostly cross-linguistic polysemy)	dick/thick	**PA**: Wenn Du immer Hamburger isst, wirst du bald **dick**. dick (i) = fat **PB**: Letzte Woche habe ich ein sehr **dickes** Buch gelesen. dick (ii) = thick (true friends)

The pupils were instructed to translate the German word as it appears in the sentence, and were told to rather write something than nothing. They were given 15 minutes to complete the task, which was intended to put them under a certain time pressure. The translation task, the German sentence contexts and the instructions were thought to rather encourage lexical transfer from German.[9] In addition, the German-English translation task was generally more difficult for the 14 out of 72 informants whose first language was not German, because their knowledge of German is likely to be more limited, and their overall performance was lower compared to the speakers with Swiss German and/or High German L1.[10] These less than ideal testing conditions and their likely impact have to be kept in mind when considering the results.

The hypothesis that partial false friends would be more difficult and therefore result in more errors was not confirmed although the percentage of false friend errors was higher for the partial false friend group, as expected. However, the number of correct answers was lower for the total false friends, and some of them proved to be real traps,

---

9 Conditions that would be less inviting for transfer would give the sentence contexts in English with gaps, and only provide the missing word in German.

10 Their performance was at roughly 70% compared to 75% according to a success index that compared the correct answers – including wrong spellings – and the number of false friends. The possible influence of L1s other than German could not be considered.

probably because the items were generally less known than the partial false friend items. As there is conflicting evidence, the results of this study are preliminary and have to be treated with caution. It was (and still is) difficult to predict which false friends will be most problematic for learners of English in a German-speaking environment, and to determine the possible reasons for their errors. Apart from the type of semantic relation the false friend is involved in, the frequency of the items in the L2 lexicon has to be taken into account. Ideally the frequency of the items in the materials (textbooks, etc.) learners were exposed to should be determined, in order to know if the informants are likely to be familiar with them.[11] Both the British National Corpus (= BNC) frequency of the English false friend terms and their frequency in *Langenscheidt's Grundwortschatz Englisch* will be considered in the following attempt at explaining why some of the examples led to more false friend errors than others.

3.1 Cross-linguistic homonymy

The cases of cross-language homonymy and polysemy will be dealt with here irrespective of whether they were originally classified as partial or total false friends in the study. Most cases of cross-linguistic homonymy corresponded to the most basic type (A.1.a) outlined above. However, some of the most problematic examples, i.e. *Golf/golf* and *Bank/bank*, involved internal homonymy in L1 and/or L2 (type A.2.a/b, see Table 4.3 for an overview). They were both classified as partial false friends by Breitkreuz (1991) because the same German word form corresponds to two different L2 lexemes, but we have classified them as cases of cross-linguistic homonymy with intralingual homonymy in L1 because the German words are semantically unrelated, although one of them corresponds to the English term as a true friend. Nevertheless, the formal identity of the L1 terms was likely to create confusion, especially in *Golf/golf*, where the English translation equivalents are also formally very similar and about equally frequent. Whereas almost half of the informants translated the German word *Golf* (in *Golfkrieg*) with the English false friend *golf*, the word *gulf* was used to refer to the sport in 3 occurrences.

Bank/bank, which involves internal homonymy in both L1 and L2, proved to be a stumbling block for one third of the pupils although *Bank* ('Geldinstitut') was correctly translated as *bank* by almost all informants. It has to be noted that *bank* is generally more frequent than *bench*[12] (known by 44% of the informants), although both items belong to the 2,000 most frequent words in English.

---

11 It would have been useful to know in what way these lexical items were taught and learnt, but this information is difficult to gather and was not available in the present case.
12 Frequency in the BNC: *bank*: 17,596 vs. *bench* 1,947 (without plural).

Table 4.3 False friend pairs involving cross-linguistic homonymy

Cross-linguistic homonymy: False friend pair	False friend errors (N = 72, 100%)		Related potential false friends	BNC frequency of English term
Golf/golf (PA09) homonymy in L1	34	(47%)	*gulf* 3	3,389
schmal//small (TA13)	32	(45%)		43,118
Tablett//tablet (TA16)	27	(38%)		1,264
Flur//floor (TA07)	26	(36%)		10,916
Bank/bank (PA02) homonymy in L1 and L2	24	(33%)		17,596
Mappe//map (TA09)	8	(11%)		4,088
sparen//spare (TA15)	5	(7%)		662
Meinung//meaning (TA10)	5	(7%)		8,039
brav//brave (TA05)	5	(7%)		1,748
Engel//angle (TA06)	5	(7%)		2,438
Angel//angle (TA01)	0	(0%)	*Angel* 2 (spelling)	2,438
Sender//sender (TA14)	0	(0%)		230
wer//where, wo//who (TA17)	0	(0%)		>100,000
also//also (TA02)	0	(0%)		>100,000
bekommen//become (TA04)	0	(0%)		>60,000

In *Tablett//tablet* (A.1.b), the deceptive close phonetic-graphemic similarity of the unrelated German words *Tablette* and *Tablett* complicated matters and apparently caused confusion, which is also reflected in wrong spellings of the last consonant (10 occurrences of **tablett[e]* or **tabletts*), and the large number of blanks. Whereas most informants correctly translated *Tablette* as either *pill* or *tablet*, almost 40% of the informants rendered *Tablett* with the false friend *tablet*, and *tray* was only known by relatively few pupils. These examples suggest that the existence of very similar or identical (homonymous) L1 words, especially if coupled with formal similarity or homonymy in L2, seems to rather increase the likelihood of false friend use despite the unrelated meanings. This situation is comparable to cross-linguistic polysemy with polysemous L1 words that also have the same form but related meanings.

The semantically unrelated false friends of the basic type of cross-linguistic homonymy (A.1.a) that led to most errors were *schmal//small* and *Flur//floor*, with 36% and 45% of false friends (see Table 4.3). In both cases, the English false friends (*small* and *floor*) seem to have been better known than the translation equivalent, and were correctly used in the B sentence by over 60% of the informants. The correct translation of *schmal*, English *narrow,* was only used by few informants. Although both *small* and *narrow* are among the 2,000 most frequent English words, *small* is generally much more frequent[13] and often taught earlier in textbooks, and *narrow* seems to be rather less known. With *Flur//floor,* the situation is similar. The majority of pupils probably used *floor* as a false friend because they did not know the translation equivalents of *Flur,* i.e. *corridor, hall(way)* or *landing,* which are much less frequent than *floor* and not usually taught in the first years[14]. Only few informants knew *corridor,* some used *hall,* but nobody chose *landing*; and there was a considerable number of blank answers. Thus if the false friend term is very frequent, i.e. much more frequent than the actual translation equivalent, the danger of it being used as a false friend seems to be greater.

Other instances of cross-linguistic homonymy that resulted in the use of a few false friends were English *map* for German *Mappe, meaning* for *Meinung, brave* for *brav, spare* for *sparen* and *angle* for *Engel.* Whereas *map* and *bag* as well as *meaning* and *opinion* are equally frequent words, most pupils did not know the rather infrequent *spare* and were thus less tempted to substitute it for the more frequent verb *save*[15]. The case of *brave* is more complex, as two thirds correctly used English *brave* for *tapfer,* but German *brav* was most often translated by *nice,* or was not known. So most informants were not tempted to use *brave* as a false friend despite (or because of) their familiarity with it. In *Engel//angle* the main difficulty was the spelling of the ending (*–le* vs. *–el*), whereas in *Angel//angle,* most informants did not know the English word *(fishing) rod,* and *angle* was not used. Instead there were two uses of *angel,* which looks even more similar to the German word than *angle.* The English word *sender* was not used as a false friend instead of *(radio) station,* but most informants unnecessarily also avoided it as a translation of *Absender.* Finally, typical beginners' mistakes of German-speaking learners did not occur at all, i.e. *become* was not used for *bekommen,* or *where* for *wer* (or alternatively *who* for *wo*). The words involved in these false friend pairs are very frequent and usually taught at an elementary stage, and the pupils seem to have learnt their lessons well in these cases.

3.2 Cross-linguistic polysemy

Most of the examples of partial false friends in the study fall into the category of cross-linguistic polysemy with internal polysemy in L1 and usually involve cognates (see Table 4.4). The general problem in these cases is overgeneralisation of the meaning of the polysemous L1 term, and the overuse of the phonetically or graphemically similar L2 word. The most problematic example of this type was *schwimmen/swim,* where the polysemous German word *schwimmen* is expressed in English either by *swim* to denote

---

13 BNC frequency: *small* 43,118 vs. *narrow* 4835.
14 BNC frequency: *floor* 10,916 vs. *corridor* and *landing* (including verb forms) 1922 each. Neither *corridor* nor *landing* occur in *Langenscheidts Grundwortschatz Englisch,* which involves the 4,000 most frequent words.
15 BNC frequency: *spare* 662 vs. *save* 7,350.

an active movement in water, usually by a person, or by *float* or *drift* to describe a passive state, usually of an object (which can also be rendered by German *treiben*). The large majority of the informants underdifferentiated in English by using the well-known *swim* (used correctly in the control sentence by all of them) instead of *float,* which was only known by three pupils.

Table 4.4 False friend pairs involving cross-linguistic polysemy

Cross-linguistic polysemy false friend pair	False friend errors (N = 72, 100%)		Related potential false friends		BNC frequency of false friend	
schwimmen/swim (PA12)	57	(79%)				4,728
Fotograf//photograph (TA08) morphologically related	31	(43%)	cf. PA08			2,595
Braut/bride (PA04)	29	(40%)				1,088
Brust/breast (PA05)	28	(39%)	chest	4		1,615
borgen/borrow (PA03) polysemy of both L1 terms	24	(33%)	lend	35 (49%)	borrow lend	4,191 3,787
Straße/street (PA15)	22	(31%)				18,865
Mörder/murder (TA11) morphologically related	20	(28%)				5,604
Strom/stream (PA16) multiple polysemy in L1	18	(25%)				2,504
Baracken//barracks (TA03)	17	(24%)				624
Rente//rent (TA12)	16	(22%)				3,313
dick/thick (PA06)	15	(21%)				4,531
älter/older (PA01) only *elder* false friend (PB01)	6	(8%)			older elder	8,731 1,335
Fotografie/photography (PA08) morphologically related	5	(7%)	cf. TA08			1,124
Kanal/canal (PA10) polysemy in L1 and L2	4	(5.5%)	channel	17 (24%)		2,108
See/sea (PA13)	3	(4%)				12,632
Fleisch/flesh (PA07)	2	(3%)				2,347
Mann/man (PA11)	2	(3%)				58,860
wenn/when (PA17)	0	(0%)				>200,000
Seite/side (PA14)	0	(0%)				32,365

The morphologically related false friend pairs *Fotograf//photographer* and *Fotografie/photography*[16] have to be classified as cases of cross-language polysemy because they are semantically closely related, although Breitkreuz (1991) put them in different groups on formal grounds. They can be represented thus:

B.2/3.a

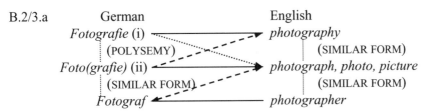

The pair *Fotograf//photograph* proved to be a special trap, as the false friend terms never exactly correspond in form and meaning (i.e. they are total false friends) despite their morphological resemblance. There were about as many false friends as correct answers. In contrast, *Fotografie* and *photography* partly correspond in meaning. However, *photography* was only used as a false friend in the plural **photographies* to translate *Fotografien*, whereas the singular was rather avoided and the equally frequent words *picture* or *photo* were used by most informants. Numerous spelling errors involving the use of German *f* and *–ie* instead of English *ph* and *–y* confirm that both of these false friends are also spelling problems.

Like *Fotograf//photograph*, the false friend pair *Mörder//murder* was put into the category of total false friends by Breitkreuz because the German words *Mörder* and *Mord* are not identical on the formal level. Yet clearly they are semantically and morphologically related nouns that belong to the same word family (B.2). Both languages use the same morphological stem, but have created different derivations (Barnickel 1992: 249). Whereas the nouns *Mord* and *murder* respectively express the criminal action of killing somebody, *Mörder* and *murderer* refer to the agent. Apart from the fact that *murder* was erroneously used to denote the agent in 28% of the answers[17], the morphological similarity coupled with a similar meaning led two learners to invent the English root **murd* for *Mord* by deducting the supposed noun suffix *–er* from *murder,* which they thought was the agent.

There were several examples involving polysemy in L1 (B.3.a) in which between 30 and 40% of false friends occurred. The *Braut/bride* pair probably lead to errors because of the rather old-fashioned use of German *Braut* (meaning *Verlobte*), and the low frequency of the translation equivalent *fiancée*[18], which was used by none of the informants. They were either not aware that the meaning of *Braut* was different in this

---

16 The "polysemy" between the two meanings of *Fotografie* is of a special kind, linking an event with the different semantic roles associated with it. Magnusson and Persson (1986: 2–6) call it "categorial hyponymy" for the different "facets" connected to an event.
17 *murderer* also happens to be less frequent (BNC frequency: *murderer* 768 vs. *murder* 5,604).
18 BNC frequency of *fiancée* 68, the lowest frequency of all English items involved as false friends or translation equivalents in the study.

context, or did not actively know *fiancée*. The learners' insecurity is also reflected by 26% blank answers.

A further difficult false friend pair was *Brust/breast*, where *breast* was used instead of *chest*. Although *chest* has a wider meaning denoting a body part of both men and women (while *breast* only denotes the female organ in contemporary non-poetic usage), *breast* was overused because of its closer formal similarity with *Brust*. Yet *chest* was also used instead of *breast* by four informants. The two English lexemes involved are not only semantically closely related, but also phonetically similar, differing only in their initial consonant clusters, /br-/ and /tʃ-/). This may have confused a few learners who used the spelling *brest that formally approaches *chest*.

Probably the most complicated false friends pair was *borgen/borrow*, which involves the polysemy of both German terms *borgen* and *leihen*, which can each be represented by *borrow* and *lend*. This results in quite a complex situation:

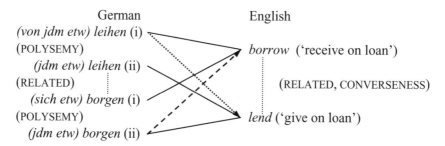

What makes this false friend pair particularly difficult is the fact that in English, the relation of temporarily giving something to somebody can only be expressed by *lend* (or *loan*), and the act of temporarily receiving something only by *borrow;* in other words, *lend* and *borrow* are converses, or relational opposites. In contrast, the German words *borgen* and *leihen* can each be used to express either relation, depending on the grammatical structure used (Table 4.5).

Table 4.5 The actions of temporarily giving and receiving something, as expressed in English, German and Swiss German

	GIVE		RECEIVE	
giver/lender	**Person X**	⟶	**Person Y**	receiver/borrower
English	LEND		BORROW	
German	(jdm etw) borgen		(sich etw) borgen	
	(jdm etw) leihen		(von jdm etw) leihen	

Thus German-speaking learners have to become aware of this difference and learn to avoid the formally similar English term in some cases. The informants were often not aware of the more restricted use of the English lexemes, and used *borrow* instead of *lend* in one third of the answers. However, *lend* was even more often erroneously used instead of *borrow* in half of the answers in the B sentence. It might also be considered a false friend, as it has a certain formal similarity to *leihen*, especially in its Swiss German form *(us)lehne* /'usle:nə/ (cf. High German *entlehnen*). This probably also explains the five uses of *lean*.

Most remaining cases of cross-linguistic polysemy exhibit internal polysemy in L1 (B.3.a). Regarding *Straße/street*, almost 60% of the pupils knew the correct answer, but about one third overused *street* because *Straße* has a much wider meaning in German. In English, *road* is the more general word, denoting large traffic routes that connect different places and often lead across the countryside. The word *street* usually refers to narrow public roads in a village, town or city, especially those used intensively by pedestrians in urban areas. Learners have to be aware of the criteria involved in differentiating *street* and *road* in English.

Strom/stream and *Kanal/canal* involve multiple polysemy in L1 and polysemy in L2 (B.3.b). *Strom* has four meanings in German, most of which are rendered by different words in English:

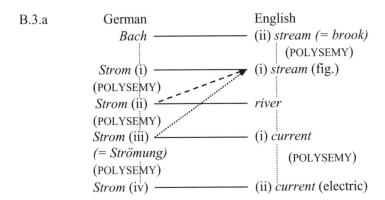

The false friend *stream* might be used by learners instead of both *river* and *current*, although only the former sense was tested. Two pupils translated *Strom* (ii) by *current* whereas one quarter of the informants used the false friend *stream* (which corresponds to *Strom* only in its figurative meaning), despite the fact that *river* is more frequent and usually taught first[19]. *Kanal/canal* on the other hand involves three polysemous senses in German, and polysemy of the English word *channel*, which resembles the false friend *canal* in spelling and also in meaning:

---

19 *River* belongs to the 2,000 most frequent words in *Langenscheidts Grundwortschatz*, and is taught with the German equivalents *Fluss* and *Strom*. BNC frequency: *river* 9,169 vs. *stream* 2,504.

B.3.b

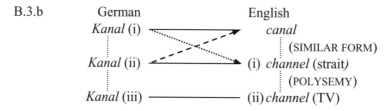

There were only few uses of the false friend *canal*, but about one quarter of the informants translated *Kanal* (i) as *channel*, which can also be considered a false friend because of its formal resemblance with both *Kanal* and *canal*. The fact that the English words can be confused is demonstrated by hybrid spellings combining features of *canal* and *channel*, e.g. **chanal* (4), **chanel* (7).

Baracken//barracks and *Rente//rent* also caused problems, with over 20% of false friends each. They were classified as total false friends by Breitkreuz (1991), but they are semantically related co-hyponyms, with *Baracken* and *barracks* designating 'some kind of very basic accommodation' and both *Rente* and *rent* denoting 'payment or transfer of funds'. Yet the more specific meanings differ in German and English, and this could have contributed to the difficulty of keeping them apart. *Baracken* means 'huts, shacks' whereas English *barracks* denotes buildings for accommodating soldiers (German *Kaserne*). In addition, *barracks* is a rather infrequent word that is not usually taught in textbooks[20] and cannot be expected to be well-known at this level. Most informants translated *Baracken* with the false friend **barack(s)* which also caused spelling problems. In the B sentence, none of the informants knew *barracks* for *Kaserne*, but one third created **casern(e)* based on the L1 word form, whereas the rest left a blank. Both **baracks* and **casern(e)* can be regarded as lexical borrowings, i.e. creations of analogous forms in English out of ignorance of the translation equivalents. In *Rente//rent*, about 25% of the informants each used the false friend *rent* and the correct answer *pension*, whereas over half of the subjects correctly translated *Miete* as *rent* in the B sentence. Thus *rent* is rather better known than *pension*, also because the verb *to rent* may be known. Yet some pupils apparently knew neither of these, as over one third of the informants left a blank in both sentences.

The false friend pair *dick/thick* was less problematic, as it involves frequent words. Most informants correctly used *fat* to describe a plump person. Although both *thick* and *fat* were acceptable modifiers of *book*, the former was used more often, but the majority chose *big*, which (like *fat*) rather denotes size in general.

With *älter/older*, the actual false friend turned out to be *elder* instead of *older*, contrary to Breitkreuz's (1991: 22f) presentation. Not only is *elder* phonetically more similar to *älter*, but it is also more restricted in use, denoting superiority in age among siblings only, and cannot even be used as a comparative before *than*. Although *elder* is "more formally correct" in the sibling context, as Breitkreuz (1991: 22) points out,

---

20 *barracks* has a BNC frequency of 624 (one of the lowest frequencies of all words involved in the study) and does not occur in *Langenscheidts Grundwortschatz*.

older is also acceptable in *my older sister* in current use, and consequently is not a false friend in this context. In contrast, *elder* is a false friend if used instead of *older* in all other contexts, which was the case in six instances.

The two pairs *wenn/when* and *Fleisch/flesh* were unproblematic in respect of false friends; yet they are interesting cases, because it was not the false friend that tended to be overused, but *if* (16.5%) and *meat* (30.5%) respectively. The English word *meat* is rather more frequent than *flesh* and usually taught earlier[21], and thus more closely associated with German *Fleisch* in the learners' minds. *When* is usually learnt first as the translation of German *wann* or *als*, and only later do pupils learn to distinguish between the temporal and conditional meanings of German *wenn* expressed by English *when* and *if* respectively. This also means learning to avoid the similar-looking *when* whenever a conditional meaning is intended, which may have resulted in an "over-avoidance". Further unproblematic false friend pairs were *Seite/side*, *Mann/man* and *See/sea*, where the false friend terms as well as the translation equivalents *(page, husband, lake)* are highly frequent words that are usually taught very early.[22]

4. Conclusion

We have taken a semantic view of false friends and classified them according to the criterion of semantic relatedness between words in different languages into the two major categories of cross-language homonymy and polysemy respectively. By adopting this perspective, we have overcome some of the limitations of an earlier classification into partial vs. total false friends, and shown the semantic and formal complexity involved in cross-language lexical relations. We have also seen that false friends have to be viewed in relation to true friends in many cases. However, our semantic classification is not unproblematic and has its pitfalls. It is sometimes difficult to determine whether two words are semantically related, especially if there is some sort of co-hyponymy, a remote historical connection, or a partial overlap of sub-meanings in the two languages. It is therefore sensible to differentiate further and postulate different degrees of semantic relatedness. Nevertheless the broad categories of cross-language homonymy and polysemy are useful as a first step towards a classification according to semantic relatedness.

The results of the pilot study with German-speaking learners of English indicate some factors that seem to encourage difficulties in production. Errors often coincide with identical forms in L1 due to internal polysemy or homonymy, or very similar forms in L1 and/or L2, and sometimes both. Thus formal similarity in general – i.e. not just between the false friend terms themselves – certainly plays an important role. Semantic

---

21 In *Langenscheidts Grundwortschatz* the word *meat* belongs to the first 2,000 words, the word *flesh* to 2,001–4,000. The BNC frequency is higher for *meat* (3,519) than for *flesh* (2,347).

22 All of these words are listed among the 2,000 most frequent words in *Langenscheidts Grundwortschatz*. BNC frequencies: *side* >32,000, vs. *page* >10,000; *man* >58,000 vs. *husband* >10,000; *sea* >12,000 vs. *lake* 3,879.

relatedness can add to the confusion, but on its own does not seem as influential on learners' behaviour as linguists might expect. In language processing, the formal level seems to be very influential if words are similar across languages. As is known from vocabulary acquisition research, word frequency is an essential factor to be considered, especially the frequency of items in the textbooks students are exposed to, as it indicates how likely learners are to be familiar with them. The fact that some false friend terms were more frequent than the correct translation equivalents may have increased the likelihood of their use as false friends. Further empirical research in this area is certainly necessary to take account of learners' perceptions of semantic correspondences.

Bibliography

Breitkreuz, H. 1991. *False Friends. Stolpersteine des deutsch-englischen Wortschatzes.* Reinbek bei Hamburg: Rowohlt.
Barnickel, K.-D. 1992. Trügerische Verwandte: Überlegungen zu einer Erweiterung des false friends-Begriffs. In: Mair and Markus 1992. 247–251.
Cambridge International Dictionary of English. 1995. Cambridge: Cambridge University Press.
De Groot, A. M. B. 2002. Lexical representation and lexical processing in the L2 user. In: Cook, V. *Portraits of the L2 User.* Clevedon: Multilingual Matters. 32–63.
Fanning, H. 1992. Falsche Freunde in verschiedenen Sprachen: Ein Vergleich des Deutschen, Englischen und Russischen. In: Mair and Markus 1992. 271–280.
Gläser, R. 1992. False friends in LSP vocabulary – with special reference to foreign language teaching. In: Mair and Markus 1992. 281–291.
Helliwell, M. 1989. *Can I become a beefsteak? Trügerische Wörter zum Nachschlagen und Üben. Deutsch – Englisch.* Berlin: Cornelsen & Oxford University Press.
Kluge, F. 1963. *Etymologisches Wörterbuch der deutschen Sprache.* Berlin: de Gruyter.
Kroschewski, A. 2000. *'False friends' und 'true friends'. Ein Beitrag zur Klassifizierung des Phänomens der intersprachlich-heterogenen Referenz und zu deren fremdsprachen-didaktischen Implikationen.* Frankfurt am Main: Lang.
Lado, R. 1957. *Linguistics Across Cultures. Applied Linguistics for Language Teachers.* Ann Arbor: The University of Michigan Press.
Langenscheidts Grundwortschatz Englisch. Ein nach Sachgebieten geordnetes Lernwörterbuch mit Satzbeispielen. 1995. Berlin, München, Wien, Zürich: Langenscheidt. [13th edition].
Magnusson, U. and Persson, G. 1986. *Facets, phases and foci: studies in lexical relations in English.* Umeå: Almqvist and Wiksell.
Mair, C. and Markus, M. (eds.) 1992. *New Departures in Contrastive Linguistics.* Vol. I. Innsbruck.
Siegrist, O. K. 1992. False friends in Varietäten des Englischen mit Bezug auf die Ausgangssprache Deutsch. In: Mair and Markus 1992. 337–341.
Weinreich. U. 1968. *Languages in contact: findings and problems.* The Hague: Mouton. [2nd edition; 1st edition 1953: New York: Publications of the Linguistic Circle of New York].
Welna, J. 1977. Deceptive words. A study in the contrastive lexicon of Polish and English. *Papers and Studies in Contrastive Linguistics* 7: 73–84.

Appendix

Code	FF pair	German Sentence	Translation/ true friend	False friend
PA01	älter/older, elder	Mein **älterer** Bruder hat mich heute angerufen.	elder, older	(older)
PB01	älter/older, elder	Meine Freundin ist **älter** als ich, aber ich bin größer als sie.	older	elder
PA02	Bank/bank	Sie setzten sich im Park auf eine **Bank**.	bench	bank
PB02	Bank/bank	Ich muss zur **Bank** gehen und Geld abheben.	bank	–
PA03	borgen/ borrow	Kannst du mir dein Fahrrad **borgen**?	lend	borrow
PB03	borgen/ borrow	Kann ich das Buch für eine Woche **ausleihen**?	borrow	lend
PA04	Braut/bride	Das ist Sarah, meine **Braut**, die ich bald heiraten werde.	fiancée, (girl-friend)	bride
PB04	Braut/bride	Die **Braut** sah wunderschön aus in ihrem weißen Kleid.	bride	–
PA05	Brust/breast	Der Mörder nahm ein Messer und stach ihm in die **Brust**.	chest	breast
PB05	Brust/breast	Der Arzt sagte ihr, dass sie **Brust**krebs hat.	breast	(chest)
PA06	dick/thick	Wenn du immer Hamburger isst, wirst du bald **dick**.	fat	thick
PB06	dick/thick	Letzte Woche habe ich ein sehr **dickes** Buch gelesen.	thick	–
PA07	Fleisch/flesh	Sie isst kein **Fleisch**, weil sie Vegetarierin ist.	meat	flesh
PB07	Fleisch/flesh	Das Seil schnitt ihm ins **Fleisch**.	flesh	–
PA08	Fotografie/ photography	Hast Du eine **Fotografie** von deinem Freund?	photograph, photo, picture	photo- graphy
PB08	Fotografie/ photography	Meine Schwester hat **Fotografie** studiert.	photography	–
PA09	Golf/golf	Im **Golf**krieg verschmutzte das Öl Wasser und Luft.	Gulf	golf
PB09	Golf/golf	Er spielt sehr gern **Golf**.	golf	(gulf)
PA10	Kanal/canal	Die Nachrichten kommen um 20 Uhr auf dem ersten **Kanal**.	channel	canal
PB10	Kanal/canal	Zwischen beiden Seen hat es einen **Kanal** für Schiffe.	canal	(channel)

PA11	Mann/man	Ihr **Mann** ist Bob Lovejoy, der berühmte Filmstar.	husband	man
PB11	Mann/man	Siehst du den kleinen **Mann** dort drüben?	man	–
PA12	schwimmen/ swim	Siehst du die Flasche, die dort im Wasser **schwimmt**?	is floating	is swimming
PB12	schwimmen/ swim	Sie gingen **schwimmen**, weil das Wetter schön war.	swimming	–
PA13	See/sea	Leider gibt es in der Nähe von Basel keinen **See**.	lake	sea
PB13	See/sea	Meine Großmutter wohnt in der Nähe der Nord**see**.	(North) Sea	(see)
PA14	Seite/side	Öffnet eure Bücher auf **Seite** 45!	page	side
PB14	Seite/side	In Großbritannien musst du auf der "falschen" **Seite** fahren.	side	–
PA15	Straße/street	Auf der **Straße** nach Brighton hat es viel Verkehr.	road	street
PB15	Straße/street	Die **Straßen** der Innenstadt sind sehr eng.	streets	–
PA16	Strom/stream	Der Mississippi ist einer der längsten **Ströme** der Welt.	rivers	streams
PB16	Strom/stream	Er sah einen endlosen **Strom** von Menschen vorüberziehen.	stream	–
PA17	wenn/when	**Wenn** du willst, komme ich mit dir.	if	when
PB17	wenn/when	**Wenn** es dunkel wird, gehen wir nach Hause.	when	–
TA01	Angel//angle	Er ging mit seiner **Angel** zum Fluss.	(fishing) rod/pole	angle
TB01	Angel//angle	"Das ist ein rechter **Winkel**", sagte der Mathelehrer.	angle	–
TA02	also//also	Unser Lehrer kam nicht, **also** gingen wir nach Hause.	so, therefore, hence	also
TB02	also//also	Da war **auch** ein Mann, der aus Schottland kam.	also, too	–
TA03	Baracken/ barracks	Viele Brasilianer leben in **Baracken** ohne Wasser und Strom.	huts, shacks	barracks
TB03	Baracken// barracks	Die Soldaten müssen am Abend wieder in die **Kaserne** zurück.	barracks	–
TA04	bekommen// become	An Weihnachten **bekomme** ich immer viele Geschenke.	get, receive	become
TB04	bekommen// become	Henry möchte Pilot **werden**.	become, be	–
TA05	brav//brave	Die Kinder meiner Schwester sind sehr **brav**.	well-behaved, good	brave
TB05	brav//brave	Helden im Märchen sind immer sehr **tapfer**.	brave, courageous	–

TA06	Engel//angle	Sie ist kein **Engel**, auch wenn sie so aussieht.	angel	angle
TB06	Engel//angle	Versuch, die Sache von einem anderen **Blickwinkel** zu sehen.	angle, point of view	–
TA07	Flur//floor	Sie traf ihren Nachbarn auf dem **Flur**.	landing, corridor, hall	floor
TB07	Flur//floor	Helen liegt auf dem **Boden** und liest ein Buch.	floor, ground	–
TA08	Fotograf// photograph	Er möchte **Fotograf** werden.	photographer	photograph
TB08	Fotograf// photograph	Sie hat mir einige ihrer **Fotografien** gezeigt.	photo(graphs), pictures	photograph –y /*–ies
TA09	Mappe//map	"Ich will eine neue Schul**mappe**", sagte Greg.	(school)bag	map
TB09	Mappe//map	Ich kann die Straße auf der **Karte** nicht finden.	map	(card)
TA10	Meinung// meaning	Seine **Meinung** interessiert sie nicht.	opinion, view	meaning
TB10	Meinung// meaning	Dieses Wort hat noch eine andere **Bedeutung**	meaning	–
TA11	Mörder// murder	Der **Mörder** von Kennedy hiess Lee Harvey Oswald.	murderer, (killer)	murder
TB11	Mörder// murder	Der Kommissar ist überzeugt, dass es **Mord** war.	murder	–
TA12	Rente//rent	Bald bekommt er seine **Rente**.	pension	rent
TB12	Rente//rent	Wieviel **Miete** müssen sie bezahlen?	rent	–
TA13	schmal//small	Ein **schmaler** Weg führt den Hügel hinauf.	narrow	small
TB13	schmal//small	Wir sind eine **kleine** Familie mit nur einem Kind.	small	–
TA14	Sender// sender	Die meisten britischen Radiosendenr senden bereits um 6 Uhr.	(radio) stations	sender
TB14	Sender// sender	Auf dem Brief stand: "**Absender**: Mrs Greenpickle"	sender, "from"	–
TA15	sparen// spare	Wir müssen nicht nur Geld, sondern auch Energie sparen.	save, economise	spare
TB15	sparen// spare	"Bitte **verschone** uns!", flehten die Leute den Piraten an.	spare	–
TA16	Tablett//tablet	Sie brachte Tee auf einem silbernen **Tablett**.	tray	tablet
TB16	Tablett//tablet	Der Arzt hat mir **Tabletten** gegeben.	tablets, pills	–
TA17	wer//where	**Wer** hat Präsident Kennedy erschossen?	who	where
TB17	wer//where	**Wo** ist meine Tasche?	where	who

Problems of adverbial placement in Learner English and the British National Corpus

Chris Gledhill

A tricky problem for French learners of English is to know where to put adjuncts in relation to the verb, as can be seen in these examples[1] taken from undergraduate essays:

NNS11 Another strategy would be to change ?<u>completely</u> the distribution network.
NNS19 The Pronunciation Unit has ?<u>as well</u> an important diplomatic role.
NNS23 That's why the advertisers thought about putting ?<u>in the centre</u> a picture of a top model.

The primary aim of this paper is to explore the constraints on adjuncts which lead us to interpret these examples as awkward or ungrammatical. A second aim of this paper is to explore whether adjuncts occur in free combination in sentences or occur as chunks, parts of longer lexical patterns, on the basis of their behaviour in a corpus of texts, i.e. the *British National Corpus*. In this paper I use "adjunct" to refer to lexical and grammatical adverbs (such as *completely, also*) as well as prepositional phrases and other expressions which function as adverbials (e.g. *as well, in the centre*).

The syntactic features of adjunct placement are well documented in the comprehensive grammars of English (Jacobson 1964, Quirk et al. 1985, Huddleston and Pullum 2002). Apart from the large number of studies in generative grammar, adjuncts are generally discussed in terms of their placement in the sentence according to such criteria as prosodic detachment and thematic structure (Moignet 1961, Nøjgaard 1968, Dulbecco 1999, Van Belle 2000, Carlson et al. 2001). Specific adverbs, such as the specifier *only* have also been widely studied, because they present problems of semantic scope (Ballert 1977, Risanen 1980, Viitanen 1992, Cairncross 1997, Clement 1998, Frosch 1997, Van Belle 2000). More recently, there have been a handful of studies on adjuncts from a phraseological point of view, for example van der Wouden (1997), who examines collocations of negative polarity, and Lysvåg (1999), who looks at the phraseology of *famously*, as in the expression *to get on famously*. As far as I know, there has been no comparative analysis of adjunct positions in English and French from a phraseological perspective, and there has been little or no analysis of adjuncts in terms of contrastive error analysis (Sylviane Granger, personal communication).

Part of the reason for the lack of phraseological research on adjuncts is that they are not considered to enter into any significant lexical patterns. For example, even some of the best-known proponents of the idiom principle, Hunston and Francis, rule out ad-

---

[1] Examples taken from student essays are signalled as NNS (non-native speaker). Unacceptable features are symbolized by *. Questionable features are symbolized by ?. The hash symbol # (used later in this paper) indicates invented examples.

verbial modifiers in lexical patterns, stating that "On the whole [...] patterns of adverbs are hard to capture ... [and since] there is no parallel to complementation patterns, adverbs can be better described in positional terms" (2000: 43). The perspective I wish to pursue here challenges this assumption. This paper is thus divided into two parts. In the first, I discuss the role of adjuncts in general. In the second, I examine problems of adjunct placement for intermediate level French students of English.

1. The grammatical features of adjuncts

ADJUNCT is a functional term for any word or phrase which modifies a clause or another phrase in terms of quality or quantity. Adjuncts are generally said to have three basic properties. Firstly, they are categorically unrestricted and can be realized by grammatical adverbs, lexically derived adverbs, prepositional phrases, or even noun phrases and clauses, as in

#1 Next week, Jim can drive, if he's up to it.

Secondly, since there is no special restriction on the number of modifiers of any phrase or clause, some adjuncts give the impression of being optional as well as freely cumulative. Thus we can have

#2 Jules cooked the barbecue happily ... on the patio ... at three o'clock ... in the dark.

Thirdly, adjuncts are claimed to be syntactically mobile.[2] A basic distinction is typically made between clause-level adjuncts, mobile at the level of the clause, as in

#3 Jim will drive <u>tomorrow</u> / <u>Tomorrow</u> Jim will drive.

and VP-level adjuncts, mobile at the level of the verb phrase:

#4 Jules enjoyed his soup <u>enormously</u> / Jules <u>enormously</u> enjoyed his soup.

A test to distinguish between the two types is that clause-level adjuncts can be extracted by clefts, so we can have

#5a It's <u>tomorrow</u> that Jim will drive.

On the other hand, VP-adjuncts resist clefting, so we cannot say:

#5b It's *<u>enormously</u> that Jules enjoyed his soup.

(all examples from Huddleston and Pullum 2002).
In addition to these syntactic features, there are two fundamental notions which are crucial to understanding how adjuncts find their positions in the clause, namely scope and thematic structure. Scope is a restriction on the semantics of another phrase. Ac-

---

2 Some adjuncts do however appear to be obligatory (Goldberg and Ackerman 2001: their example is *this book reads well*). There also appears to be a pragmatic limit to the types of adjunct that can be stacked together (we cannot easily say *Jim also ?as well cooked the barbecue happily ?easily*).

cording to the generative school of syntax, a clause-adjunct is said to have scope over the finite or modal part of the clause (thereby expressing a speech act), while a VP-adjunct has scope over the predicate (expressing manner) (Jackendoff 1972, Kayne 1975, Ballert 1977, Pollock 1989, Müller and Riemer 1998, Alexiadou 1997, Ernst 2002, but this has been questioned by Cinque 1999). Furthermore, variable scope adverbs, such as frequentatives *(often, always)*, have wide scope in pre-finite position, as in

> #6a Medicine regularly wasn't available.
> ('there was a constant lack of medicine')

and narrow scope in post-finite position as in

> #6b Medicine wasn't regularly available.
> ('there was an intermittent lack of medicine')

The notion of scope is used to explain why there is a preference for comments to come before mood adjuncts. Thus we have:

> #7a They had luckily already left.

but not

> #7b They had *already *luckily left.

Finally, scope is used to explain what are known as 'bounding effects'. For example

> #8a She ran for 10 minutes.

is acceptable but not

> #8b She ran *in 10 minutes,

because *in 10 minutes* is an unbounded duration which cannot be the scope for an unbounded event (*She ran*).

Functional linguistics examines similar phenomena, but from a different perspective. Halliday (1985: 81) points out that positional variation corresponds to major divisions in the clause, notably the Theme-Rheme boundary (a textual division) or the Mood-Residue boundary (a division of intonational units). In the following diagram, we can see that *however* does not have any significant difference in meaning in pre-finite or post-finite position, while *just* expresses variable scope at each boundary:

	Theme		Rheme
#9a	Such men	however	*don't make good husbands*
		just>	

	Mood		Residue
#9b	Such men don't	however	*make good husbands*
		>just	

Halliday concludes from this that conjunctive adjuncts such as *however, that is, surely*, operate at the textual (Thematic) level of the clause, outside the Mood-Residue system.

They can thus occur at any boundary (initially and finally, between Theme and Rheme, or between Mood and Residue). A similar analysis can be applied to prosodically detached items, such as non-restrictive relative clauses, continuatives (*yes* and *no*), vocatives *(Sir, Madam)* and comment adjuncts *(frankly, really* or *no doubt)*.

It seems therefore that there are two major factors which account for the positional variation of a great number of adjuncts in English, namely scope and thematic structure. However, in the following section I examine the possibility that lexical factors may also have a part to play.

2. Adjuncts between Verb and Object

In general English grammar, it is often noted that adjuncts cannot occur in the sequence Verb + Adjunct + Object (henceforth V + A + O). As Ernst puts it:

> Any theory must account for a number of basic word order facts for English complements and post-verbal adjuncts. First, adjuncts do not occur between the verb and a nonheavy direct object [Noun Phrase]. (Ernst 2002: 207)

In a similar vein, Huddleston and Pullum (2002: 102) stipulate that there is a ban on post-verbal adjuncts, and regularly use it as a diagnostic test. For example, they argue that the copular uses of *is* are auxiliary verbs, because only auxiliaries allow frequency and modality adjuncts in post-verbal position as shown in #11b:

Lexical verb   #10a   He always **looks** miserable.
                    #11a   They probably **go** by bus.
Auxiliary verb #10b   He **is** always miserable.
                    #11b   They **have** probably gone by bus.

Generally speaking, adjunct position is explained either by a grammatical relationship to the clause (frequentative, modal, etc.) or to the verb (auxiliary, modal, etc.). This is after all a tried and tested way of doing things in traditional grammar, especially if we assume that an adverb is something which attaches to a verb (i.e. ad + verb). What is less clear from the traditional account is the extent to which adjunct placement may depend on the lexical interdependence of the adjunct with other parts of the clause. This perspective was succinctly expressed by Pawley and Syder:

> A *lexicalized sentence stem* is a unit of clause length or longer whose grammatical form or lexical context is wholly or largely fixed; its elements form a standard label for a culturally recognized concept, a term in the language. Although lexicalized in this sense, most such units are not true idioms but rather are regular form-meaning pairings. (Pawley and Syder 1983: 191–192)

According to this phraseological perspective, we must expect to find at least some adverbials in lexicalized sentence stems. An examination of *briefly* in the *British National Corpus* appears to provide us with a phraseology of this sort:

BNC1   We now turn to **examine** briefly the influence of sex.
BNC2   Finally, we **considered** briefly the meaning of an equilibrium in macroeconomics.

BNC3 In the last chapter, I have **discussed** briefly the most general principles of individuation.
BNC4 It might be helpful if I were to **outline** briefly the history of the STUCC.
BNC5 It may help to **summarise** briefly the current positions.

These concordance lines show us that *briefly* is used with a limited set of verbs, meaning roughly to 'restate in written form'. Although *briefly* could occur with any verb in theory, its use is restricted to VERBAL PROCESS + *briefly* as a lexical collocation. But it is also worth pointing out that these examples all occur at a very precise stylistic moment in a text, a "rhetorical move" to use Swales's (1990) term. The adverb *briefly* therefore has a very specific pragmatic function as a hedging device in academic writing. It is this stylistic dimension which distinguishes between *discuss briefly* as a recurrent lexical collocation and *discuss briefly* as a lexicalized sentence stem, or phraseological unit.

It might be argued that instances of Verb + Adjunct + Object (V + A + O) occur in order to avoid stylistic heaviness, where the adjunct precedes a long or complex complement. However, if we accept that adverbs such as *briefly* have lexical patterns, we must ask whether this is the case in other V + A + O patterns. In order to do this, I examined a sample of 750 sequences of the pattern V + A + O using *Wordsmith* (limited to grammatical and lexical adverbs and not all types of adjunct). The most frequent adverbs to emerge from this search appear in Table 5.1.

Table 5.1 The ten most frequent adverbs in Verb + Adjunct + Object position

only	150	directly	23
exactly	87	briefly	17
precisely	40	probably	14
accurately	20	merely	13
seriously	27	almost	13

It is not surprising to find *only, exactly* and *precisely* at the top of the list, since they are specifiers. Specifiers regularly occur in V + A + O position as pre-modifiers of the noun group complement, as in *they won only one game*. More significantly, Table 5.1 shows that grammatical adverbs[3] occur in V + A + O position, but not very frequently. This is probably because conjunctive adjuncts (such as *also, as well*) or mood-oriented adjuncts (such as *already, sometimes*) are attracted to other positions in the clause. Thus

---

3 Grammatical adjuncts, sometimes known as 'intensifiers' or 'degree adverbs', are a class of adverbials which signal abstract information, such as proximity, intensity, or comparison *(almost, more, very)*. They do not usually form phrases, but instead principally function as specifiers in adverbial or and adjective phrases.

the only grammatical adverbs to be frequently used in V + A + O position appear to be modal comments *(only, almost)*.

3. 'The Three Fs': figures, formulae and phrases

In this section I argue that all of the adverbs in Table 5.1 are involved in various forms of collocational pattern, ranging from metaphorical figures of speech, to more fixed types of lexical formulae and phrases (this three-part typology was first presented in Gledhill 2000). In order to do this; let us look a little more closely at some of the most frequently encountered adverbs in Verb + Adjunct + Object position in the *British National Corpus*. Firstly, several adverbs contribute to figures of speech where the adverbial expresses the typical way in which the language encodes the speaker's attitude towards quantification, as in *broaden considerably, strengthen modestly, reduce significantly:*

BNC6 It is extremely difficult to **gauge** accurately the dimensions of the shroud ...
BNC7 Smoking by women appears to **reduce** significantly the chances of successful pregnancy.

The basic role of these adverbials is to provide semantic reinforcement for the predicate in question. In other cases, the adverbial and complement form a rather more fixed form of lexical formula, where the adverbs in V + A + O are all necessary components of the expression. This is the case of *precisely* in the expression *do precisely the opposite*:

BNC8 The technique sets out to **do** precisely the opposite.

Here the verb is semantically light and the weight of lexical meaning is effectively carried by both the adjunct and complement. A similar case involves the expression *take seriously* in the sense of 'consider':

BNC9 They have **taken** seriously the aspirations of the masses.

I would claim that *take seriously* is a complex verb group. The reasoning for this follows Halliday's (1985) analysis of separable phrasal verbs, such as *put down,* where the adverbial is treated as part of the predicator in a complex verb group. In this case, the particle contributes to the predicational content of the clause. A comparable analysis has been proposed by Allerton (2002), who describes the adverbials in *live abroad, last long* as "adverbial elaborators". The expression is not a stretched verb (in Allerton's terms), since there is no single equivalent lexical verb. But the adverb in *take seriously* contributes more than the adverbs in the expressions *gauge accurately* or *reduce significantly:* it contributes to the predication of the verb and cannot be omitted. In other words, the verb is semantically light and the adverbial is an obligatory part of a fixed lexical expression.

Needless to say, there are a number of examples where there appears to be no lexical or phraseological link between the verb and adverb, as in:

BNC10 We **saw** probably a total of 24 different young men from a professional model agency.

On first inspection this looks like a classic case of an adverb preceding a 'heavy' NP complement. However, if we look a little more closely at the corpus data, the adverb *probably* frequently occurs in V + A + O position, especially with verbs of identity:

BNC11 Britain **became** probably the most open market in the world.
BNC12 The increased metabolism of glutamine by the distal colon in ulcerative colitis **seems** probably a response to inflammation and consequent hyperplasia ...

or with *to have* and relational verbs denoting possession or attribution:

BNC13 He **had** probably the nicest nature of any dog I ever owned, and possessed the loveliest eyes, brown in colour, and he was my dog definitely.
BNC14 Cloke (1977b, p. 19) **provides** probably the most useful definition: ...

The only material process verbs followed by *probably* have a quantity as their complement, as in:

BNC15 Erm I just **moved** probably a half a pace so PC would get exactly the same view as myself.
BNC16 Er in the good old days when we used to go to shows we **spent** probably a hundred and thirty to two hundred pounds a year ...

It is noticeable that the complement in each of these examples, even those with material verbs, is not quite the same as the traditional notion of direct object. At this point we need to appeal to Halliday's distinction between two types of complement: Goal and Range[4]. A Goal corresponds to the traditional notion of object complement, which is an affected participant of a material process verb (as in *take an umbrella*). Range on the other hand expresses the extent of application of the verb, but is not materially affected by the process (as in *take a bath*). Halliday gives the following definition of Range:

> The Range is [...] the scope, type, extent, quality or quantity of the process or simply a restatement of the process itself in a nominal form. (Halliday 1985: 149)

In other words, the Range can re-express a circumstantial (as in *climb up the mountain*) as a direct object complement *(climb the mountain)*. Or the Range can re-express a process (as in *to curtsey*) as a direct object complement *(drop me a curtsey)*. Returning to our examples with *probably*, in each case the adjunct is not interrupting Verb + Goal but Verb + Range. In example BNC10 above we are dealing with a Mental Process verb; such verbs always take Phenomenon (i.e. Mental Goal) as their complement. Likewise, the complements of the relational process verbs we saw in BNC11–14 are not materially affected Goals either, but either re-express the subject *(became the most open market)* or re-express the process itself *(provide a definition)*. Similarly the apparent exceptions BNC15–16 are not Material Goals but express the scope of the process

---

4 Initial capitals are used in Hallidayan grammar to signal functions.

(to spend a hundred and thirty pounds, to move a half a pace), in other words they are Range items. It seems therefore that modal adjuncts such as *probably* can occur between Predicator + Range, but not between Predicator + Goal.

To summarize, I have argued in this section that many common uses of adjuncts in V + A + O position can be explained in terms of their role in a phraseological unit, i.e. as a lexical phrase, figure, or formula. In more complex cases, as with *probably*, there is a more general process at work which allows comment adjuncts to intervene between a verb and its complement (usually a complement with the grammatical role of Range rather than the traditional object complement). In the next section, I compare these lexical properties of adjuncts with the difficulties of adjunct placement experienced by French students of English.

4. Adjunct problems in student essays

The initial aim of this study was to establish a typology of errors in English produced by undergraduate students at the Université Marc Bloch, Strasbourg. To find a sample, I selected four pass-graded exam essays from three groups of Francophone students (two second-year language groups and one first-year language group). These twelve essays answered comprehension questions about three newspaper articles. The results are summarized in Appendix 1, where each category of error is accompanied by some prototypical examples. The composition of each category is more important than its relative weight in this small sample, but it is interesting to note that the students made more errors of a phraseological nature than grammatical errors in such traditional categories as morphology and modals. However, what really caught my eye was the smaller category of syntax, which is dominated by problems of adjunct position. All of the syntactic errors of adjunct placement are given in the Appendix 2. There are several reasons why adjunct placement may pose such a problem for learners. Firstly adjunct placement is not widely taught and so there is virtually no awareness of the problem. Secondly French can very freely place adjuncts in post-verbal position, and this happens to be one of the most identifiable differences between English and French word order, a feature which is well-documented in the literature of generative syntax (as discussed in Roberts 1997: 30–40, Ouhalla 1994: 303–310, Jones 1996: 339–347, Cook and Newson 1996: 213–214 and Gledhill 2003: 81–86).

Most of the adjuncts that my students had problems with were functional or grammatical adjuncts, and only three of the 30 errors involved circumstantials. Dividing the list of 30 into Halliday's main adjunct categories (see Appendix 2), I selected one modal comment adjunct (*above all* NNS9–10), one modal mood (*always* NNS2–4), one conjunctive (*also* NNS17–18) and one circumstantial (*in the centre* NNS23–25). These were then compared in turn with occurrences in the *British National Corpus*. The main question to be asked was: does the typical phraseology of these adjuncts in the corpus help us to explain why errors NNS1–30 are felt to be wrong?

4.1 Modal comment adjunct: *above all* ...

As a comment adjunct, *above all* frequently occurs in clause-initial Theme position (675 instances out of a total of 2230), as in

BNC17   Above all, it strengthens bones and prevents brittle bone disease.

Although placement between verb and complement is infrequent, it does occur and there is therefore no general reason to reject the following student errors:

NNS9   when they do *above all everything,
NNS10 ... to accept *above all students from public schools.

Looking at the BNC, however, we can see that all the corpus examples involve relational verbs, or the lexical phrase *require above all* + complement:

BNC18   To clean up dirty land efficiently and cheaply will **need**, above all, pragmatism and moderation.
BNC19   But the fact that they did not impose formal constraints upon royal power **reflected** above all their overriding interest in the maintenance of a strong central state.
BNC20   This **required**, above all, substantial tax cuts to foster hard work, enterprise and saving.
BNC21   To be able to take action ahead of time **requires** above all the freedom to do so, unfettered by exchange-rate restrictions.
BNC22   Hence the teaching of adults **requires**, above all, an understanding of adults as learners ...

So the essential problem with NNS9–10 is that *above all* is incompatible with the semantics of *accept* and *do*, which are respectively mental and material events, while *be, have, require, need, depend on* express relational states. The typical patterns of the verbs *do* and *accept* also seem to militate against my students' errors. As a lexical verb, *do* does allow adjuncts in V + A + O position in lexical formulae such as *do precisely that, do just that*, as well as in 'extended adverbials' such as *do nicely, do badly*. Similarly, over a third of the uses of *accept* are with circumstantials of the type *accept + for the time being, temporarily*, or with emphatic modal adjuncts *accept + unquestioningly, without question*. Thus *accept* is used with adjuncts which express temporal, mental or verbal modality rather than the quantificational modality expressed by *above all*.

4.2 Mood adjunct: *always* ...

Always is a mood adjunct of usuality, and as such is associated with the finite element of the clause. Using *Wordsmith*, we find that of 44,432 instances of *always* in the BNC, there are only a tiny handful of examples of *always* in V + A + O, namely with the verbs *seem* (49), *provided* (9, as a complex subordinator: *provided always that*), *remember* (5, in imperatives) and *remain* (3 instances). As we saw with *probably,* the small set of verbs which express relational or mental processes readily allow V + A + O position. For example:

BNC23 Conrad **remains** <u>always</u> the European observer of the tropics, the white man's eye contemplating the Congo and its black gods.
BNC24 Wilcox **remained** <u>always</u> the showman, often directing his movies even though, like Saville in the same role, he was always more competent than gifted.
BNC25 … Frederick II **remained** <u>always</u> the executor of Frederick William I.

This pattern contrasts with our two student errors, where the verbs express material processes: *get *<u>always</u> cheap food* and **do *<u>always</u> higher profits*. The second expression is particularly awkward because of the collocational error with *do*. Even if we correct this to *make ?always higher profits*, there still appears to be a problem. In fact there is only one example of *make + always + Object* in the corpus, and it happens to be a quote from a well-known non-native speaker of English:

BNC26 'Very interesting,' says [Jean-Paul] Gaultier, 'I make <u>always</u> the same thing.'

It is this type of usage which contributes to what might be called the "phraseological accent" displayed by French speakers of English, and it is ironic that it should crop up in a corpus which was originally designed to exclude non-British forms of English!

The grammatical rule therefore seems to be that *always* is prohibited from intervening between a material process and its complement, and this is valid for both Goal and Range complements. The explanation for this may be that if the adjunct itself expresses the scope of the verbal process, it clashes with any Range complement. Halliday himself states that adjuncts which themselves express material scope, such as *steadily*, cannot readily intervene between verb and Range, as in

#12a   She climbed ?steadily the mountain.
#12b   She climbed steadily up the mountain.

This can only be repaired by repositioning the adverb or by re-expressing the Range item as a prepositional adjunct.
Our third error with *always*,

NNS4   Some students have not *<u>always</u> the most obvious abilities.

is more complex, since *have* is a relational process verb and should freely allow adjuncts in V + A + O position. I only found seven examples of *have + always + Object* in the corpus, including:

BNC27 Though I **haven't** <u>always</u> enough to do.
BNC28 The symphonies are full of difficulties and in those days the orchestras **had not** <u>always</u> the resources we have today.
BNC29 The noble owner has built of brick, … so that he **has** <u>always</u> a dry walk, …

These examples appear to be stylistically marked, or come from archaic or literary sources. However, BNC27 sounds perfectly normal, and there appears to be no other natural place for the adjunct in this example. If we compare these with *always + have + Object* in the corpus, we generally find a large number of light verb constructions with Range complements, as in *always* + *have the chance to, have the opportunity to, have the time to* or figurative stretched verbs such as *always have the last laugh*. Examples of the sequence *have* + *always* + Object are less frequent and tend to express possession of material items rather than attributes (*has always a dry walk* (= a dry walkway), *haven't always enough to do*). Thus it appears that the awkward status of student error NNS4 is due to the fact that the post-verbal use of *always* is restricted to *have* as an auxiliary verb. This restriction applies to mood adjuncts like *often* and *sometimes*, but not to comment and conjunctive adjuncts, as we have seen for *probably* and *also* (see sections 2 and 3.3).

4.3 Conjunctive adjunct: *also* ...

There are over 123,000 instances of the conjunctive adjunct *also* in the BNC. The concordancer shows that the only verbs with significant instances of *also* to their immediate right are *be* and *have*, modals such as *will* and *can*, and verbs such as *seem* (39), *report* (16) and *find* (6 instances). As with modal comments such as *probably*, conjunctive adjuncts can be freely placed between a verb and its complement:

BNC30 That approach has also the **benefit** of introducing several British names.
BNC31 Mary ... is very domesticated but has also a **capacity** for managing other people's affairs.
BNC32 A Ministry Centre has also the **opportunity** to establish far closer links by his staff and ...
BNC33 ... has also the **responsibility** for providing an environment in which each individual is able to fulfil his obligations.
BNC34 The tradesmen had also the **satisfaction** of knowing that they had saved the cricket club.

It is noticeable that in each instance we have a Range complement followed by a post-modifying clause (in fact the Range item is a nominalized process, usually expressing the subject's 'potential for action'). But how do we explain the following error?

NNS18 The BBC plays *also an important role.

This appears to be a problem of lexical collocation. Of 1220 instances of *play* + *role* in the corpus, the only adjuncts which [occur between verb and object] are *only* (in eleven examples of *play only a minor role*), *even* and *exactly* (with one example each). As mentioned before, these are specifying adjuncts relating to the following noun group:

BNC35 Evolutionism **played** only a minor **role** ...
BNC36 ... neutrality would be preferable to them to a series of regional alliances in which the Western powers **play** even a marginal **role**.
BNC37 It is only fair to add that some lawyers **play** exactly the opposite **role**, ...

In contrast, the *BNC* has nine examples of the expression *also have an important role* and 18 of *also play an important role*, with no examples of *have *also an important role* or *play *also an important role*. What explanation can we offer for this restriction? One reason may be that we are dealing with what Halliday calls 'Entity Range'.

An Entity Range does not express the verbal process (as in *have a bath*), but expresses its scope *(climb a mountain)*. Thus the main difference is that expressions such as *have the benefit of, have the responsibility for* (BNC30–34) involve a Process Range, whereas *have/play a role* (BNC35–37) involve an Entity Range. A further difference is that in each Process Range (BNC30–34), the complement is post-modified by an embedded clause which carries the subject of the main clause. But the Entity Range in *have/play a (significant) role* involves modification of the noun with no further embedding. Generally speaking then, as we saw above for *climb ?steadily a mountain*, we cannot place adjuncts between a verb and its Entity Range. On the other hand, it seems that adjunct placement between a verb and its Process Range is possible because the adjunct is not interrupting the process and a complement as such. Furthermore, it seems that the first ('light') verb in Process Range cases functions more like a Finite element than a full lexical Predicator.

Turning to

NNS17 But we soon notice that the customer gets *also in this situation.

the strangeness of this expression lies with the collocation of *?get + in a situation* rather than with the adverbial *also*. The BNC shows two possible phraseologies with *get*. The first is *get + into a situation* + relative clause *(You will rapidly get into a situation where you cannot cope)*. The second more productive phraseology involves *get + in a situation* with an obligatory reflexive pronoun, i.e. *get oneself into* (105 instances) or *get oneself in* (33 instances) + a negative situation *(trouble / a mess / a difficult situation)*:

BNC38 ... you'll **get yourself** in all sorts of difficulties ...
BNC39 How could she have **got herself** into a mess like this?
BNC40 If you have **got yourself** in this situation and cannot get back ...
BNC41 ... had no intention of telling his brother how he'd **got himself** into this situation.
BNC42 Kate would never **get herself** into this sort of situation.

In either phraseology, it could be argued that the prepositional phrase *into a (difficult) situation* is the Entity Range of the verb, i.e. a lexical expansion of a material process verb, where *get oneself* is the finite element of a complex verb group. As we saw with *play a role*, our student's problem comes from the fact that the adverb *also* cannot be used between the main verb Predicator and its Entity Range, even when the verb seems 'light' and looks like it might allow an adverbial expression to be inserted between V + O.

4.4 Circumstantial adjunct: *in the centre ...*

Prepositional phrases such as *in the centre, in the 60's* and *in the university,* as we have in errors NNS23–25, are prototypical circumstantial adjuncts:

NNS23 That's why the advertisers thought about putting *in the centre a picture of a top model.
NNS24 De Gaulle vetoed *in the 60's the entry of the UK in the Common Market.
NNS25 Actually the dons don't want *in the university weaker students.

In French, circumstantials occur relatively freely between verb and complement, including all the major types of verbal process, as in the following example:

CF4 Déjà, il pense à **créer** dans toutes les facultés économiques une section de management.
[Already, he is thinking of creating in all Economics departments a management section.]

In English, adjuncts in the sequence V + A + O are restricted to complex (or 'heavy') complements after a form of the verb *to be*. The only exception to this involves the verbs *find* and *keep*. Most senses of *find* involve location and time circumstantials, with a large number relating to passages in a text, and a smaller number with *find* as an appreciative mental process. An example of each of these uses is given here:

BNC43 I **found** in the bottom of the freezer some pork that I didn't know we had.
BNC44 ...; the Romanian people can be confident that it will always **find** in the Soviet people a reliable ally, a useful partner, and a true friend.

The verb *keep* also allows for prepositional phrases, where the adjunct expresses a complex verb or 'Process Range' as opposed to a circumstantial function, as can be seen in the following:

BNC45 The Right will clearly expect Mr Hamilton to **keep** in check some of Mr Heseltine's more interventionist policies.
BNC46 ... that children below the age of seven years did not structure their stories or explanations coherently, nor did they **keep** in mind the extent of the listener's ignorance.

5. Adjuncts in English and French

If nothing else, the data I have presented so far cast doubt on the notion that adjuncts do not occur in English in the structure (lexical) Verb + Adjunct + Object. The corpus data demonstrate that post-verbal placement of an adjunct is possible, although subject to certain lexical restrictions. Consequently, not a single one of the student errors I have examined are contraventions of any 'rule' which might ban Verb + Adjunct + Object in English. Instead, my students' errors are essentially lexico-grammatical, in that they contravene the general patterns of transitivity associated with various verbs and their complements.

In this final section, I examine why students transfer what is essentially a French syntactic pattern to English and I attempt a generalization about the restriction of word orders in both languages. In current generative theory, it is assumed that complements accompany verbs in what is known as the "VP-shell". This structure works for English, but not for French which allows adjuncts freely in post-verbal position, as in example

#13 Je mange souvent des pommes (cf. I eat *often apples).

Discussing the wayward behaviour of this adjunct in French, Carnie says that "in this sentence the adjunct **surprisingly** appears between the head of VP and its complement" (2002: 192, my emphasis). This is echoed by Roberts who in his introduction to generative theory states that:

> We certainly don't want to say that X'-theory allows French to have a different hierarchical structure inside VP as compared with English. Whatever the final verdict is on parameters of linear order, everyone agrees that hierarchical structure should not differ across languages ... (Roberts 1997: 32)

This stipulation is a generally adopted one in generative theory, but there are several reasons why we need to question it. Firstly, there is considerable evidence to suggest that complements and adjuncts exist on a continuum and therefore differences in linear order cannot be due to simple differences between complement-adjunct order. Various intermediate categories have been proposed, as we have seen with Halliday's (1985) notion of Range, Goldberg and Ackerman's (2001) obligatory adjuncts, or Gisborne's (2002) predicative complements. Secondly, it is generally agreed in typological studies that grammatical items and (especially) adjuncts are highly contingent features of language (Croft 1991). In most of these studies, adverbials and adjuncts are considered to be the least 'universal' of any of the traditional parts of speech. It is strange then to see that in standard generative accounts of adjunct placement, it is assumed that adjuncts and complements form wholly distinct categories. For example, Ernst considers that the following examples are ungrammatical because of the restriction that (to re-quote him) "adjuncts do not occur between the verb and a nonheavy object" (2002: 207):

#14   The shakers made *skilfully boxes.
#15   The city council blocked *frequently their proposals.

The transitivity roles in each of these examples are not mentioned in the analysis proposed by Ernst, although it is clear that in #14–15 the adjunct is interrupting a Process + Goal. So while not inaccurate, Ernst has not quite given us the whole picture: he ought to have pointed out that (non-scopal) adjuncts can interrupt a Process + Range. Since the generative description of English is so incomplete, it would be more useful to establish what the differences are between English and French word order rather than stipulating a single basic parameter.

One explanation may be that post-verbal position is a grammaticalized zone in English, a feature which would be compatible with Harris's (1978) treatment of the corresponding pre-finite position in French. It is well-documented that the pre-finite position in French is the preferred zone for the accumulation of clitics (i.e. morphological pronouns and negatives, as in *Je ne le lui en parlerai pas*). As a consequence, it is not normally possible for adjuncts to be positioned in this zone, especially between the subject pronoun and verb (as discussed by Jones 1996, Korzen 1996, Gledhill 2003). This means that in French, the post-verbal or V + A + O zone is freed up, and we therefore find a variety of different structures which would be more marked in English, for example indirect objects:

#16   Il donna à Jean une grande gifle
       [He gave to John a great slap]

manner adverbs:

#17   Jospin a tancé vertement son Ministre
       [Jospin criticized strongly his Minister]

adverbs of time:

#18   Je mange toujours des pommes
       [I eat always apples]

grammatical negatives:

#19   Il ne prendra jamais sa retraite
       [He will take never his retirement]

and so on.

6. Conclusion

There are of course very many syntactic or stylistic reasons why adjuncts may sometimes be placed in post-verbal position, not least of which are semantic scope, prosodic detachment and thematic structure. However, I have argued here that the transitivity relationship between verb and its complement and between the verb and the adjunct are also important factors. Furthermore, the analysis conducted here suggests that there are collocational restrictions in the use of adjuncts, and that a number of adjuncts appear in Verb + Adjunct + Object position because they form a phraseological unit in which the adjunct is effectively part of the predicate structure of a complex verb group. This appears to be the case with lexical phrases of the type *take seriously, do precisely that*. The phraseological approach adopted here challenges the generative assumption that adjuncts are modifiers, simply inserted after the creation of a core clause or VP-shell. In other words, this approach contradicts the commonly held belief that adjuncts are optional and unrestricted.

The purpose of this paper has been to re-evaluate the rule of thumb which states that adjuncts and prepositional phrases in English cannot interrupt the verb and its complement. By using corpus data as opposed to relying on invented examples, it is possible to establish that examples of Verb + Adjunct + Object occur in English. It has also been possible to use standard corpus methodology to explain a little more objectively why certain learners' errors appear to be awkward. Indeed, this is the kind of approach that Granger (1993) has long campaigned for in research on learner corpora.

Bibliography

Alexiadou, A. 1997. *Adverb Placement: a Case Study in Asymmetric Syntax*. Amsterdam: John Benjamins.
Allerton, D. J. 2002. *Stretched Verb Constructions in English*. London: Routledge.
Ballert, I. 1977. On semantic and distributional properties of sentential adverbs. *Linguistic Inquiry* 8 (2). 337–351.

Blasco-Dulbecco, M. 1999. *La dislocation en français contemporain: étude syntaxique*. Paris: Honoré Champion.
Cairncross, A. 1997. Positional variation of the adjunct only in written British English. *Journal of English Linguistics* 25. 59–75.
Carlson, K., Clifton, C., Jr. and Frazier, L. 2001. Prosodic boundaries in adjunct attachment. *Journal of Memory and Language* 45. 58–81.
Carnie, A. 2002. *Syntax: a Generative Introduction*. Oxford: Blackwell.
Clement, D. 1998. Wie frei sind die Adjunkte? Plädoyer für eine differenzierte syntaktische Beschreibung der Adjunkte am Beispiel der durch während eingeleiteten Adverbialsätze im Deutschen. *Deutsche Sprache* 26 (1). 38–62.
Cook, V. J. and Newson, M. 1996. *Chomsky's Universal Grammar: an Introduction*. 2nd ed. Oxford: Blackwell.
Croft, W. 1991. *Syntactic Categories and Grammatical Relations*. Chicago: Chicago University Press.
Cinque, G. 1999. *Adverbs and Functional Heads. A Cross-Linguistic Perspective*. Oxford: Oxford University Press.
Ernst, T. 2002. *The Syntax of Adjuncts*. Cambridge: Cambridge University Press.
Frosch, H. 1997. VG-Adverbiale: Prädikatmodifikation und Komplementbezug. *Sprachtheorie und Germanistische-Linguistik*. 7–26.
Gisborne, N. 2002. The complementation of verbs of appearance by adverbs. In: Bermúdez-Otero, R. et al. (eds.), *Generative Theory and Corpus Linguistics: A Dialogue from 10 ICEHL*. New York: Mouton De Gruyter. 53–76.
Gledhill, C. 2000. *Collocations in Science Writing*. Tübingen: Gunter Narr Verlag.
Gledhill, C. 2003. *Fundamentals of French Syntax*. Munich: Lincom Europa.
Goldberg, A. and Ackerman, F. 2001. The Pragmatics of Obligatory Adjuncts. *Language*. 77 (4). 799–814.
Granger, S. 1993. The international corpus of learner English. In: Aarts, J., de Haan, P. and Oostdijk, N. (eds.), *English Language Corpora: Design, Analysis and Exploitation*. Amsterdam: Rodopi. 56–69.
Halliday, M. A. K. 1985. *Introduction to Functional Grammar*. London: Edward Arnold.
Harris, M. 1978. *The Evolution of French Syntax: a Comparative Approach*. London: Longman.
Huddleston, R. and Pullum, G. 2002. *The Cambridge Grammar of the English Language*. Cambridge: Cambridge University Press.
Hunston, S. and Francis, G. 2000. *Pattern Grammar – A Corpus-Driven Approach to the Lexical Grammar of English*. Amsterdam: John Benjamins.
Jackendoff, R. S. 1972. *Semantic Interpretation in Generative Grammar*. Cambridge, MA: MIT Press.
Jacobson, S. 1964. *Adverbial Positions in English*. Uppsala: Tofters Tryckeri Ab.
Jones, M. A. 1996. *Foundations of French Syntax*. Cambridge: Cambridge University Press.
Kayne, R. 1975. *French Syntax and the Transformational Cycle*. Cambridge, MA: MIT Press.
Korzen, H. 1996. L'unité predicative et la place du sujet dans les constructions inverses. *Langue française* Sept. 1996, 59–82.
Lysvåg, P. 1999. ... who famously contributed to corpus linguistics. A study of famously in the BNC. In: Hasselgård, H. and Oksefjell, S. (eds.), *Out of Corpora: Studies in Honour of Stig Johansson*. Amsterdam: Rodopi. 61–68.
Moignet, G. 1961. *L'adverbe dans la locution verbale. Etude de psycho-systématique française*. Québec: Presses de l'Université Laval.
Müller, N. and Riemer, B. 1998. *Generative Syntax der Romanischen Sprachen*. Tübingen: Stauffenburg Verlag.
Nøjgaard, M. 1968. L'object direct et l'ordre des mots en français. *Le Français moderne* 36 (1). 1–18.
Ouhalla, J. 1994. *Introducing Transformational Grammar*. London: Edward Arnold.
Pawley, A. and Syder, F. H. 1983. Two puzzles for linguistic theory: Nativelike selection and nativelike fluency. In: Richards, J. C. and Schmidt, R. W. (eds.), *Language and Communication*. London: Longman. 191–226.
Pollock, J.-Y. 1989. Verb movement, Universal Grammar and the structure of IP. *Linguistic Inquiry* 20 (3). 365–424.
Quirk, R., Greenbaum, S., Leech G. and Svartvik, J. 1985. *A Comprehensive Grammar of the English Language*. London: Longman.
Risanen, M. 1980. On the position of only in Present-Day English. In: Jacobson, S. (ed.), *Papers from the Scandinavian Symposium on Syntactic Variation. Stockholm Studies in English 52*. Stockholm: Almqvist & Wiksell. 63–76.
Roberts, I. G. 1997. *Comparative Syntax*. London: Edward Arnold.

Swales, J. 1990. *Genre Analysis: English in Academic and Research Settings*. Cambridge: Cambridge University Press.
Van Belle, W. 2000. Object condition adjunct and its equivalents in French. *Leuvense Bijdragen* 89. 277–288.
van der Wouden, T. 1997. *Negative Contexts. Collocation, Polarity and Multiple Negation.* Routledge: London.
Viitanen, T. 1992. *Discourse Functions of Adverbial Placement in English Clause-Initial Adverbials of Time and Place Descriptions*. Åbo: Åbo Akademis Förlag.

Appendix 1

ERROR ANALYSIS:
TWELVE ADVANCED LEARNERS OF ENGLISH

Error Type	Typical example	Marginal example	Quantity	%
Lexical phraseology	V+N They want to *do a profit	They are interested in this issue *in a political view	138	38.5
Morphology	N+V The United Kingdom *want to have their *propers laws	... one must have excellent *result throughout *his life	57	15.9
Syntax	V+ADV they mix *sometimes two words together	... it's all easier for them	54	15.1
Lexico-grammar	UNC These studies aim to show that *the social background isn't linked *with *a wide knowledge	They don't have *so much subsidies *than in France	48	13.4
Lexical choice	*the Speakeasy system has the obvious advantage *to be a first *help device	* ... it is not world-wide spread	29	8.1
Auxiliary / Modal	The antagonism *has been lasting since Azincourt	All that a user *should do is click *to a button	12	3.4
Anaphor / Cohesion	The problem is that as *it has been explained in this text	*They are 22% also receive the classification	10	2.8
Spelling	*british Universities	People can climb in the *hierarchia and *is able to succeed	10	2.8
			358	100%

Appendix 2

ERRORS OF PREDICATE – ADJUNCT SEQUENCE

Modal: mood

1. NNS1 This would allow customers to get *already accustomed to the local gastronomy.
2. NNS2 This allows customers to get *always cheap food.
3. NNS3 The wish of a great deal of supermarket chains to *do *always higher profits can explain the difference ...
4. NNS4 Some students have not *always the most obvious abilities, ...
5. NNS5 So much that they finally aren't able *anymore to buy anything.
6. NNS6 ... they mix *sometimes two words together.
7. NNS7 British leaders seem *often involved in a struggle.
8. NNS8 ... seems to be very *often involved in a deadly hunt.

Modal: comment

1. NNS9 ... when they do *above all everything
2. NNS10 There is a tendency for Oxford University to accept *above all students from public schools
3. NNS11 Another strategy would be to change *completely the distribution network.
4. NNS12 The role of the BBC's pronunciation unit *allows presenters and commentators to pronounce *correctly foreign words.
5. NNS13 ... it seems *even to be the contrary.
6. NNS14 We *impossibly can use English spelling to represent *fairly names.
7. NNS15 Most of the time, there are *only not so relevant *faultes, ...
8. NNS16 If you're looking for the city *'Lyon' and ask *it in *the *english way, you could be *perhaps *set to the zoo.

Conjunctive

1. NNS17 But we soon notice that the customer gets *also in this situation.
2. NNS18 ... the BBC plays *also an important role.
3. NNS19 The Pronunciation Unit has *as well an important diplomatic role.
4. NNS20 They think that the prices should be able to attract *as well customers.
5. NNS21 There is *here a new weapon to take against the government.
6. NNS22 ... the Speakeasy system is *for those reasons an advantage.

Circumstantial

1. NNS23 That's why the advertisers thought about putting *<u>in the centre</u> a picture of a top model.
2. NNS24 De Gaulle vetoed *<u>in the 60's</u> the entry of the UK in the Common Market.
3. NNS25 Actually the dons don't want *<u>in the university</u> weaker students.

Other Adjunct Errors

1. NNS26 ... a 'watchdog' is an organization which has *<u>for goal</u> to verify Supermarket's behaviour.
2. NNS27 ... the watchdog is an organization who has *<u>for assignment</u> to defend consumers.
3. NNS28 ... a policy of integration that was *<u>for the British</u> difficult to accept
4. NNS29 They are supposed to train pupils *<u>better</u> to compete university entrance.
5. NNS30 They keep *<u>up-to-date</u> a database which allows presenters to see the current word pronunciation.

Corpora and language teaching: what learner corpora have to offer

Nadja Nesselhauf

Corpora, i.e. systematic collections of naturally occurring text stored on computer, can be fruitfully used in the field of language teaching in various ways.[1] While native speaker corpora have been increasingly exploited in this field, the exploitation of other types of corpora is only starting. Learner corpora, i.e. corpora consisting of language produced by (foreign or second language) learners, are a type of corpus with a high potential in this area, as they allow a systematic analysis of the typical difficulties of certain learner groups (for a more detailed definition of learner corpora see section 2). The aim of this article is to investigate in some detail what learner corpora have to offer to the area of language teaching, in particular as compared to other types of corpora.[2] Both the contribution that learner corpora have already made and some as yet largely unused possibilities will be discussed. As up to now hardly any learner corpora have been compiled for languages other than English, only the impact on ELT (English language teaching) will be considered here.

The first section of this paper provides a brief overview of the types of corpora (besides learner corpora) that either have influenced or have the potential to influence language teaching. In the second section, the field of learner corpora is surveyed, by examining what (types of) learner corpora have been compiled to date and by discussing the general potential and limitations of this type of data. The third section investigates how results from learner corpus analyses have been integrated in to ELT material of different kinds; the limitations of the approach are also briefly discussed. In the fourth and final section, the possibility of using learner corpora directly in the ELT classroom, in an approach often referred to as "data-driven learning", is explored.

1. Corpora and language teaching

Native speaker corpora are the type of corpus that has had the greatest impact by far on language teaching. In addition to these and to learner corpora, there are some other types of corpora that can also be exploited for language teaching, in particular multi-

---

1 A wider definition of corpora also includes text collections stored otherwise, but such collections are not considered in this article.
2 Other papers which discuss the relationship between learner corpora and language teaching, and on which the present paper partly draws, are Granger 1998, Granger 2002 and Nesselhauf 2004.

lingual corpora and textbook corpora (see below).³ The greatest impact of native speaker corpora on language teaching to date has been on dictionaries. In fact, there is hardly any monolingual English dictionary today which is not at least to some degree based on the analysis of native speaker corpora. The dictionaries that are most consistently corpus-based, and also pioneering in this respect, are the Cobuild dictionaries, most importantly the *Collins Cobuild English Dictionary* (1995). An example entry from this dictionary illustrates how it has been influenced by the reliance on corpus data in its compilation:⁴

> **perform** [...]   ♦♦♦♦◊
> 1 When you **perform** a task or action, especially a   VERB
> complicated one, you do it. *We're looking for peo-*   V n
> *ple of all ages who have performed outstanding acts*
> *of bravery, kindness or courage ... His council had*
> *had to perform miracles on a tiny budget ... Several*
> *grafts may be performed at one operation.*
> 2 If something **performs** a particular function, it   VERB
> has that function. *A complex engine has many*   V n
> *separate components, each performing a different*
> *function.*
> 3 If you **perform** a play, a piece of music, or a   VERB
> dance, you do it in front of an audience. *Gardiner*   V n
> *has pursued relentlessly high standards in perform-*   V
> *ing classical music ... This play was first performed*
> *in 411 BC ... He began performing in the early fifties,*
> *singing and playing guitar.*
> 4 If someone or something **performs well**, they   VERB
> work well or achieve a good result. If they **perform**
> **badly**, they work badly or achieve a poor result. *He* V adv
> *had not performed well in his exams ... England per-*
> *formed so well against France at Wembley ... 'State-*
> *owned industries will always perform poorly,' John*
> *Moore informed readers ... When there's snow and*
> *ice, how's this car going to perform?*

First of all, the number of black diamonds next to the entry gives information about the frequency of the word (five black diamonds denote very high frequency, four denote fairly high frequency, words with five or four black diamonds making up about 75% of the reference corpus). The individual senses of each word are also ordered according to frequency, so that in the example above, the more abstract or more general senses of

---

3 Other types of corpora which can also be used in (second and foreign) language teaching such as corpora of second language varieties of English (e.g. large parts of the ICE-corpus, see Nelson 1996) or ELF (English as a Lingua Franca) corpora (see for example Seidlhofer 2000) will not be discussed in this paper. What will also be disregarded is the influence of corpora on L1 teaching, for example on the basis of child language corpora, see (Leech 1997: 19*f*).

4 The original version of this dictionary (1987) was based on a 20 million word corpus; its successor, the 1995 edition was based on a 200-million-word collection, now referred to as *The Bank of English*. This corpus contains both British and American English and both spoken and written text types.

perform appear before the sense of 'performing a play, a piece of music, or a dance'. A further consequence of the corpus-based compilation is the emphasis on typical patterns, such as "**perform** a task or action", where in particular *task* is a highly frequent collocate of *perform*, or the extra entry for *perform well* and *perform badly*. The decisions of which words, meanings, and phrases were included in the dictionary were also made on the basis of their frequency. In addition, the examples provided are all retrieved from the corpus and not invented. Finally, information on usage and style is also based on corpus-evidence, such as in the entry of *so-and-so*:

> 2 People sometimes refer to another person as a **so-and-so** when they are annoyed with them or think that they are foolish. People often use **so-and-so** in order to avoid using a swear word. Used in informal English. *All her fault, the wicked little so-and-so.*   N-COUNT PRAGMATICS

Reference grammars of English have, to differing degrees, also been improved by incorporating results based on corpus-analyses. Two grammars which have been particularly strongly influenced are the *Collins Cobuild English Grammar* and the *Longman Grammar of Spoken and Written English* (Biber et al. 1999), the former being more geared towards learners of English than the latter. In these grammars, many or even all examples are drawn from corpora, and there is an increased emphasis on lexico-grammatical information and on frequency information.

In addition to the influence of corpus linguistics on reference materials, there has also been some influence on textbooks:

> Corpus data has provided a much more objective basis for vocabulary selection, has led to greater attention to word combinations of all types (collocations, prefabs or semi-prefabs) and has also greatly improved the description of genre differences. (Granger 2002: 21)

An example of a textbook informed by corpora to a great degree is, *Exploring Grammar in Context* (Carter et al. 2000). This book incorporates a large number of authentic texts, and grammatical features are often illustrated in the context of more than a single sentence. In addition, grammar rules are often introduced not explicitly but by presenting a large number of patterns from which this rule can be inferred by the learner. This type of approach, in which the learners induce patterns from authentic corpus data, can also be used independently from textbooks in an approach commonly referred to as "data-driven learning" (Johns 1991). There is thus some overlap between corpus-based textbooks and the use of corpora or evidence from a corpus directly in the language classroom. An example of data-driven learning is given below, where the aim is to teach the difference in semantic prosody (i.e. typical semantic environments) of the two – otherwise semantically similar – expressions *on the brink of* and *on the road to*.[5]

---

5   This example together with the relevant concordance lines was retrieved from http://www.geocities.com/tonypgnews/ddl_30.htm (16.11.03). To reflect linguistic reality even more closely, it might be appropriate to additionally include some instances of *on the road to* with a negative prosody in these example concordance lines, as expressions such as *on the road to tragedy* or *on the road to chaos* also sometimes occur (cf. e.g. British National Corpus, J37 964 and CG0 294).

Rather than stating this difference in abstract terms, learners are presented with concordance lines (i.e. lines from a corpus with the expression in question) from which the difference can then be inferred:

Bosnian peace talks in Geneva were	on the brink of	collapse today. Reports out
The Soviet economy is poised	on the brink of	disaster, output is falling
that Kirghizia and Uzbekistan are	on the brink of	war. Troops have been sent
night. The 42-year-old actor is	on the brink of	death with spine and head in
designed to save species teetering	on the brink of	extinction can have a dramatic
lines of conflict in Eritrea are	on the brink of	starvation and some of the
Ken Rutherford (61) put the side	on the road to	victory with a match-winning
home believing he had put the world	on the road to	peace and prosperity. Dreams
years after Lithuania's first steps	on the road to	independence. Dayva said she
firmly to support Hungary	on the road to	democracy and stability and
Worse, it was IBM that put Gates	on the road to	riches, by handing him its
a diet guaranteed to put anyone	on the road to	good health and blokes will

Three further possible types of application of native speaker corpora and corpus results to language teaching, which do not, however, appear to be particularly widespread at the moment, are syllabus design, language testing and correcting. One of the few syllabuses strongly influenced by corpus linguistics is Willis's "Lexical Syllabus" (Willis 1990), in which the progression is based on the frequency of lexical items and lexical patterns rather than on grammatical structures, as in traditional syllabuses. The potential of corpora in language testing has been discussed in particular with respect to the self-testing made possible by corpus-based CALL programs, where the corpus provides a large number of authentic test samples (Leech 1997: 16*ff*). As a help in correction, native speaker corpora are particularly useful to non-native teachers, who can turn to them when other reference materials do not provide sufficient evidence as to whether or not a learner production is acceptable or not (Mukherjee 2002: 138*ff*). More generally, corpora "might be treated as a reference tool, which could be looked up to provide examples and therefore clarify doubts on particular problems which had arisen in other language activities" (Aston 1996: 205). This activity is then again close to data-driven learning, which illustrates that the different types of corpus application differentiated in this section in reality shade into each other.

In contrast to native speaker corpora, multilingual corpora and textbook corpora have not yet had any significant impact in the field of language teaching. But some applications have been suggested, and some beginnings have been made. Multilingual corpora are corpora consisting of more than one (native) language, the subcorpora either consisting of the same text types or even of the same (translated) texts (this latter type being sometimes referred to as "parallel corpora"). With such corpora, comparative studies are possible which allow to identify potential areas of difficulty for the language learner by comparing the learner's L1 with the language to be learnt.[6] One of

---

6 Note, however, that without additional learner corpus analysis, only potential but not necessarily real areas of difficulty can be identified with multilingual corpora.

the rare examples of teaching materials that have been created on the basis of an analysis with a multilingual corpus is the "Chemnitz Internet Grammar", which consists of a reference grammar and exercises focussing on areas where English and German differ substantially.[7] As with native speaker corpora, data-driven learning is also possible with parallel corpora, with the help of a so-called parallel concordancer, which enables the learner to obtain concordance lines of the same clause or expression in different languages on the same screen for direct comparison (cf. Barlow 2000).

Textbook corpora, which are corpora containing certain (or all) texts of a foreign language textbook or textbook series, can be used to compare the input that learners get in the classroom to the input they would get in natural communicative situations. As there are only very few corpora of this type to date, and analyses based on textbook corpora are only starting to emerge (e.g. Römer forthcoming), this type of corpus has not had any discernible impact on the field of language teaching to date. But while authentic language is not necessarily the best input for the learner, textbook corpora can help uncover areas where there are radical and pedagogically unnecessary differences between the language the learner is exposed to in the book and actual speech and writing; such results can then lead to a modification of the language used in textbooks.

2. Existing learner corpora and their potential

Before the field of learner corpora can be reviewed, a clarification of the concept appears necessary. According to the general definition of corpora given at the very beginning of this paper, a learner corpus could be defined as a systematic computerized collection of naturally occurring texts produced by learners. There are two problems with this definition. First, what are naturally occurring texts and secondly, who counts as a learner of a language? When these questions are addressed, it turns out that the concept of the learner corpus is a prototypical concept, with some learner corpora being more and others less typical. With respect to the naturalness of texts, the question is whether texts that (foreign) learners produce in or for the language classroom are to be counted as natural. A question connected with this is to what degree the texts can have been elicited. Collections of texts elicited in the classroom with a small degree of control (such as essays where only the topic had been given) are usually considered typical learner corpora, while those elicited with a high degree of control (such as retellings of picture stories) are considered learner corpora only by some researchers. Second language texts are usually considered as stemming from learners if the person in question either learns the language in a country where the L2 has no official function, or learns the language (as an immigrant or visitor) in a country where it is spoken natively. The term "learner" is also sometimes applied to non-adult speakers of the L2 in countries where the L2 has some kind of official function. Varieties spoken by adult

---

7 Cf. http://www.tu-chemnitz.de/phil/InternetGrammar/publications/info/grammar.htm (16.11.03).

speakers in countries where the language has an official function (such as Kenyan English) are not usually considered learner varieties, however, and corpora containing such varieties are therefore not usually referred to as learner corpora.

In what follows, only typical learner corpora will be discussed. While many learner corpus projects have been started in recent years, the number of those that have actually been completed or of which at least parts can be used is still comparatively small. One of the reasons for this is that, with very few exceptions, learner corpus compilation only started in the 1990s, about 30 years after the first native speaker corpora were compiled. The probably largest learner corpus to date, the HKUST (Hong Kong University of Science and Technology) learner corpus contains around 25 million words; typically, currently existing learner corpora contain between 200,000 and 500,000 words. For comparison, the largest native speaker corpora currently contain a hundred million words and more, although there is a large number of one million word native corpora as well. While the language represented in almost all existing learner corpora is English, the L1 (first language) of the learners varies greatly. Most learner corpora contain only productions from one native language group; fairly large-sized learner corpora are available for example for Chinese (HKUST and TeleNex Student Corpus), Swedish (the Uppsala Student English Project), Japanese (Corpus of English by Japanese Learners), Hungarian (Janus Pannonius University Corpus), and Polish (Polish Learner English Corpus; cf. Nesselhauf 2004, for a description of these and other learner corpora). There are also a few learner corpora which contain language from learners with several different L1s. Two of them, the Longman Learner Corpus (LLC) and the Cambridge University Press (CUP) Learner Corpus are not strictly controlled for text types (and, as they are owned by publishing houses, not generally available for research). One of the most important and widely used learner corpora to date, the ICLE corpus (International Corpus of Learner English), contains the same or comparable text types for all its subcorpora; it contains language from learners with more than 10 different language backgrounds.[8] Most of the learner corpora existing today contain language from intermediate or advanced learners; there are also some which include texts from learners at different levels. Truly developmental learner corpora, in which texts from the same learners at different levels are included, do not appear to have been compiled yet, however. As to the type of language that is recorded, the overwhelming majority of learner corpora includes exclusively written language; a few record (either exclusively or in addition to written language) spoken language. One example of a spoken learner corpus project is LINDSEI, the Louvain International Database of Spoken English Interlanguage (cf. De Cock 1998). For a few of the learner corpora, so-called native speaker control corpora have also been compiled. These are native speaker corpora designed in the same way as the learner corpus, i.e. of the same size, containing the same types and proportions of text types, etc.

---

8 For more information about ICLE, see http://www.fltr.ucl.ac.be/FLTR/GERM/ETAN/CECL/cecl.html (12.12.03).

Learner corpora are not the only type of data on the basis of which learner language can be investigated, of course. Learner language was also collected before the advent of computers, and in particular in the 60s and 70s error collections were highly popular in an approach usually referred to as "error analysis". More experimental data than is included in typical learner corpora can also serve for the analysis of learner language, such as data from elicitation tests where the learner has to provide words that have been blanked out. Compared to these other types of learner language analysis, the analysis of learner corpora has a number of inherent advantages, however. In contrast to pure error collections, learner corpus data allows the investigation of how often a certain feature is used appropriately in addition to how often it is not. This is important, as a feature that has been used inappropriately, say, 5 times in a given amount of text cannot be considered to have the same degree of difficulty if it is at the same time used appropriately 50 times as if it is used appropriately only once or twice. If a native speaker control corpus is available, overuse and underuse (i.e. the question of whether certain features are used with much greater or lower frequency by a certain learner group than in comparable native speaker language) can also be investigated with a learner corpus but not with a collection of errors. Compared to any kind of collection of learner language which is not computerized, learner corpora have the advantage of sometimes simplifying the analyses because certain features can be searched for automatically.[9] The computerization of the data also simplifies its distribution. The results from a learner corpus study can therefore be compared and verified much more easily than if each researcher bases their studies on data collected individually for this purpose. Compared to more experimental data such as judgement tasks or multiple choice tests, (more or less) real production data is examined in learner corpus studies, which means the learners' problems in actually producing the second language are investigated and not their more abstract knowledge of certain features. In addition to these advantages, depending on the type of corpus, some learner corpora also allow the investigation of the role of extralinguistic factors on production, such as years of acquisition or age, as well as the comparison of learner production on different proficiency levels, with different L1s and the production problems that occur in different text types.

Despite the great potential of learner corpora, this type of data naturally also has some limitations. For example, it is not possible to investigate comprehension with a learner corpus, and neither is it possible to determine how certain a learner is about an expression he or she has produced. If a certain feature does not occur in a (part of a) learner corpus, this does not allow any conclusions about the learners' competence, as it might be merely by coincidence (or due to non-linguistic reasons) that the feature in question was not used. Finally, though not impossible in principle, an investigation

---

9 It has to be pointed out, however, that learner corpus analysis can rely less on automatic extraction of elements than native speaker corpus analysis, because of the usually large number of misspellings and other kinds of mistakes that occur in learner language. What can often be done, however, is to check after a manual analysis whether all relevant instances of the phenomenon in question have actually been extracted.

into the role of certain learner characteristics such as motivation and into the role of input and interaction in second language acquisition is hardly feasible with most of the learner corpora existing to date.

3. Learner corpora and pedagogic material

Because there are comparatively few existing learner corpora, and many are of a rather modest size, the number of comprehensive studies based on such corpora is not very large either. Consequently their influence on pedagogic material is rather limited at this point in time. The main exception to this are learner dictionaries, as for some of them systematic learner corpus research has been carried out (by publishing houses) and the results have been used to compile or improve them. Four dictionaries in particular have been heavily influenced by results from learner corpus analysis:

> *Longman Language Activator* (1993)
> *Longman Dictionary of Contemporary English* (1995)
> *Longman Essential Activator* (1997)
> *Cambridge International Dictionary of English* (1995)

In addition, the *Longman Dictionary of Common Errors* (1987), a collection of words and expressions that learners frequently misuse, has also been compiled on the basis of learner corpus analysis. These dictionaries are based on the Longman Learner Corpus and the Cambridge University Press Learner corpus, which both comprise around 10 million words, each from learners of a number of different L1s and of different levels and text types. Two examples of how learner corpus analysis has contributed towards these dictionaries are given below, the first from the *Longman Essential Activator*, the second from the *Longman Dictionary of Common Errors*. Both entries not only give the correct form of an expression that is frequently misused but also warn the user against the most frequent inappropriate use:

> **mention** [v T] to talk about someone or something, but without giving details or saying very much about them: *He mentioned something about a party, but didn't say when it was.*
> + *(that): I forgot to mention that I won't be in tomorrow.*
> *mention where/who/what etc.: Did they mention where they were going?*
> Don't say 'mention about something'. Say **mention something**.

> **demonstration** × Many demonstrations have been made in recent years in protest against the level of pollution.
> √ **Many demonstrations have been held in recent years in protest against the level of pollution.**
>
> **hold/stage a demonstration** NOT **make**

While a number of dictionaries have thus greatly profited from learner corpora, there has been hardly any influence on reference grammars, with the exception of an online grammar created in a project for teachers of English in Hong Kong, called Tele-Gram.[10] TeleGram is a grammatical description of English geared towards Hong Kong learners of English and based on the TeleNex Student Corpus which contains several million words of texts from the learner group in question. In addition to providing the rules for certain grammatical phenomena, the database also presents typical problems of Hong Kong learners, which were revealed by the analysis of the learner corpus. Examples of typical problems extracted directly from the corpus are also given[11]:

! **Students' problems**
Omitting the auxiliary in passive voice

This problem involves students using transitive verbs as if they were ergative. Some students omit the relevant form of the verb *be*, with the effect that the verbs look as though they are being used as ergative verbs:

*He found the heroin in my bag so I [^] **arrested** in the airport.*
(TeleNex Students)

[…]

For further information about passive voice in general, see Using passive voice: Overview.

For further information about ergative verbs, see Using transitive and intransitive verbs: Using ergative verbs.

As with grammars, teaching material based on learner corpus analysis is only starting to emerge, and the material currently available is online material. One example is TeleTeach, which resulted from the same project as TeleGram and contains teaching material for teachers of English in Hong Kong. The material was also created for those areas with which Hong Kong learners of English were found to have most difficulties. Another example of teaching material is an interactive CALL program also designed for Chinese-speaking learners of English called AutoLANG (see Milton 1998 and http://home.ust.hk/~autolang/). The target group is advanced learners, and the program mainly contains proof-readings exercises, in which the learner is asked to identify and explain common errors hidden in texts; additional information and exercises on frequent mistakes are also provided. An example is given below. The text that the learner is supposed to correct contains a simple verb which should be replaced by a prepositional verb in order to make the sentence appropriate. If the learner asks for additional information on this type of mistake, a box containing the following information pops up:

Missing Preposition

An example of a frequent error in preposition omission is the confusion between "search" and "search for". Try to understand the difference between these two expressions by studying the following correct and incorrect sentences:

---

10 See http://www.telenex.hku.hk/telec/pmain/opening.htm (16.11.03).
11 See http://www.telenex.hku.hk/telec/sgram/ti_sspr8.htm (16.11.03).

√New graduates may encounter difficulties when they search for a job.
× New graduates may encounter difficulties when they search a job.
√At some airports the Customs officials search travellers.

Click here for practice in using prepositions.
Click here for a list of expressions commonly confused by learners of English.

On language testing and on syllabuses, finally, the impact of learner corpora has also been very slight. A suggestion of how to use results from a learner corpus study for language testing is made in Hasselgren (2002). She finds that "smallwords" such as *well* and *sort of* are indicators of fluency in learner language and therefore suggests testing learner fluency by testing learners' use of these words. As to syllabuses, there appears to be only one project at the moment where the results from learner corpus analysis have led to a modification of the syllabus. On the basis of a 500,000 words corpus containing texts from university students with L1 Hungarian, Hórvath redesigned a course teaching writing skills to Hungarian students of English with increased focus on their particular problem areas (Hórvath 2001).

While the main potential of learner corpora for the improvement of pedagogical materials therefore lies in their capacity for revealing typical areas of difficulty and typical mistakes, a word of caution is in order. For native speaker corpus analysis, a direct application of the results to language teaching according to the formula "more frequent = more emphasis in teaching" has often been criticized for being too simplistic and slighting other pedagogical considerations (Widdowson 2000). A similar danger lies in directly applying results from learner corpus analyses to language teaching, only this time according to the formula "more liable to mistakes = more emphasis in teaching". Certainly, both factors, the factor of frequency of a feature as well the factor of difficulty for the learner, should be taken into account when selecting features for teaching. In addition, other factors might have to play a role as well, such as disruptiveness for the listener/reader of certain inappropriate features (cf. Nesselhauf forthcoming). In any case, as for every other type of application of theoretical results, it is important to critically reflect on the implications the results of a learner corpus analysis have for the design of language teaching materials.

4. Learner corpora in the classroom

A data-driven learning approach to teaching as described in section 1 is also conceivable on the basis of learner corpora if it is accepted that negative evidence can aid language learning.[12] If this is true, and there is evidence that it is (Ellis 1994: 639*ff*), learners should profit from inductive learning with learner corpus data in a similar way as they appear to profit from such learning with native speaker corpora. An important

---

12 This assumption also underlies most of the teaching materials based on learner corpora, as warnings against common mistakes are often included there.

difference, however, is, that if learners analyse lines from a learner corpus they should always at the same time be provided with examples of the same phenomenon in native speaker production. In order not to confuse learners it also seems particularly desirable when working with non-native speaker concordance lines in the classroom that teachers carefully select which features to study and if necessary edit out unnecessary or confusing instances. Features that are particularly suited to classroom concordancing are two-word or three-word patterns that learners often misuse, such as the complementation of nouns, verbs, and adjectives, and other words and expressions which can be identified as inappropriate from their direct environment. More abstract grammatical features such as tense and aspect, on the other hand, are not particularly suitable for this kind of treatment. Two examples of suitable features are given in Figures 6.1 and 6.2.

Figure 6.1 *Economical* in the French subcorpus of ICLE (16 out of 50 occurrences)

```
              ɉ at things and in political, economical and social str
              ˙ies have to reinforce their economical and social col
               even if they agree with an economical and political E
              ʝ92 aims at increasing the economical and political s
              ǝ a Europe as strong in its economical and social pol
              eing European. Secondly, economical and political u
              s very much influenced by economical and political n
              ll lose it because of some economical and social me
              ich is more ambiguous, in economical and political fi
              uge changes especially in economical and social spl
              ʌe can go further than the economical aspect and m
              ˥ed in connection with the economical aspect, freedc
              ɘnt EEC countries. But the economical aspects of Eu
              rmonization only keeps to economical aspects. How
              ɟurope was a political and economical chaos. Severɑ
              l mean that a political and economical collaboration
```

In Figure 6.1, the use of the word *economical* in the French subcorpus of ICLE (International Corpus of Learner English, cf. above) is displayed. Students can investigate the frequent confusion of *economical* with *economic* by learners on the basis of these concordance lines and a native speaker corpus such as the BNC.[13] Tasks that could guide the student through this exercise are, for example, a comparison of the coordination of *economical* and *social/political* and of *economic* and *social/political* in the BNC. They will find there that while *economic* is coordinated with *social* (in a span of 3) over 2,000 times and with *political* over 1,200 times, *economical* is never coordinated with *social* and only 3 times with *political*. Similarly, some of the nouns that are used

---

13 BNC stands for British National Corpus. It contains 100 million words of modern British English of various text types (cf. http://www.hcu.ox.ac.uk/BNC; 12.12.03).

with *economical* in the learner corpus, such as *chaos, aspect(s)* or (in the results not displayed) *interest* and *policy* could be investigated as to their co-occurrence with *economical*, yielding the result that most of the nouns the learners used do not occur with *economical* but occur fairly frequently with *economic*. It does not seem unlikely that exercises such as these make a more lasting impression on the learners than merely being told (probably not for the first time) that the two words do not mean the same in English.

A second example of data-driven learning material based on a learner corpus is the complementation of *reason* by a preposition in the Spanish subcorpus of ICLE. Figure 6.2 gives the results of a search for *reason*, with the irrelevant instances (such as *reason that*) edited out.

Figure 6.2 *Reason for/of* in the Spanish subcorpus of ICLE (irrelevant instances removed)

```
           piece "Les misérables". The reason for his change of mir
           ve got to wonder what is the reason for it. I suppose, the
           edy and perhaps that is the reason for their bad depictic
         x equality is one of the great reason for fights in most pla
           develop properly. The main reason for this deliberate lim
          ning is done for us. The only reason for such a thing is th
       onsideration, go to the other reason for defense this who
         regard the oil business as a reason for the involvement o
        ves well in prison there is no reason for letting him free. A
         a translator or a lawyer? The reason for companies to ask
             oney. We can think that the reason of the creation of the
         all finish in divorce. The last reason of discrimination is tl
         : way to obtain a job. For the reason of lack of experience
          sm constitutes an important reason of conflicts in our so
          e money has been the main reason of many mischiefs d
         castle who doesn't know the reason of the young man's a
          n religion represents another reason of distinction. Some
```

If *reason of* and *reason for* are compared in the BNC, the learner will discover not only that *reason for* is almost ten times as frequent as *reason of*, but that *reason of* occurs predominantly in the phrase *by reason of*, and that, therefore, in all the examples from the learner corpus, *for* would have been the appropriate preposition.[14] Again, it does not seem unreasonable to suspect that insights of this kind are longer-lasting than a mere presentation of the fact that the appropriate preposition after *reason* is *for*.

Data-driven learning with learner corpora has only been attempted by very few teachers so far, but those who have tried it report it to be motivating for the students

---

14 Learners well versed in concordance analysis might discover that, in addition, *reason of* is used a few times in the BNC to state the reason itself after the preposition. One instance of this use also occurred in the learner corpus but was edited out, in order to not confuse the learners.

(cf. e.g. Horváth 2001). The approach can also enhance learners' attitude towards mistakes, as mistakes are not considered as an evil that is to be avoided but rather as something that can be discovered. Like data-driven learning with native-speaker corpora, the approach also enhances learner autonomy, as the learners are no longer merely presented with what is inappropriate and what appropriate, but can actively and (at least partly) independently of the teacher make their own inferences. Some limitations of the approach are that it is only feasible with fairly advanced students and that some time needs to be spent first on introducing learners to the work with concordance lines before the approach can be profitably exploited. As mentioned before, not all problematic language points lend themselves to this type of data-driven learning, and to avoid confusing learners, it is necessary to carefully prepare the features to be investigated, and in many cases also of the concordance lines presented. Finally, there is a danger of focussing on what is inappropriate rather than on what is appropriate, which can be counteracted, however, by focussing on the appropriate expressions in follow-up exercises. Although the potential of data-driven learning with learner corpora is only starting to be recognized and to be implemented, if applied prudently, the advantages certainly outweigh the disadvantages.

Learner corpora therefore have a great deal to offer not only for the improvement of syllabuses and other pedagogic material but also directly in the classroom. Whereas the latter influence may take place immediately, provided there is a teacher who is willing and capable of trying out data-driven learning with a learner corpus and a learner corpus of the L1 in question is available, the increase in the influence of learner corpora on most pedagogic material will take place only slowly, as comprehensive analyses of large learner corpora are necessary first. By no means, however, should the influence of learner corpora replace that of other types of corpora. Ideally, different types of corpora (native speaker corpora, bilingual corpora and learner corpora) should play a role in the classroom, and results from different types of corpora should complement each other in helping design improved teaching materials.

Bibliography

Aston, G. 1996. Involving learners in developing learning methods: exploiting text corpora in self-access. In: Benson, P. and Voller, P. (eds.), *Autonomy and Independence in Language Learning*. London: Longman. 204–214.
Barlow, M. 2000. Parallel texts in language teaching. In: Botley, S., McEnery, T. and Wilson, A. (eds.), *Multilingual Corpora in Teaching and Research*. Amsterdam and Atlanta: Rodopi. 106–115.
Biber, D., Johansson, S., Leech, G., Conrad, S. and Finegan, E. 1999. *Longman Grammar of Spoken and Written English*. Harlow: Pearson Education.
Cambridge International Dictionary of English. 1995. Cambridge: Cambridge University Press.
Carter, R., Hughes, R. and McCarthy, M. 2000. *Exploring Grammar in Context. Grammar reference and practice upper-intermediate and advanced*. Cambridge: Cambridge University Press.
Collins Cobuild English Dictionary. 1995. London. Harper Collins.
De Cock, S. 1998. A recurrent word combination approach to the study of formulae in the speech of native and non-native speakers of English. *International Journal of Corpus Linguistics* 3 (1), 59–80.
Ellis, R. 1994. *The Study of Second Language Acquisition*. Oxford: Oxford University Press.

Granger, S. 1998. The computer learner corpus: a versatile new source of data for SLA research. In: Granger 1998. 3–18.
Granger, S. (ed.) 1998. *Learner English on Computer*. London: Longman.
Granger, S. 2002. A bird's-eye view of learner corpus research. In: Granger et al. 2002. 3–33.
Granger, S., Hung, J. and Petch-Tyson, S. (eds.) 2002. *Computer Learner Corpora, Second Language Acquisition and Foreign Language Teaching*. Amsterdam/Philadelphia: Benjamins.
Hasselgren, A. 2002. Learner corpora and language testing: smallwords as markers of learner fluency. In: Granger et al. 2002. 143–173.
Horváth, J. 2001. *Advanced Writing in English as a Foreign Language. A corpus-based study of processes and products*. Pécs: Lingua Franca Csoport.
Johns, T. 1991. Should you be persuaded – Two examples of data-driven learning materials. *English Language Research Journal* 4, 1–16.
Leech, G. 1997. Teaching and language corpora: a convergence. In: Wichmann, A., Fligelstone, S., McEnery, T. and Knowles, G. (eds.), *Teaching and Language Corpora*. London and New York: Longman. 1–24.
Longman Dictionary of Contemporary English. 1995. London and New York: Longman.
Longman Essential Activator. 1997. London and New York: Longman.
Longman Language Activator. 1993. London and New York: Longman.
Milton, J. 1998. Exploiting L1 and interlanguage corpora in the design of an electronic language learning and production environment. In: Granger 1998. 186–198.
Mukherjee, J. 2002. *Korpuslinguistik und Englischunterricht. Eine Einführung*. Frankfurt: Lang.
Nelson, G. 1996. The design of the corpus. In: Greenbaum, S. (ed.), *Comparing English Worldwide: The international corpus of English*. Oxford: Clarendon. 27–35.
Nesselhauf, N. 2004. Learner corpora and their potential in language teaching. In: Sinclair, J. (ed.), *How to Use Corpora in Language Teaching*. Amsterdam: Benjamins. 125–152.
Nesselhauf, N. (forthcoming). *Collocations in a Learner Corpus*. Amsterdam: Benjamins.
Römer, U. (forthcoming). Comparing real and ideal language learner input: The use of an EFL textbook corpus in corpus linguistics and language teaching. In: Aston, G. and Bernardini, S. (eds.), *Corpora and Language Learners*. Amsterdam: Benjamins.
Seidlhofer, B. 2000. Mind the gap: English as a mother tongue vs. English as a lingua franca. *Vienna English Working Papers* 9 (1). 51–68.
Sinclair, J. (ed.), 1995. *Collins Cobuild English Grammar*. London: Harper Collins.
Turton, N. D. and Heaton, J. B. 1987. *Longman Dictionary of Common Errors*. Harlow: Longman.
Widdowson, H. G. 2000. On the limitations of linguistics applied. *Applied Linguistics* 21 (1), 3–25.
Willis, D. 1990. *The Lexical Syllabus. A new approach to language teaching*. London and Glasgow: Collins.

Error Analysis with computer learner corpora: a corpus-based study of errors in the written German of British university students

Ursula Weinberger

In the early 1970s Error Analysis was considered a useful method of studying learner language, but by the mid 1970s severe criticism of the methodology and the scope of the studies had led to a quick decline in its popularity. In the late 1990s Dagneaux et al. (1998) introduced "Computer-aided error analysis" – a new technique in the analysis of learner errors which they hoped would give a "new impetus to Error Analysis research, and re-establish it as an important area of study" (Dagneaux et al. 1998: 163). One purpose of this article is to give a brief overview of the principles of error analysis, the criticism that led to its decline in the 1970s and how Computer-aided Error Analysis can improve the investigation of learner errors in such a way that it becomes a fruitful method for Applied Linguistics. The second purpose is to present a pilot study applying Computer-aided Error Analysis to a corpus of written German produced by British university students. For this, a corpus of approximately 30,000 words was collected from students at Lancaster University, UK. A specially designed tagset was then used to annotate the corpus according to a comprehensive error classification. After that the corpus was analysed for distribution of errors across categories as well as error patterns within categories, which revealed some interesting results concerning areas of persistent difficulty.

1. Error Analysis and Computer-aided Error Analysis

1.1 Traditional Error Analysis in context

In order to understand how the new approach of Computer-aided Error Analysis (CEA) can improve Error Analysis (EA) in such a way that it becomes a useful method for Applied Linguistics, it is important to understand the context of the original EA studies within the wider context of theoretical second language acquisition frameworks and research paradigms.

Error Analysis as a method of studying learner language had its peak in the early 1970s[1]. Raabe (1980: 65) points out that the general evaluation of errors, and in particular second language learner errors, somewhat mirrors the research history of second lan-

---

[1] Studies of learner errors had been conducted before this time (e.g. French. 1949. *Common Errors in English*. Oxford: Oxford University Press). These studies, however, lacked any systematic methodology and had no great impact on language pedagogy at the time.

guage acquisition. Before the emergence of EA as a research approach errors were at best dismissed as "a matter of no particular importance" (Corder 1967: 162) if not considered annoying and distressing.

This view was sustained well during the heydays of behaviourism and linguistic structuralism in the 1950s and 1960s. In accordance with the behaviourist postulate that learning in general, and consequently language learning, is essentially a matter of habit formation, second language teaching took up approaches like the Audiolingual Method focusing primarily on pattern drills and the avoidance of errors at all cost, so that learners would not acquire 'erroneous' language habits. Researchers at the time carried out extensive Contrastive Analysis studies in order to find out which features of a second language would pose difficulties for learners with a certain first language in order to adjust teaching accordingly. It was soon realized, however, that Contrastive Analysis could only account for about 30% of learners' errors and was dismissed by teachers as uninformative and inaccurate (James 1998: 4*f*).

Finally, CA was also criticized as being grounded in outdated theoretical bases when behaviourism was superseded by theories of cognitive learning. This 'cognitive revolution' with the idea that learning is a cognitive process where the learner actively forms hypotheses about the foreign language and develops and employs cognitive learning strategies thoroughly changed the way errors were viewed. The person who undoubtedly laid the foundations for a systematic approach to EA was Pit Corder. He really brought the "significance of learner errors" (Corder 1967) to the attention of second language acquisition research. He stresses that errors are significant in three ways:

(a) They provide teacher and learner with valuable feedback about what the learner has or has not yet learned.
(b) They give indications to the researcher as to what strategies learners use in their discovery of the foreign language.
(c) They are important for learners as a way of testing their hypotheses about the foreign language.

The core idea behind EA was to reverse the negative perception of errors as "annoying and distressing" and to acknowledge errors as evidence for the learners' developing interlanguages. "In error analysis, 'error' has a positive import with a function in learning strategy." (Svartvik 1973: 9)

In the course of applying the theoretical assumptions into workable research studies, a general procedure for EA evolved which essentially includes the following steps (Ellis 1994: 47–72):

(i) Collection of samples of learner language
(ii) Identification of errors
(iii) Description of errors
(iv) Explanation of errors

It was soon realized, however, that all of these steps entail a number of problems that need to be addressed if EA is supposed to be useful as an analytical tool with implications for language pedagogy.

1.2 Criticism against Error Analysis

The way in which EA studies were carried out in the early 1970s evoked severe criticism, which falls into two groups. The first concerns methodological weaknesses, the second limitations in scope.

Methodological weaknesses became apparent in nearly all stages of the EA procedure. In terms of data collection the accusation was that many EA studies were based on heterogeneous learner data, because not enough attention was paid to consistent sample design criteria, which rendered those studies "difficult to interpret and almost impossible to replicate" (Ellis 1994: 49). Design criteria that should be controlled for include factors such as spontaneous vs elicited experimental data, longitudinal vs cross-sectional data, medium (spoken vs written), learners' L1, level of proficiency and learning situation (second vs foreign language learning).

Where the identification of errors is concerned, the problem of what constitutes an error is most prominent. If, as I suggest, we accept Lennon's (1991: 182) rather astute definition of error as "a linguistic form, [...] which, in the same context would in all likelihood not be produced by the learner's *native speaker counterparts*", this at least takes into account the fact that what a learner utterance should be measured against is not a standard norm or variety of the L2, but an utterance of a native speaker who has a similar level of education, is of the same age group, socio-economic class, gender, etc.

There are, however, still three variables in terms of which the utterance can be deviant (Enkvist 1973: 20):

grammaticality: is the utterance grammatically correct?
acceptability: is the utterance acceptable with respect to the linguistic context?[2]
appropriateness: is the utterance appropriate in its communicative context? (This notion is closely connected to 'communicative success'.)

While it should be less difficult to objectively assess grammaticality (for example with reference to a descriptive grammar of the L2), acceptability and appropriateness are more subject to the discretion of the person judging the utterance, and this introduces an unwanted notion of subjectivity and inter-rater variability into error-identification.

Finally, the biggest problems arise on the levels of error classification and explanation. Most error taxonomies used in the traditional EA studies have been accused of being subjective or fuzzy and lacking the ability to describe errors comprehensively. They were usually either based on linguistic categories (such as syntax, morphology and vocabulary) or on target modification (i.e. errors are classified according to the way they alter the surface structure of an utterance in comparison to the correct L2 form). Categories within the latter taxonomy are for instance omission, addition, misformation, and misordering. These two types of classification (linguistic categories and target modification) were employed in an either/or fashion depending on the intended

---

2 James (1998: 71) lists as grounds for unacceptability deviations like "failure to fit intended context, reference to inconceivable situation, flouting customary collocation, producing unusual grammar of phonological configuration, upsetting the balance of sentence parts".

research aims, thus failing to provide a comprehensive picture of the types of errors. On top of that some of the taxonomies confused error description with error explanation. While the former is considered a linguistic matter, the latter is essentially a psychological matter. Scholfield (1995: 189*f*) gives an example of a taxonomy consisting of the categories "spelling errors", "grammatical errors", "vocabulary errors", and "L1-induced errors". Since L1-induced errors can in fact be manifest in spelling, grammatical and vocabulary deviations, the overlap in the categories makes this taxonomy inadequate.

The second criticism levelled against traditional EA concerns limitations in scope; in other words, EA fails to provide a comprehensive picture of the learner's language because it concentrates on the errors in learner language and therefore neglects all those instances where the learner actually produces correct utterances. This is especially true of many of the studies of the 1970s, which, having extracted the errors, discarded the rest of the data. The approach also fails to capture instances of avoidance, where learners avoid structures they feel they have not yet mastered sufficiently and are therefore insecure about using. And finally, none of the early EA studies could provide information about progress in learning, as they gave only a static picture of L2 learning at a certain point in the learning process – which sometimes was not even defined in the sample design criteria.

1.3 Computer-aided Error Analysis

Looking at the points of criticism in the previous section, it does not seem surprising that the usefulness of EA studies for Applied Linguistics and language teaching soon became questioned and finally led to a sharp decline in the popularity of EA already by the mid 1970s. But, although the traditional EA studies of the early 1970s may be justly criticized, the fact that this criticism pertains to methodology and scope indicates that these are not problems inherent to the EA approach as such. Its principal ideas have not been proven obsolete, but the methodological weaknesses have to be addressed. Data collection procedures must involve recording and monitoring as many variables as possible that may influence the learners' performance and thus the data. In terms of error categorization, larger corpora of learner errors can help to develop more precise categories that are extracted from the data itself rather than being the result of expectations and speculations on the part of the researcher. As for the limitations, it is true that EA merely accounts for errors in learner language. This, however, is only a drawback if EA is the only type of analysis that is carried out on a corpus of learner language. Raabe (1980: 67) suggests subsuming 'error' under the broader category of DEVIATION ("Abweichung") in order to accommodate for other interlanguage phenomena, such as avoidance, over-/underrepresentation, lexical inconsistencies, reductions, or low complexity. Moreover, it has to be pointed out that Corder (1971) had earlier emphasized the importance of examining learner language in its entirety.

In the 1970s, however, such studies were normally carried out without the help of computers, so that there were either small amounts of data or unmanageable amounts of manual work. This might also be a reason why that decade saw a shift in the focus of interlanguage research away from the product of learner performance and towards the mental processes of second language acquisition (SLA) and the acquisition of competence as a psychological function. Within this paradigm, the actual product was considered to have only indirect connections with the underlying processes.

Today, after decades of substantial development in computer technology, computers possess such advanced data storage and processing capabilities that it now seems worthwhile to utilize data-driven corpus[3] techniques for data-oriented investigations into learners' production. After all, as Leech emphasizes in the preface to Granger's *Learner Language on Computer*,

> it is time that some balance was restored in the pursuit of SLA paradigms of research, with more attention being paid to the data that the language learners produce [...]. (1998, xvii)

And just as traditional EA was eventually put forward as a valuable starting point for learner language investigations, Dagneaux et al. (1998: 163) now suggest using computer learner corpora for "reinventing [EA] in the form of computer-aided error analysis (CEA)".

Their study (Dagneaux et al., 1998) is one of the first and most thorough CEA studies to date. They used a 150,000 word corpus of the French component of the ICLE (International Corpus of Learner English) together with similar learner data taken from an intermediate proficiency level. This may seem small in terms of current native speaker corpora, but in comparison to former EA studies, these are considerably larger data samples from a considerably higher number of informants. This addresses one of the points of criticism listed above. In the data collection process careful attention was paid to strict design criteria. Variables concerning both the learners and the language learning situation were carefully recorded and controlled. The corpus therefore consists of a fairly homogeneous body of data, which tackles the criticism of heterogeneity of data successfully. In order to address difficulties with error identification and description, pairs of native speakers of French and English worked together identifying and subsequently tagging the errors with the help of a specially designed software tool. A comprehensive error tagging manual had been compiled together with guidelines on how errors should be classified in order to achieve the highest possible consistency in error annotation. The corpus was then analysed for progress rate between intermediate and advanced level students along a range of grammatical and lexical variables.

After explaining the principles and methods of Error Analysis and Computer-aided Error Analysis, I now demonstrate how they can be put into practice. I will therefore present a CEA pilot study of learner German, which was conducted as part of my MA dissertation.

---

3 By using the term 'corpus' I refer to 'computer corpus' in the sense of a textual database in machine-readable form (cf. definition in Leech 1991).

2. Computer-aided Error Analysis in practice

2.1 Design of the pilot corpus

The time constraints involved in compiling the corpus made it necessary to strike a careful balance between what would be ideal in terms of design criteria or corpus size and what was realistically obtainable. I nevertheless tried to adhere to the strict design criteria that have been identified as relevant to learner production and were employed for the ICLE corpus.

The data was collected from two different groups of undergraduate students of German at Lancaster University: one group was first year students (group A), the other group final-year students (group B). Two types of data were obtained: the first type contains untimed compositions of variable length voluntarily submitted by first and final year students for the corpus (i.e. essays, short commentaries, etc. which are regularly produced for language classes); the second type is made up of exam scripts from the first and final year students' end of year exams. The corpus is thus divided into four subcorpora:

Table 7.1 Details of the Pilot Corpus

Subcorpus	No. of informants	No. of texts	Words
A exam (Aex)	22	22	3847
A untimed (Aun)	7	26	7236
B exam (Bex)	14	28	6762
B untimed (Bun)	6	19	9850
Total:			27,695

The size and shape of the corpus suggest that it should only be used as a pilot corpus to discover some potential trends and tendencies in error patterns and learner language, which would then have to be probed in larger scale investigations. However, the data within the subcorpora is quite homogeneous. With respect to language variables the data is consistent for the following factors: medium, text-type, technicality of texts, topics, and task setting. With respect to learner-related features the following factors were controlled and kept consistent within the subcorpora: age, L1, learning context, proficiency level, and L2 experience.

2.2 Error annotation

One of the lessons that was to be learned from the criticism of traditional EA studies was that error taxonomies need improving. To be captured comprehensively, errors need to be categorized not only along one dimension (e.g. linguistic categories), but according to a flexible, multidimensional error taxonomy. An attempt at such a taxonomy was made by Dagneaux et. al (1998) for their study. For the present study, however, a new tagset had to be devised. This was, first of all, because none of the existing tagsets for errors in German seemed comprehensive and detailed enough, and secondly because new tagsets for CEA studies are all developed for English learner corpora. Since there are specific error types which figure prominently in learner German (e.g. adjective declension) but do not occur at all in learner English, it was necessary to 'sculpture' the tagset to fit all these error types.

The notion of sculpturing the tagset is intended to indicate that the taxonomy was not fully completed at the start of the error annotation process. Rather, I started the annotation with the main categories, adding and revising more detailed layers of description as I progressed. This obviously meant several rounds of re-tagging parts of the corpus.

The result of these proceedings is a corpus annotated for errors according to a multidimensional hierarchical error taxonomy. It is multidimensional in that it captures errors along three of the dimensions Raabe (1980: 76) identified for linguistic error description, i.e. linguistic category, affected parts of speech (POS) + relatable functions (e.g. tense), and target modification. These dimensions are structured into a hierarchical taxonomy with:

– linguistic categories at the first level
– affected POS at the second level
– sub-classes of the linguistic categories at the third level

and finally, where appropriate,

– target modification or other additional information (e.g. whether a word order error occurs in a main or subordinate clause) at the fourth level.

This not only allowed a relatively easy incorporation of new error types derived in the course of the annotation effort, but also made the tagset very flexible in that various subcodes can be combined freely to describe errors more comprehensively.

Each error in the corpus was tagged with a code that categorizes it on all levels, so codes or part of codes can be searched using a text retrieval tool. The tag is comprised of two-letter codes for the individual categories in a string from first to last level.

So a tagged error would look like this:

*Die Erklärung für <**MoArInGn**> **diese** Phänomen ist einfach.

indicating that it is a morphological error (**Mo**) on an article (**Ar**) which is incorrectly inflected (**In**) with respect to the gender (**Gn**) of the noun it refers to. Once the corpus had been fully annotated in this way, various types of analysis were possible.

126 Ursula Weinberger

3. Analysis results

3.1 Overall error frequencies and progress from A to B groups

Since the investigation into the corpus was intended to be of a heuristic nature, a top down approach was taken towards analysing it. That is to say the investigation started off with the overall distribution of errors across the main categories and significant differences between the two levels of proficiency, proceeding further within the categories where there seemed to be interesting patterns.

The overall distribution of errors is depicted in Figure 7.1:

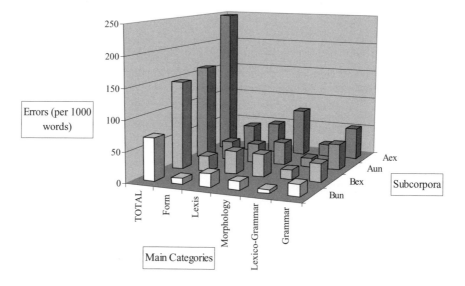

Figure 7.1 Distribution of errors in the main categories across the four subcorpora

Figure 7.1 shows that error frequencies in practically all categories decrease steadily from first year exams to final year untimed essays. However, exams impose very different conditions on the students than untimed compositions with access to language resources such as dictionaries. It was therefore not thought to be feasible to compare exam groups to untimed groups. For the following analysis comparisons will therefore only be drawn for Aun/Bun and Aex/Bex respectively.

Since the aim was to assess differences between groups in terms of statistical significance, the Mann-Whitney U-Test was carried out on the A and B group as a whole. This revealed that there is genuine progress between the first and final year students – an expected but reassuring fact.

Figure 7.2 also shows that in terms of overall frequencies **lexis, morphology and grammar** rank highest in all four groups, so these seem to be the main problem areas. However, taking into account the percentages by which error frequencies decrease between Aun/Bun and Aex/Bex reveals another interesting point.

Figure 7.2 Decrease Rates in error frequencies in main categories from Aex to Bex and Aun to Bun

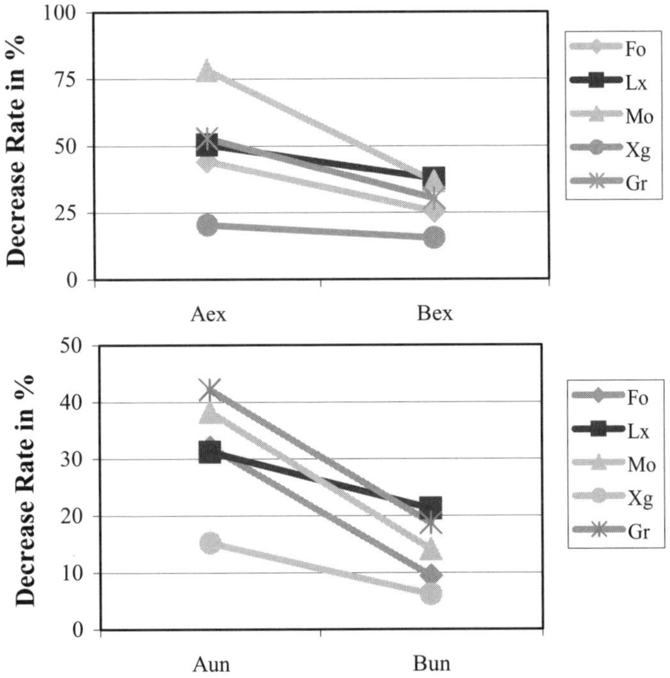

Figure 7.2 makes it clear that for both types of data, it is lexical errors that decrease the least from the first year to the final year group. If this is combined with the information in Figure 7.1, it becomes evident that the lexical error category starts out in the top three in terms of overall frequencies. Moreover it is the category that decreases least between the A and B groups, so that lexical errors actually end up as the biggest category in terms of overall frequencies for both Bex and Bun. I would therefore suggest that, while morphology and grammar errors rank high in terms of overall frequencies and therefore can be called 'problem areas', it is lexical errors that represent the most persistent area of difficulty. Continuing the top-down approach from main categories into sub-categories, it therefore seems worthwhile to investigate the category of lexical errors in more detail.

3.2 Lexical Errors

The subcategories of Lexical Errors can be represented thus:

Table 7.2 Category "Lexical Errors" with subcategories (taken from the error annotation tagset)

Level 1 Main categories	Level 2	Level 3		Level 4
Lexical (Lx)	Parts of Speech	Choice Non-existent	(Ch) (Nx)	–

The Lx-category does not contain many subcategories, so the first analysis within this category was carried out on level 3, which is to find out whether more errors occur due to the wrong choice of an existing word or to the creation of non-existent words. As Figure 7.3 shows, choice-errors outnumber non-existent word errors by a large amount.

Figure 7.3 Subcategories of lexical error: Choice vs. Non-existent

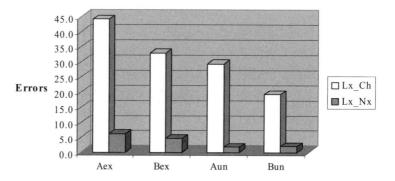

The next point of interest that follows on from this result is whether there are any particular word classes where students chose an inappropriate (or even made-up) word more often than in other word classes. For this, a table which displays lexical error of choice (tag: Lx_Ch) split up into the various parts of speech (level 2) was produced.

Figure 7.4 Breakdown of lexical errors of Choice into parts of speech (with only the most prominent categories displayed)

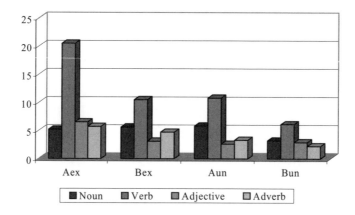

Figure 7.4 shows that verbs make up by far the largest group of lexical choice errors in all four subcorpora. The advantage of the computer corpus is that one can draw up a concordance of all instances of inappropriately chosen verbs in context (tag: LxVr) in order to find out whether there are any further patterns in what the nature of these verbs would be. For this, non-existent word errors were included again.

Looking at the individual concordances soon makes it clear that many lexical errors with verbs are due to wrong prefixes on the verbs, as in examples[4] (1) to (5):

(1) An den Universitäten behauptet man, dass Frauen seit 30 Jahren <LxVrCh> **entmutigt** werden, weiter zu studieren.
(2) Meine Meinung nach ist es wichtig, daß die Schule einen Lernort bleibt, um die Ausbildung unserer Kinder zu <LxVrCh> **versichern**.
(3) Heutzutage studieren mehrere Frauen bei der Universität als vor 30 Jahren. Die Frauen glauben nun, daß zu <LxVrCh> **verheiraten**, keine Bildung ist.
(4) … man ist noch nicht völlig <LxVrCh> **aufgewachsen** oder sozusagen entwickelt.
(5) Verdacht gegenüber das Gefahr für die Gesundheit wird <LxVrNx> **ausäußert**.

A count of all individual instances of wrong prefixes revealed that up to 36.1% of lexical errors with verbs and 13.4% of the total lexical errors are due to wrong prefixes (Table 7.3).

Table 7.3 Percentage of wrong prefixes on verbs in relation to lexical errors on verbs and lexical errors in total

Subcorpus	wrong prefix	total LxVr-errors	% wrong prefix out of **LxVr**	% wrong prefix out of **total Lx**
Aex	26	83	**31.3**	13.4
Bex	16	79	**20.3**	6.3
Aun	21	82	**25.6**	9.3
Bun	22	61	**36.1**	10.5

For teaching purposes such results can provide useful feedback, which in turn can have consequences for syllabus design. The matter of prefixes on verbs in German appears to be one where students are easily confused and make quite a lot of errors. It may therefore be worthwhile to pay special attention to verbs with different prefixes and practise them repeatedly, perhaps with a native speaker corpus, which the students can explore, e.g. for different prefixes that one particular verb can take and their different meanings in context.

4. Conclusion

Despite the controversies surrounding earlier EA studies and error annotation, it emerges from studies like the one presented here that error analysis can benefit greatly from the use of tools and methods of a computer-based approach, thus making it a more valuable

---

[4] Only LxVr errors are marked, other error tags have been deleted for clarity.

technique for studying learner language. In addition to that, applying corpus techniques to learner language research also allows non-error focused studies on interlanguage phenomena such as avoidance, over- or underuse of certain lexical or grammatical constructions, low complexity, etc. Through this a more comprehensive and reliable approach to investigating second language acquisition can be created. The study presented in this paper has aimed to explain how CEA can be put into practice and the results should have showed that CEA produces results that are relevant for language teaching.

Unfortunately, research in this area almost exclusively focuses on English as a foreign language. Corpus-based research on other languages, like German in this case, however, can serve two purposes. As pointed out before, it can provide new insights into the interlanguage(s) of learners of German, which can be applied to teaching material design. But additionally, through extending corpus research to learner languages other than English, a comparison of results across languages can yield new information about universal, L1- and L2-independent features of learner language, which in turn can advance our theoretical understanding of stages of language learning. For example, this study revealed lexis as the category of most persistent difficulty. The Dagneaux et al. (1998) study for French learners of English also identified lexis as an area of great difficulty even for advanced learners. Similarities like these seem to be worth investigating further, and the more different native-speaker and annotated learner corpora are available, the easier and more fruitful these investigations will become. This would suggest the need for extensive international collaboration in corpus research and broad access to a wide variety of corpora.

Bibliography

Corder, P. 1967. The significance of learners' errors. *IRAL*, 5: 161–167.
Corder, P. 1971. Describing the language learner's language. *Interdisciplinary Approaches to Language*, CILT Reports and Papers 6. 25–37.
Dagneaux, E., Denness, S. and Granger, S. 1998. Computer-aided error analysis. *System* 26: 163–174.
Ellis, R. 1994. *The Study of Second Language Acquisition*. Oxford: Oxford University Press.
Enkvist, N. E. 1973. Should we count errors or measure success? In: Svartvik 1973. 16–23.
French, F. G. 1949. *Common Errors in English*. Oxford: Oxford University Press.
Granger, S. (ed.) 1998. *Learner Language on Computer*. London, New York: Longman.
James, C. 1998. *Errors in Language Learning and Use. Exploring Error Analysis*. London, New York: Longman.
Leech, G. 1991. The state of the art in corpus linguistics. In: Aijmer, K. & Altenberg, B. (eds.), *English Corpus Linguistics*. London, New York: Longman. 8–29.
Leech, G. 1998. Learner corpora: what they are and what can be done with them. Preface to Granger 1998. xiv–xx.
Lennon, P. 1991. Error: some problems of definition, identification and distinction. *Applied Linguistics* Vol. 12/2: 180–196.
Raabe, H. 1980. Der Fehler beim Fremdsprachenerwerb und Fremdsprachengebrauch. In: Cherubim, D. (ed.) *Fehlerlinguistik*. Tübingen: Niemeyer. 61–94.
Scholfield, P. 1995. *Quantifying Language*. Clavedon: Multilingal Matters.
Svartvik, J. (ed.) 1973. *Errata. Papers in Error Analysis*. Lund: Gleerup.

The comprehension and acquisition of metaphorical and idiomatic phrases in L2 English

Judith Wieser

In Second Language Acquisition (SLA) and Applied Linguistics, vocabulary was long neglected mostly because of a focus on grammar and sound in both the structuralist and the Chomskyan frameworks, and because of the difficulty of teaching lexis, given that most syllabi are organized around grammar (Coady 1997: 273, Gass and Selinker 2001: 372). Today the importance of the lexicon in second language acquisition is recognized. In the past 25 years, the difficulties involved in learning and teaching vocabulary have been investigated, and vocabulary acquisition has become an increasingly popular field of research. Communicative approaches to language teaching have emphasized meaningful interaction and thus assigned the lexicon a more prominent role. Recent impulses have also come from psycholinguistic research into the bilingual lexicon and language processing by multilingual speakers. Although many teachers still do not see the need for vocabulary teaching, on the assumption that words are learnt naturally (Coady 1997: 274), vocabulary acquisition research has influenced the ways in which vocabulary is being taught today.

Vocabulary knowledge is now considered a prerequisite to achieving a high proficiency in any second or foreign language (henceforth L2). Nation (2001: 20) estimates that educated native speakers of English know around 20,000 word families, and language learners need to acquire a vocabulary of about 15,000 to 20,000 words in order to read a text "with minimal disturbance from unknown vocabulary". Laufer (1992) found that an L2 learner has to acquire about 3,000 word families (approximately 4,800 words) to reach a critical threshold in reading ability. Yet not all words are of equal value to language users. It is generally recommended that learners initially focus on the most frequent 2,000 words[1], which cover more than 80% percent of the tokens in an average text. Over time, speakers can then acquire specialized academic and technical vocabulary according to their needs and gradually build up their knowledge of thousands of low-frequency words, which make up the largest proportion of words in a language, by using various learning strategies (Nation 2001: 9–21).

In L2 vocabulary acquisition, expressions with a metaphorically extended meaning represent a particular obstacle to learners because of their partly opaque meanings. They are usually quite infrequent as individual items, but often make a substantial semantic contribution to a text, and are typical of native-like language use. Despite this, the acquisition of metaphorical and idiomatic phrases in a second language has not often

---

1   The most well-known list of the most frequent 2,000 word families is West's (1986) *General service list of English words*.

been dealt with explicitly in SLA research. The more frequent vocabulary items are usually given priority, and metaphorical expressions are left to the initiative of more advanced learners. Yet it is a legitimate concern to examine how metaphorical phrases can be understood and acquired by L2 learners, as recent publications testify (Beissner 2002, Boers 2000, Arnaud and Savignon 1997, Wray 2002).

In this paper, I examine how lexical units with a metaphorically extended meaning are comprehended and acquired in L2 English.[2] I will discuss cognitive linguistic theories of metaphor and present some recent findings from the fields of SLA, corpus linguistics and psycholinguistics. After providing a definition of metaphors and idioms and dealing with metaphor comprehension in L1, I will show to what extent the representation and processing of metaphorical and idiomatic phrases need to be viewed in the light of recent research into lexical chunking. Finally I will give a brief overview of the most relevant findings in L2 vocabulary acquisition research and make suggestions how metaphorical expressions can be learnt and taught.

1. What is metaphor?

Metaphor was long regarded as a stylistic device mainly found in literary language. Yet research in cognitive linguistics has revealed that metaphor is a broader linguistic and cognitive phenomenon on which much of our everyday language use is based. The term METAPHOR is generally used in two different ways. On the one hand, it refers to a linguistic expression (word or phrase) with a metaphorically extended meaning. On the other hand, metaphor is a cognitive mapping process that underlies metaphorical expressions. For example, *Sermons are sleeping pills* is a nominal metaphor of the 'A is B' type (Glucksberg 2001: 34*f*). The linguistic term that is used metaphorically, *sleeping pills*, is the VEHICLE as it conveys a meaning that is different from its denotation, and the referent that is described, *sermons*, is called the TOPIC. An original metaphor involves an unconventional act of reference: on reading or hearing the above sentence, we soon recognize that the vehicle term is not used with its literal denotation. In order to interpret the metaphor, the hearer must establish some kind of similarity between the metaphor vehicle and the unconventional referent (topic) by discovering the GROUNDS, i.e. the features shared by topic and vehicle terms. We have to ask ourselves in what respect a *sleeping pill*, a kind of medicine, resembles a *sermon*, a religious speech. Which relevant properties of the vehicle term *sleeping pills* have been transferred to a relevant dimension of the topic term *sermons*? While the shape or colour of the pill will not be of importance in the present context, its effect or function of inducing sleep corresponds with the possible effect (though not the intended function) of a sermon (Fig. 8.1). In that way, the similarity between the source domain of *sleeping pill*

---

2   I will focus on comprehension and only occasionally refer to production. The terms "acquire" and "learn" will in most cases be used as synonyms, but explicit or implicit learning will be distinguished where necessary.

(MEDICINE) and the target domain[3] of *sermon* (SPEECHES) can be established (Glucksberg 2001, Goatly 1997, Langlotz 2004).[4]

Figure 8.1 Metaphor as cognitive mapping process

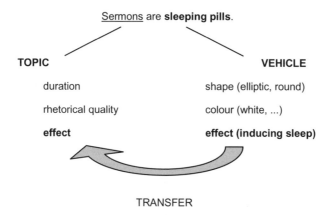

Metaphor is such a common phenomenon that most of the metaphors used in everyday language are no longer recognized as such. Their extended meanings have become lexicalized alongside the literal word meanings of polysemous words. For example, the English noun *mouse* literally denotes a small rodent, but can also refer to a timid person or to a pointing device for computers (metaphorical extensions). These metaphors can be termed "inactive" if the underlying metaphorical extension can still be activated, as with the polysemous meanings of *mouse*, or "dead" if the extension can no longer be recognized, as with homonyms like *pupil* that were once related (Goatly 1997: 32, Langlotz 2004: 45*f*).

Apart from single words, many noun and verb phrases have become conventional metaphor vehicles through repeated use, so that their metaphorical meaning has been lexicalized, and their form is at least partly fixed or "fossilized". Conventional metaphors like *spill the beans* or *hot potato* can be termed "inactive" because they are at least partly semantically transparent, whereas idioms in the narrow sense like *kick the bucket* or *red herring* are semantically opaque "dead" metaphors because they have lost their link to the literal meaning – the grounds of the metaphor have become obscured[5]. In contrast, innovative metaphors like *sleeping pill* are "active" as they have not been lexicalized.

---

3 Lakoff and Johnson (1980) use the terms "source domain" (vehicle) and "target domain" (topic).
4 The metaphor vehicle is often a noun, but can also take the form of an adjective or a verb, a phrase or even a whole sentence (Goatly 1997). In contrast to the 'A is B' type, the topic usually has to be supplied by the hearer.
5 Cowie and Mackin (1991: xii*f*) use the terms "figurative idiom" for partly transparent metaphors and "pure idiom" to refer to opaque metaphors.

Figure 8.2 Continuum of metaphoricity

```
    transparent              semi-transparent              opaque
◄── ─ ─ ─ ─ ─ ─ ─ ─ ─ ─ ─ ─ ─ ─ ─ ─ ─ ─ ─ ─ ─ ─ ─ ─ ─ ─ ─ ─ ─ ──►
```

innovative metaphor	**conventional metaphor**	**idiom**
innovative	conventional	conventional
active	inactive	dead
e.g. *sleeping pill*	e.g. *hot potato*	e.g. *red herring*

Metaphors can thus be classified according to their degree of semantic transparency, i.e. the degree to which the relation between their literal and metaphorical meanings can still be established, and be arranged on a continuum of metaphoricity (Fig. 8.2), with the three categories "innovative metaphor", "conventional metaphor" and "idiom" representing the most typical stages. The first category also involves the variable of rarity or originality. In this paper, the focus will be on conventional metaphors and idioms that form multi-word units, i.e. consist of at least two words.

2. Metaphor comprehension in L1

It was long assumed that metaphors are processed more slowly than literal expressions. According to Searle's (1979) literal-first hypothesis, the literal meaning of metaphors is always retrieved first and only rejected if it does not make sense in context. However, recent empirical research by Glucksberg (2001: 22*ff*) and others has shown that for metaphors of the 'A is B' type, literal and metaphorical interpretations are generated in parallel, and metaphorical meanings are usually available from the beginning of processing. They are derived automatically in context, and consequently cannot be suppressed. Relying on research into saliency by Giora (1999), Beissner (2002: 79*f*) concludes that it is not the literal meaning that is automatically processed first, but the meaning that is most salient due to its familiarity, conventionality and frequency, and this can be the literal or the metaphorically extended meaning. Thus novel metaphors can be understood as fast as comparable literal expressions if their metaphorical meaning is equally salient in the speaker's mental lexicon. The non-literal sense of conventional metaphors is even more salient, as it has been lexicalized as such and may be more frequent and/or familiar than its literal sense.

There has been a long-lasting controversy over how idioms are stored and retrieved. The conclusions reached partly depend on the definition of idioms as analysable or unanalysable units. If idioms are defined as non-compositional metaphorical phrases, there are basically two options. The idioms list hypothesis assumes that idioms are stored in a special list which is separate from the rest of the lexicon, and their retrieval requires a specific idiom processing mode which is only applied after a literal analysis has failed. In contrast, the lexical representation hypothesis by Swinney and Cutler (1979: 525) states that idioms are stored in the lexicon as units and retrieved like words.

No special processing mode is required, but as soon as the first word of the unit occurs, the idiomatic meaning of the string as a whole is computed in parallel with the literal meaning. The idiomatic meaning becomes available earlier as the word-by-word analysis of the idiom takes more time. Recent evidence suggests that the lexical representation hypothesis is more likely and no special idiom mode is required. In terms of the categorization given in section 1, this type of processing would mostly apply to opaque idioms.

Researchers who adopt a broader definition of idiom that includes partly transparent conventionalized metaphors usually argue for the analysability of idioms in processing, partly because of their motivation by metaphorical concepts (Cacciari 1993, Gibbs 1995, Glucksberg 1993). A statement by Gibbs (1995: 98*f*) exemplifies this view:

> Research in cognitive linguistics and experimental psychology supports the idea that idioms retain much of their metaphoricity. Many idioms are partly motivated by pervasive, preexisting metaphorical concepts that can account for significant aspects of the linguistic behaviour of idioms as well as for the acquisition and comprehension of idioms.

Cognitive linguistic research has shown that many expressions traditionally termed "idioms" are partly semantically analysable, and allow for a certain degree of creative manipulation or variation according to the needs of language users (see Langlotz 2003). Glucksberg (2001) also takes an analytic approach by postulating "phrase-induced polysemy". Words used in frequent idioms develop a phrase-specific idiomatic meaning that is stored in the lexicon. Following this view, the semantic qualities of idiom constituents contribute to the overall figurative meaning, and many idiomatic phrases are not stored as units because they are still partly analysable. However, Gibbs (1995: 101) emphasizes that idioms differ with respect to their analysability, i.e. the degree to which their parts contribute to their overall meaning. This observation corresponds to our broad distinction between partly transparent conventional metaphors and opaque idioms, with the former still being analysable.

Tabossi and Zardon (1993) suggest that an idiomatic phrase is processed literally up to the "idiom key", i.e. the point at which it is recognized as an idiom. Their empirical results indicate that the idiomatic meaning only becomes available (i.e. is retrieved) after the idiom key – usually a content word – is read or heard. This could also apply to the retrieval of the non-literal meaning of conventional metaphorical phrases.

Based on the definition of metaphor types given in section 1, the following broad assumptions about metaphor comprehension in L1 can be made, taking examples (1) to (4) as a starting point:

(1) Life is **a box of chocolates.**[6] (Goatly 1997: 8*ff*)
(2) Her invention is a **gold mine.** (Glucksberg 2001: 44)
(3) He **burnt his fingers** with that deal.
(4) Her remark was **a red herring.**

---

6 It was originally used in the form of a simile in the film *Forrest Gump*: "Life is like a box of chocolates; you never know what you're going to get."

Innovative metaphors like *a box of chocolates* in example (1) have not been lexicalized, so that the literal meaning is salient and the metaphorical meaning has to be actively constructed by establishing a similarity between vehicle and topic.

With conventional metaphors, like *gold mine* and *burn one's fingers* in examples (2) and (3), the metaphorical meaning will be activated in parallel with the literal meaning and chosen because it fits best in the given context. If the metaphor is frequent, the metaphorical meaning is likely to be more salient than the corresponding literal meaning (Beissner 2002: 82). This could apply to idioms as well as conventional metaphors. If speakers are not familiar with a conventional metaphor, however, they will have to actively interpret it as an innovative metaphor, and this will probably be successful because of its partial transparency or analysability. The metaphorical meaning of the polysemous compound *gold mine* as denoting a source of wealth can be traced back to a place where gold is found, and the verb phrase *burn one's fingers*, expressing (financial) suffering due to one's foolish behaviour or meddling, is still related to physical suffering after carelessly touching a hot surface.

With opaque idioms like *red herring* in example (4) the non-literal meaning is usually salient and activated first, even in literal contexts, as soon as the idiom key is reached. According to Beissner (2002: 81), the literal meaning is not likely to be activated in idiomatic contexts. Yet if opaque idioms have not been learnt, the active construction of their meaning is likely to be unsuccessful because of their lack of transparency.

As will be seen in section 4, L2 learners are generally less likely than native speakers to know lexicalized metaphors and idioms and therefore more often have to engage in active interpretation. This is partly due to the way in which lexical units are processed and represented in the lexicon.

3. From words to lexical chunks

Research findings in psycholinguistics and corpus linguistics have challenged the generativist account of syntax that proposes a single, grammatically based processing system. According to Wray (2002: 12, ix*f*) Chomskyan linguists assume that words are stored as individual items that are then combined according to syntactic rules to generate an utterance, and that likewise, language is fully analysed into words in comprehension. Idioms are traditionally regarded as an exception or anomaly because their meaning is non-compositional, i.e. cannot be derived directly from the analysis of their parts.

However, it seems that generative theory has overemphasized the linguistic potential for novelty by neglecting performance. Bolinger (1975) pointed out that the rule-based approach to language is not always justified because much language use is not very creative, but rather repetitive and based on lexical elements to a high degree. Pawley and Syder (1983) followed suit by observing that not all grammatical structures that are possible according to generative rules occur with equal frequency or are judged to be equally idiomatic by native speakers. They propose that language users store hundreds of preconstructed clauses to achieve fluent and idiomatic (native-like) language use. Sinclair (1987) finally drew a distinction between the open choice principle, which corresponds to the traditional analytic view, and the idiom principle, which he characterises as follows:

> The principle of idiom is that a language user has available to him or her a large number of semi-preconstructed phrases that constitute single choices, even though they might appear to be analysable into segments. (1987: 320)

Words that regularly co-occur are selected together, and frequent words are often delexicalized if they occur in phrases, i.e. they lose their meaning to the overall unit. This implies that the co-occurrence of words is often restricted, and that words do not occur in random distribution, but in regular combinations ("unrandomness"). In contrast, the open choice principle involves the creative generation of language according to linguistic rules. The idiom principle normally takes precedence over the open choice principle unless a more detailed analysis is required.[7]

Recent research in corpus linguistics and psycholinguistics has shown that words often occur in the same combinations, and many vocabulary items are multi-word units rather than single words. These units are alternatively referred to as "lexical chunks" (Lewis 1993), "lexical phrases" (Nattinger and DeCarrico 1992), or "formulaic sequences" (Wray 2002), and generally include different types of phrases:

(a) everyday routine formulas, e.g. *I see, you know*
(b) preconstructed clauses, e.g. *(I'm) sorry to keep you waiting*
(c) collocations, e.g. *large amount, make amends*
(d) conventional metaphors and idioms, e.g. *spill the beans, (be a) hot potato*

Chunking[8] is a general cognitive principle. Chunks are created whenever sequences of letters, morphemes or words are coded as a group because they frequently co-occur or form regular patterns. As language users typically work with meaningful groupings of items, chunks are central to language knowledge. Thus chunking can be regarded as a learning mechanism that affects different levels of language acquisition:

> Learning vocabulary involves sequencing the phonological properties of the language: the categorical units (whether these be phonemes or syllables), syllable structure, and phonotactic sequences [...]. Learning discourse involves sequencing the lexical units of the language: phrases and collocations. Learning grammar involves abstracting regularities from the stock of known lexical sequences. (Ellis 1997: 126)

Collocations, idioms and other lexical units represent one level of chunking that involves the long-term storage of associative connections between words. Collocational knowledge is therefore an essential aspect of word knowledge (Ellis 2001). Defined in a broad sense, collocations are groups of words that belong together because they

---

7 For a detailed summary see Skehan (1998: 29–41) and Nation (2001: 321–328).
8 The term "chunking" was originally coined by Miller (1956) to refer to "the development of permanent sets of associative connections in long-term memory" that "underlies the attainment of automaticity and fluency" (Ellis 1997: 124).

commonly co-occur or their meaning is not obvious from the meaning of their parts[9] (Nation 2001: 317). They are often syntactically inflexible and/or to some degree semantically unpredictable. Following this view, metaphorical and idiomatic phrases are not primarily anomalous, but represent one type of collocation or lexical chunk that is distinguished from other fixed phrases by their overall metaphorically extended meaning. Opaque idioms are the archetypal formulaic sequences, because they are syntactically frozen and impenetrable at the word level. Conventional metaphors are still partly analysable, so that strings can be active or inactive according to the speakers' perception of their compositionality (Wray 2002: 56).

Connectionist models of processing can help to partly resolve the issue whether or not idioms are stored as units. Evidence from connectionist research suggests that there are strong associative links between lexical items that frequently co-occur (Ellis 2001, Rumelhart and McClelland 1986). If units are defined with respect to lexical networks and patterns of activation, idioms and conventional metaphors can be viewed as networks of frequently co-occurring words that are closely connected and normally jointly activated, but can also be partly analysed or creatively modified if the context of use demands it.

The main advantage of storing word sequences as units in our mental lexicon is processing speed. Chunks can be processed much faster than the same number of individual words that have to be combined according to syntactic rules.[10] In line with Sinclair, Wray (2002: 12*ff*) proposes a choice between two processing strategies in her Dual Systems Approach. In analytic processing, new material is decoded bottom-up according to grammatical rules, and larger items are recreated on every single use. In holistic processing, prefabricated strings (e.g. idioms) are retrieved top-down as units. By skipping a full linguistic analysis, holistic processing allows a faster and more efficient retrieval of blocks of material. As more material can be stored in short-term memory, processing pressures are reduced, fluency is increased, and speakers have more time for conversational planning (Skehan 1998, Nation 2001: 320*ff*). Whereas holistic processing accounts for idiomaticity and fluency, the necessary creativity in combining units is guaranteed because analytic processing remains available.

Yet chunking has one limitation: memory capacity. Chunks represent a higher long-term memory load than individual words, especially if a word is represented both as a single entry and as part of one or several lexical units, giving rise to multiple storage. If too many long chunks were stored, the capacities of our long-term memories would be exceeded. As such an organization of our lexicons would not be efficient, it is assumed that only items that frequently co-occur are stored as chunks whereas infrequent word sequences are represented as individual words (Nation 2001: 320*f*). This implies that lexical items can be represented differently by different speakers, depending on how frequently they use an expression.

---

9 Note that the term "collocation" is used in a broader sense here than in example (c) and in Nesselhauf, this volume.
10 Up to seven units can be held in short-term memory at one time (Miller 1956).

4. Lexical chunks in L1 and L2

These findings about chunking by native speakers have consequences for our understanding of language learning. Language acquisition is as much based on memorizing sequences of items as on learning rules of how to combine them. Knowing the multi-word units a word forms part of is essential for language learners to achieve a high level of proficiency in a foreign language, in terms of both fluency and idiomaticity (Nation 2001, Pawley and Syder 1983). Indeed, SLA research has shown that advanced L2 speakers, like native speakers, often use strings of words that frequently co-occur.

However, L2 speakers may encounter a number of problems. Wray (2002: xi) considers formulaic language "the biggest stumbling block to sounding native-like" for intermediate and advanced learners. One of the reasons is that L2 learners tend to approach multi-word units in a way different from native speakers. In the acquisition of English as a first language, lexical chunks ("formulaic sequences") are dominant in the earliest phase (up to age 2), which is followed by a segmentation phase in which the formerly holistic units are analysed. From age 8 onwards, formulaic sequences are increasingly used for efficient storage and retrieval, although analytic processing remains available. Wray (2002) concludes that native speakers usually operate with the largest possible unit, favouring a top-down approach.

L2 learners are most likely to follow a similar pattern if they acquire lexical chunks in an L2 environment where the need to interact and be integrated is central. In most traditional classroom settings, however, idioms are rarely used in interaction, and learners' analytic approach is often reinforced by teaching. According to Wray (2002), teenage and adult learners therefore tend to focus on words as the smallest vocabulary units. Chunks are often not learnt as wholes – they are broken down into words, but not given a detailed grammatical analysis. Consequently, many learners have an incomplete memory of idioms and other lexical chunks, and feel insecure about using them. It is a challenge for L2 learners to strike a balance between the analytic and the holistic system if they want to achieve native-like selection and fluency. On the one hand, they should not underuse lexical chunks; on the other hand, they have to learn not to be too creative in producing incorrect chunks that then become fossilized in their L2 competence.

5. Relevant findings in vocabulary acquisition research

We can now consider some important findings from vocabulary acquisition research that partly explain the difficulties involved in acquiring metaphorical and idiomatic phrases and serve as a background to the recommendations for learning and teaching. Vocabulary knowledge is a complex phenomenon involving various kinds of knowledge about the form, meaning and use of a word. Ideally, the following aspects of a word have been acquired (Laufer 1997: 141, Nation 2001: 27):

- spoken and written form
- word parts: stem, affixes, common derivations, inflections
- meaning: denotation, connotations, metaphorical extensions, etc.
- lexical relations
- grammatical characteristics: part of speech, complementation, syntactic agreement features (gender, number)
- collocations
- pragmatics: referents, register, formality, frequency, etc.

It is quite demanding to know all the aspects and uses of a lexeme. In the earlier stages of acquisition, matching word form and meaning is the greatest challenge, but as learning progresses, it becomes increasingly more important to master the semantic, pragmatic and grammatical aspects of word knowledge. The learning burden of a word, i.e. "the amount of effort required to learn it" (Nation 2001: 23), depends on learners' first language background, i.e. the typological similarity between their L1 and L2, and their familiarity with aspects of vocabulary knowledge that could represent a particular difficulty.

All of the above-mentioned aspects of vocabulary knowledge have a receptive and a productive dimension. Words can form part of a speaker's 'passive' or 'active' vocabulary. A speaker may know the word form receptively when automatically recognizing a lexical item and accessing its lexico-semantic representation in listening or reading, but he or she may not be able to actively produce the form of the same item in speaking or writing. Experimental evidence has shown that receptive vocabulary is easier to learn and use for a number of reasons (Nation 2001: 28*ff*). Contrary to earlier assumptions, receptive knowledge is not automatically transformed into productive knowledge (Skehan 1998: 11*f*)[11], but the productive use of lexical items has to be practised with meaning-focused speaking and writing activities (Nation and Meara 2002). Thus the comprehension of metaphors and idioms can generally be expected to be less problematic than their production, especially because the phonological and syntactic structure of longer sequences of words is more difficult to remember actively than to merely recognize.

There has been a debate about how vocabulary is best learnt, particularly whether implicit learning of vocabulary is sufficient, or whether there is a need for explicit learning and teaching (Schmitt and McCarthy 1997: 3). Teaching methods long relied on the notion that words are learnt implicitly ('naturally') through guessing from context and do not need to be taught. Yet recently, vocabulary instruction involving both direct learning and the teaching of learning strategies has been advocated more strongly by scholars and teachers (Coady 1997: 273*f*), especially for the acquisition of word meaning. According to Ellis (1997), word form, lexical specifications, grammatical class and collocations are best acquired through implicit learning processes, whereas seman-

---

11 Krashen's (1989) comprehensible input alone is not sufficient for productive vocabulary knowledge to be acquired, although extensive reading may result in receptive knowledge of vocabulary and spelling.

tic and conceptual properties are learnt through explicit learning processes that involve the mapping of word form labels onto meaning representations. Implicit and explicit learning can interact in useful ways: the knowledge of explicitly learnt words can be consolidated by repeated exposure in context, which facilitates the acquisition of additional meanings, grammatical patterns and collocates (Schmitt and McCarthy 1997: 3). It seems therefore that a combination of both implicit and explicit learning processes is most efficient, with some aspects of vocabulary knowledge being considered more or less suitable for conscious learning.

It is generally agreed that high-frequency words should be learnt explicitly, quickly and directly (e.g. by using word cards and mnemonic techniques) as they form the basis of language use. In contrast, the huge number of less frequent words are often not considered worth learning or teaching explicitly because of time constraints (Nation 2001). However, Arnaud and Savignon (1997: 158*f*) stress that rare words often carry a high information load in a text and can constitute a major obstacle to comprehension if unknown. Therefore Nation and Meara (2002: 40) recommend providing learners with learning strategies that enable them to deal with infrequent vocabulary on their own. Guessing from context is considered the most useful strategy for acquiring less frequent vocabulary. It involves processing meaning-focused input through extensive reading or listening, and is most successful if 95 to 98% of the words in a text are known. The effectiveness of guessing is enhanced if learners are encouraged to pay attention to the unknown words through glossing, highlighting of items, or dictionary use. However, the acquisition of a word does not necessarily follow from its comprehension in context, as Arnaud and Savignon (1997: 159) observe: "when a rich context facilitates guessing, effortless access to the overall meaning of the passage may just prevent the acquisition of the lexeme."

6. Suggestions for learning and teaching

Like rare words, metaphorical and idiomatic phrases have quite low discourse frequencies as individual lexical items, despite their semantic importance. Yet findings by Arnaud and Savignon (1997) suggest that L2 speakers can reach native-like proficiency with respect to rare words, but not normally with respect to complex lexical units. Compared to native speakers, even advanced learners know fewer idioms, and do not learn them as often and as easily as single words. This is especially so if they live in a non-English-speaking environment and lack interaction with native speakers in informal contexts. In addition, metaphorical expressions are often understood if a close L1 equivalent exists, but they are not noticed[12] and therefore not acquired. Comprehension can be complicated by interference from L1 (or other L3s, etc.), although idiomatic phrases are generally less likely to be transferred because they are considered marked

---

12 According to Schmidt (1990), noticing is a prerequisite for (incidental) learning to occur.

due to their opacity. The meaning of opaque idioms is particularly difficult to determine if they have not been encountered before. In addition, multi-word units can represent a high learning burden because their form, meaning and use are not readily predictable from either L1 or L2 knowledge. Their more complex form also involves a greater memory load than single words.

In spite of these difficulties, advanced learners (especially language teachers) must acquire a large stock of complex lexical units in order to increase their receptive competence, and should also recognize variations of their canonical forms (Arnaud and Savignon 1997: 161). Frequent exposure to the L2 is desirable for the acquisition of idioms, but as this is not always possible in school contexts, learners need to have suitable learning strategies to be able to gradually acquire conventional metaphors and idioms.

Nation and Meara (2002: 44) suggest learning multi-word units mostly through extensive meaning-focused language use rather than direct study.[13] Both formal aspects of vocabulary knowledge and collocational relations are encountered in context and learnt implicitly, provided that learners pay attention to these patterns. Nation (2001: 335*f*) recommends dealing with idioms as if they were words, paying most attention to the expressions with the highest frequency and widest range of occurrence. If possible, the learning of idioms should be enriched by the explanation of their parts, history and function[14]. Thus explicit and implicit learning can be combined.

Pedagogical chunking (Lewis 1993: 122) is a widely recommended strategy that helps learners to regroup known components into larger units. Nation (2001: 336*ff*) proposes three main kinds of pedagogical chunking:

(a) fluency development
(b) memorization
(c) language-focused attention

First, learners should be encouraged to use language more fluently as this forces them to use larger units in production, i.e. to restructure knowledge into chunks. Second, the memorization of unanalysed chunks can increase fluency, especially in the early stages of learning. Finally, learners should be helped to pay attention to larger units by dividing texts containing familiar items into chunks. Beissner (2002) proposes training learners in identifying large lexical units in context, so that they can acquire syntactic patterns and collocates of familiar words along with the words. In general, words should not be learnt in isolation, but as parts of multi-word units. Yet metaphorical and idiomatic phrases should not remain unanalysed chunks, but be learnt as consisting of meaningful parts, so that their potential for variation is recognized. As learners often have difficulty in remembering the form of chunks, they must be trained to pay attention to "the precise words used to express a particular pragmatic function" (Lewis 1993: 121).

---

13 In contrast, Coady (1997) advocates learning and teaching multiword phrases explicitly because they are not learnt well through ordinary language experience.
14 These recommendations have to be seen in the context of rich instruction, cf. Nation (2001: 94–108).

Learner autonomy can be increased by the use of metacognitive strategies like pedagogical chunking that enable learners to analyse language on their own, search for regularities, and form hypotheses that are then supported or refuted by authentic L2 material (Beissner 2002: 143*ff*). Another such strategy is raising learners' metaphor awareness. Its ultimate aim is to make learners "capable of identifying metaphoric themes and of categorizing idioms independently" (Boers 2000: 564) as they encounter them in the language they are exposed to. Boers (2000: 566) lists five specific objectives in raising metaphor awareness, and suggests ways of achieving them:

(a) recognition of metaphor as a common ingredient of everyday language, by becoming aware of the figurative language one uses to describe abstract notions in L1;
(b) recognition of metaphorical themes behind many figurative expressions, by grouping the expressions under more general themes, which can be explained through reference to their experiential basis;
(c) recognition of the non-arbitrary nature of many figurative expressions, by trying to explain the meaning of partly transparent expressions;
(d) recognition of possible cross-cultural differences in metaphorical themes, by comparing figurative discourse in L2 with L1;
(e) recognition of cross-linguistic variety in figurative expressions.

Beissner (2002: 55*ff*) observes that idioms are often not taught systematically, but as independent units, and learners are usually not aware of the conceptual motivation of idioms because of their conventionality or assumed arbitrariness. Yet according to cognitive constructivist theories, the L2 lexicon is a network of conceptually motivated meanings into which new items have to be integrated. Learners should therefore be made aware of the cognitive motivation of figurative expressions. Beissner recommends learning metaphorical phrases through multiple encounters in different contexts, in which the figurative meaning can be seen as an extension of the known literal meaning. If partly transparent metaphors are related to the underlying concepts by which they are motivated, they can be made transparent and meaningful. Boers (2000: 553) suggests using recurring metaphorical themes as "an alternative type of lexical field, revealing structure and organization in a world of figurative language which may at first sight seem to be largely arbitrary". His studies, which involved language learning activities aimed at raising learners' metaphor awareness, have shown that organizing figurative expressions along metaphoric themes or source domains can facilitate the retention of unfamiliar units. For example, metaphors denoting anger can be classified and learnt according to the underlying cognitive metaphors, as shown in Table 8.1 (Boers 2000: 555):

Table 8.1 Metaphors denoting anger

ANGER IS HOT FLUID IN A CONTAINER	ANGRY PEOPLE ARE DANGEROUS ANIMALS
be boiling with anger	*have a ferocious temper*
be all steamed up	*Don't snap at me!*
be fuming	*unleash one's anger*
blow up at somebody	*bite somebody's head off*
flip one's lid	
Simmer down!	

If learners are made aware of the cognitive motivation of expressions in their first language, the comprehension and production of lexemes that are motivated in the same way in L2 is further facilitated, especially if the learners' L1 is typologically closely related to English. Learners with German L1, for instance, can draw on their knowledge of expressions similar to those listed above, such as *an die Decke gehen, kochen vor Wut* or *Wutausbruch*. According to Boers (2000: 557), transfer of familiar L1 concepts can speed up learning, although the danger of erroneous direct translations remains. Beissner (2002: 148) therefore advocates the systematic presentation and learning of metaphorical concepts that underlie lexical phrases in L1 and L2, including the different linguistic realizations or conceptualizations in the two languages. This could be enhanced by a contrastive analysis of the differences between concepts and expressions in L1 and L2, for instance by working out L2 concepts from authentic contexts and contrasting them with L1 concepts.

7. Conclusion

In this paper I have investigated how learners of L2 English can comprehend and acquire metaphorical and idiomatic phrases, and what problems they may encounter. Research in cognitive linguistics has shown that metaphor is a phenomenon underlying much of everyday language use. A large number of metaphorical expressions have become lexicalized as units with differing degrees of semantic transparency. In this paper, a broad distinction was drawn between "conventional metaphors", which are still partly analysable, and opaque "idioms". Empirical studies of processing in L1 indicate that frequent and familiar metaphorical meanings can be as salient as literal meanings and therefore, metaphors and idioms can be processed as fast as literal expressions, especially in figurative contexts. The question whether metaphorical and idiomatic phrases are stored as units (i.e. chunks) or single words has still not been completely resolved. However, psycholinguistic research suggests that there are strong associations between frequently occurring items in the speakers' lexicon. As storage as units results in faster processing, native speakers tend to work with the largest possible units in processing. In contrast, teenage and adult L2 learners often focus on single words rather than lexical units in the classroom, and consequently do not learn multi-word units properly.

Metaphorical and idiomatic phrases can represent an obstacle to L2 learning and lead to comprehension problems because of their low discourse frequency, their conventionality and partial opacity, and their status as multi-word units. These difficulties can be overcome if learners are (made) aware of the co-occurrence of words and acquire figurative expressions as lexical units. Pedagogical chunking is recommended to increase learners' awareness of the units that words form part of. At the same time, learners should still be able to recognize the contribution of the parts of a unit to the overall meaning. This is achieved by the analysis of chunks that have already been acquired, and by making learners aware of the conceptual motivation of partly transparent metaphorical expressions. As the conceptual motivation of opaque idioms has become obscured, they are most difficult to acquire, and learning them as units from context with their pragmatic functions seems to be the main option available, possibly with an explanation of their historical origin. Yet in general, partly transparent metaphorical expressions should be classified and learnt according to the underlying concepts, and compared with expressions in the learners' L1, so that their meaning can be integrated into the learners' pre-existing cognitive networks. These approaches all aim at developing learners' awareness and enabling them to deal with metaphors and idioms autonomously and to achieve native-like fluency and idiomaticity in L2 production in the long run.

Bibliography

Allerton, D. J., Nesselhauf, N. and Skandera, P. (eds.) 2004. *Phraseological Units: basic concepts and their application*. (= ICSELL 8). Basel: Schwabe.

Arnaud, P. J. L. and Savignon, S. J. 1997. Rare words, complex lexical units and the advanced learner. In: Coady and Huckin 1997. 155–173.

Beissner, K. 2002. *I see what you mean – Metaphorische Konzepte in der (fremdsprachlichen) Bedeutungskonstruktion*. Frankfurt a. M.: Peter Lang.

Boers, F. 2000. Metaphor Awareness and Vocabulary Retention. *Applied Linguistics* 21(4). 553–571.

Bolinger, D. 1975. *Aspects of Language*, 2nd edition. New York: Harcourt Brace Jovanovich. (1st edition, 1968).

Cacciari, C. and Tabossi, P. (eds.) 1993. *Idioms. Processing, Structure, and Interpretation*. Hillsdale (N.J.): Lawrence Erlbaum.

Cacciari, C. 1993. The Place of Idioms in a Literal and Metaphorical World. In: Cacciari and Tabossi 1993. 27–55.

Coady, J. 1997. L2 vocabulary acquisition: A synthesis of the research. In: Coady and Huckin 1997. 273–291.

Coady, J and Huckin, T. (eds.). 1997. *Second Language Vocabulary Acquisition*. Cambridge: Cambridge University Press.

Cowie, A. P. and Mackin, R. 1991. *Oxford Dictionary of Current Idiomatic English*. Vol. 2: Phrase, Clause and Sentence Idioms. Oxford: Oxford University Press. x–vi.

Ellis, N. C. 2001. Memory for Language. In: Robinson, P. (ed.), *Cognition and Second Language Instruction*. Cambridge: Cambridge University Press. 33–68.

Ellis, N. C. 1997. Vocabulary acquisition: word structure, collocation, word-class, and meaning. In: Schmitt and McCarthy 1997. 122–139.

Gass, S. M. and Selinker, L. 2001. *Second Language Acquisition: an introductory course*. Mahwah (NJ): Lawrence Erlbaum.

Gibbs, R. 1995. Idiomaticity and Human Cognition. In: Everaert, M., van der Linden, E.-J. et al. (eds.), *Idioms: structural and psychological perspectives*. Hillsdale (N.J.): Lawrence Erlbaum.

Giora, R. 1999. On the priority of salient meanings: studies of literal and figurative language. *Journal of Pragmatics* 31. 919–929.

Glucksberg, S. 2001. *Understanding Figurative Language: from metaphors to idioms*. New York: Oxford University Press.

Glucksberg, S. 1993. Idiom meanings and allusional content. In: Cacciari and Tabossi 1993. 3–26.

Goatly, A. 1997. *The Language of Metaphor*. London and New York: Routledge.

Krashen, S. 1989. We acquire vocabulary and spelling by reading: additional evidence for the input hypothesis. *Modern Language Journal* 73 (4). 440–464.

Lakoff, G. and Johnson, M. 1980. *Metaphors we Live by*. Chicago and London: University of Chicago Press.

Langlotz, A. 2004. What are metaphors? In: Allerton, D. J., Nesselhauf, N. and Skandera, P. (eds.) *Phraseological Units: basic concepts and their application*. (= ICSELL 8). Basel: Schwabe. 37-51.

Langlotz, A. 2003. *Idiomatic Creativity. A Cognitive Linguistic Model of Idiom Representation and Variation for English Idioms*. University of Basel (unpublished PhD dissertation).

Laufer, B. 1997. What's in a word that makes it hard or easy: some intralexical factors that affect the learning of words. In: Schmitt and McCarthy 1997. 140–155.

Laufer, B. 1992. How much lexis is necessary for reading comprehension. In: Arnaud, P. J. L. and Béjoint, H. (eds.), *Vocabulary and Applied Linguistics*. Basingstoke: Macmillan. 126–132.

Lewis, M. 1993. *The Lexical Approach: the State of ELT and a Way Forward*. Hove: Language Teaching Publications.

Miller, G. A. 1956. The magical number seven, plus or minus two: some limits on our capacity for processing information. *Psychological Review* 63. 81–97.

Nation, P. and Meara, P. 2002. Vocabulary. In: Schmitt, N. *An Introduction to Applied Linguistics*. London: Arnold. 35–54.

Nation, I. S. P. 2001. *Learning Vocabulary in Another Language*. Cambridge: Cambridge University Press.

Nattinger, J. R. and DeCarrico, J. S. 1992. *Lexical Phrases and Language Teaching*. Oxford: Oxford University Press.

Pawley, A. and Syder, F. 1983. Two puzzles for linguistic theory: nativelike selection and nativelike fluency. In: Richards, J. C. and Schmidt, R. (eds.), *Language and Communication*. London: Longman. 191–226.

Rumelhart, D. E. and McClelland, J. L. (eds.) 1986. *Parallel Distributed Processing: Explorations in the Microstructure of Cognition*. Cambridge (Mass.): MIT Press.

Searle, J. R. 1979. *Expression and Meaning*. Cambridge: Cambridge University Press.

Schmidt, R. W. 1990. The role of consciousness in second language learning. *Applied Linguistics* 11. 129–158.

Schmitt, N. and McCarthy, M. (eds.) 1997. *Vocabulary. Description, Acquisition and Pedagogy*. Cambridge: Cambridge University Press.

Sinclair, J. M. 1987. Collocation: a progress report. In: Steele, R. and Threadgold, T. (eds.). *Language Topics: Essays in Honour of Michael Halliday*. Vol. II. Amsterdam: John Benjamins. 319–331.

Skehan, P. 1998. *A Cognitive Approach to Language Learning*. Oxford: Oxford University Press.

Swinney, D. A. and Cutler, A. 1979. The access and processing of idiomatic expressions. *Journal of Verbal Learning and Verbal Behaviour* 18. 523–534.

Tabossi, P. and Zardon, F. 1993. The activation of idiomatic meaning in spoken language comprehension. In: Cacciari and Tabossi 1993. 145–159.

Turner, M. and Fauconnier, G. 1995. Conceptual integration and formal expression. *Journal of Metaphor and Symbolic Activity* 10 (3). 183–203.

West, M. 1986. *General Service List of English Words*. London: Longman.

Wray, A. 2002. *Formulaic Language and the Lexicon*. Cambridge: Cambridge University Press.

CALL and linguistics

Cornelia Tschichold

Computer-assisted language learning (henceforth CALL) is a relatively broad term for computer applications of various types, all having the aim of improving language teaching and learning. Usually, but not exclusively, the term applies to second or foreign language learning rather than to first language acquisition. The origins of CALL go back almost half a century, to a time when modern linguistics was still a young science and behaviourist theories of learning were prevalent. Behaviourist learning theories had a lasting influence on CALL and its image among teachers and learners. In contrast to behaviourism, the various successive developments in the field of linguistics and language learning during the whole period between the middle of the 20th century and the beginning of the 21st have had surprisingly little influence on CALL. Today the stimuli for CALL development come mainly from applied linguistics and language teaching methods on the one hand, and – often more importantly – from the technical progress in computer hardware and software on the other hand. Computational linguistics and its applied branch, natural language processing, have so far had relatively little impact on mainstream CALL.

In this paper, I intend to give a short overview of the history of the use of computers in language learning and teaching before looking more specifically at the contributions of two linguistic subdisciplines to CALL. An outlook towards possible future developments of the field concludes the article.

1. The history of computers in language teaching

Many authors (e.g. Bax 2003, Levy 1997, Warschauer 1996) partition the history of computers in language teaching and learning into three periods with somewhat varying beginning and end dates. The earliest period lasted from the 1950s into the 1970s or even 1980s and is characterized by a strong influence of behaviourist theories of learning on CALL. Programmed instruction was a teaching approach easily implemented on a computer and consequently, the typical exercises were of the drill-and-practice type, often involving sentence reformulation and short translation exercises. The user would typically get immediate feedback for every single answer typed in. What counted as correct and incorrect answers had to be specified in advance by the linguist-programmer, and the computer response to each answer needed to be chosen in advance as well. Technically, the period was dominated by mainframe computers, which were capable of delivering exercises to a certain number of students, who all had to be in a specialized computer lab where the terminals connected to the mainframe would be positioned. CALL exercises were wholly text-based, with (at least initially) no colour, sound or images. Only language learners who happened to study at a university with the necessary technical equipment and – even more importantly – a language teacher willing to invest the considerable amounts of time required for setting up the software and producing the exercises had the possibility of benefiting from such early CALL systems at all. While the technological limitations and the use of mainframes for CALL have since been overcome, the type of exercise dominant at that time can still be found today. An example of such a structuralist exercise (for Latin) would be the following:

Put the following verbs in the first person singular present tense.

facere

posse

venire

The second period covers roughly the last two decades of the twentieth century and is often called that of 'communicative CALL', being strongly influenced by the then fashionable trend of Communicative Language Teaching. In contrast to the earlier, more structuralist view of language, Communicative Language Teaching assumes a more clearly functional model of language, thus de-emphasizing form (e.g. morphologically correct forms) in favour of function (e.g. attaining a certain communicative goal). On the technical side, PCs had become affordable and widespread, and by the 1990s they were also capable of displaying elaborate graphics and of playing good-quality sound files. Typical CALL packages of that period make increasingly heavy use of these multimedia facilities and focus on communicative aspects of the language by privileging dialogues over grammar exercises. Most CALL programs of this type therefore use the target language as much as possible, or even exclusively, once the user is 'inside' the program, avoiding translation, and also avoiding exercises that are too obviously of the drill-and-practice type. Activities are sometimes aimed at encouraging communication with other students or stimulating writing activities. Feedback is generally more sparse, partly because some CALL producers believed that earlier CALL programs gave too much feedback too frequently, thus interrupting the learner's language flow; and partly because learners had comparatively fewer opportunities for typing in answers that could then be evaluated, due to the new technical potential for authentic language input and the emphasis Communicative Language Teaching put on it. An example of this type of CALL activity can be found in the appendix.

The third period in the history of CALL is what we are experiencing now. It has been called that of 'integrative' (Warschauer 1996) or 'integrated' (Bax 2003) CALL. On the technical side, the increasingly powerful multimedia PCs now standardly used also have internet access. Hypermedia technology allows the language learner to access web pages with practically unlimited amounts of authentic target language data, to consult large-scale on-line dictionaries for unknown words, and to listen to native speakers pronouncing the words as often as desired. Tools such as word processors and concordancers can easily be integrated into a CALL course.[1] CALL exercises thus not only offer communicative practice, but often do so with the help of large amounts of authentic language originating from a variety of sources.

Considering the whole history of CALL, the most striking changes in CALL programs have clearly arisen from the technical improvements of computer hardware and software. As a field, CALL seems to be pushed forward more resolutely by the rapid changes in computer technology than by the slower developments in other relevant fields. This has led to a large range of language teaching activities, all somehow involving the use of computers, and leaving practitioners and outsiders alike to wonder what actually constitutes a CALL activity.

2. The field of CALL today

At present there is no agreement within the community of CALL practitioners on the general aim or the boundaries of CALL as a field. Levy makes this point, which has lost nothing of its validity today, when he writes that CALL is still a very diversified field with no clear sense of direction.

> A research agenda, a path for development, or even the problems to which CALL provides the solution have not been agreed and, without this, CALL is somewhat fragmented, and moving in many different directions at the same time. (Levy 1997: 228)

Levy is not alone in calling for principles, theories and clear aims for the field of CALL. Chapelle 1997 is another widely read and cited article calling for proper research paradigms to be set up. CALL, as it is understood by many practitioners and reflected in the topics dealt with at academic conferences and in its journals, has continually widened its range, from programs delivering relatively simple grammar exercises to whole suites of tools being used in the service of language teaching. Following Hewer et al. (1999), I would like to argue, however, that not all applications of computers in the field of language learning should be subsumed under the category of CALL. When tools such as word processors, email programs or web browsers are used in a language teaching context, this is an instance of ICT (Information and Communications Technology) used in a language learning context rather than a case of 'hardcore' CALL. Such uses of computer software, though highly useful in many language teaching situations, are not the focus of this paper. In contrast to Bax (2003), I believe that the term CALL should be reserved for computer programs developed specifically for the teaching and learning of (foreign) languages or a particular aspect of them, and that it should therefore not include what is sometimes called technology-enhanced language learning (TELL), data-driven learning or concordancing (see Mair and also Nesselhauf, this volume), or

---

1 For some CALL practitioners such tools sometimes even replace programs designed specifically for second language learning.

so-called computer-mediated communication (CMC)[2], even if these techniques are successfully employed in foreign language teaching.

CALL programs (in the more restrictive sense that I prefer) can be either programs that handle text and allow teachers to fill in their content (including authoring programs[3] of varying complexity), or they can supply some set content, sometimes with the possibility of adding further content, e.g. in the form of extra vocabulary, or with access to other sources of content, e.g. web pages. Programs where the content needs to be supplied by the teacher typically produce one type of exercise and handle students' reactions to the task at hand by giving pre-programmed responses. Examples are programs for producing gap-filling and text reconstruction exercises and multiple-choice questions. Such programs have the advantage that they can be used for many languages and any level of language proficiency. Their main disadvantage concerns the time required by the teacher, or sometimes the learner, to familiarize themselves with the program and to then input all the text of the actual exercises, the correct and incorrect answers, and sometimes also the feedback texts. This type of 'content-free' program is also excluded from of this paper, as it is very restricted, providing practice for one specific type of exercise or skill only, and thus in principle allowing for many types of (text-based) learning content, from foreign languages to history or even biology. I will focus instead on CALL packages that also contain and present linguistic material to be learned by its users and that supply a number of different exercises. This is the kind of CALL program that can nowadays be found in language labs and bought in bookshops as an alternative or supplement to more traditional language courses. Descriptions and reviews of CALL packages can be found in the relevant journals (see 'Further Reading'-section, and Nesselhauf and Tschichold [2002] for a more critical evaluation of vocabulary CALL).

3. The contribution of applied linguistics

As mentioned above, during the first phase of CALL, behaviourist theories of learning were dominant. The linguistic school contemporary with behaviourism was structuralism. For structuralist applied linguists, mastering the function words and the main sentence structures of a language was the necessary first step in learning a foreign language. Only once these aspects were thoroughly mastered should learners go on to learn more than the minimal quantities of content words needed to fill the lexical slots in grammar exercises (Carter and McCarthy 1988: 40). The view that learning larger numbers of vocabulary items before the learner has a firm grasp of grammar is a waste of

---

2 The term "CMC" usually covers the use of email, on-line chatting and other computer-based, written communication. Despite making use of a written medium, CMC shows a number of linguistic features more typical of oral communication, a feature which makes it particularly attractive to teachers who subscribe to the Communicative Language Teaching approach.

3 Authoring programs provide templates for the creation of exercises. Teachers have dedicated interfaces for filling the templates that are then used to create the exercises that students can work on.

time can hardly be said to have died out even today. For a long time Chomskyan linguistics also embraced the idea that lexical items were not the central aspect of language knowledge. Many of the more traditionally oriented CALL programs still contain a large number of exercises that focus on mastering the grammatical structures of the target language by providing structured drills.

With Communicative Language Teaching came a new emphasis on the use of language in real-life situations – or students' communicative competence – over the production of the correct linguistic forms – or grammatical competence. In CALL, this focus on communicative aspects of the language was implemented through an approach that would allow learners to acquire language implicitly rather than explicitly. Thanks to the continuously increasing memory capacities of PCs and their storage media, these programs overall have a much larger quantity of target language data that can be presented to the learner, making sheer exposure to linguistic data a much more attractive option than was possible with the older programs. Often large amounts of language data were taken from existing sources, especially language courses, and supplemented by a number of easily implementable exercises, usually of the multiple-choice type. As Communicative Language Teaching ranks contact with native speakers quite high, some programs also have in-built functions that connect the learner to the World-Wide Web and encourage contacts with native speakers via email or in chatroom discussions.

The contribution of applied linguistics to CALL so far can be said to be one of moving from the earlier structure drills to encouraging delivery and display of growing amounts of linguistic material, and conversely of a movement away from trying to deal with learners' language production, an idea that was quite prominent in the earliest CALL programs. This increasing lack of true interactivity is problematic, however. Students often get only few opportunities to practise their active foreign language skills and receive (too) little feedback on their language production when using such programs. As Chapelle (1997) rightly points out, mere mouse clicks for selecting an answer to a multiple-choice question cannot be called true language interaction and probably do not train the learner's productive skills. But programs that restrict the user to mouse-click activities play it safe. There is little danger of giving wrong or otherwise unsuitable feedback to the user, a danger that can hardly be overestimated from a didactic point of view (Schulze 2003, Tschichold 1999). It could be said that the delivery of practice material in CALL programs today leaves little to be desired, but dealing with the productive skill of learners remains the big challenge.

Some theories of second language acquisition, however, would not consider this to be problematic. The so-called "no interface position" posits that instruction has no effect on language acquisition (Larsen-Freeman and Long 1991). Many CALL programs in the Communicative Language Teaching spirit suit such an approach quite well, with their clear focus on presentation of linguistic material. If, conversely, we accept the idea that instruction does influence second language acquisition, or at least its progress, we need a different kind of CALL program. According to Larsen-Freeman and Long (1991) most learners benefit from instruction, with learners' age and proficiency being two relevant factors. In other words, while all learners seem to gain from instruction, adult learners and learners at intermediate and advanced foreign language levels benefit more than young children and beginners. This "interface position" claims that there is an interface between the cognitive processing of instruction and that of acquisition, thus making the progression from consciously learnt material to unconsciously mastered material possible. This move from explicit to implicit knowledge, from controlled to automatic processing can be achieved through practice and routinization. For CALL designers, such an approach is clearly more interesting, as it accepts the general use of instruction, a feature CALL can be good at. Chapelle (1998: 23–25) lists seven hypotheses, extracted from research on instructed second language acquisition, that ought to be taken into account by CALL designers:

1. The linguistic characteristics of target language input need to be made salient.
2. Learners should receive help in comprehending semantic and syntactic aspects of linguistic input.
3. Learners need to have opportunities to produce target language output.
4. Learners need to notice errors in their own output.
5. Learners need to correct their linguistic output.
6. Learners need to engage in target language interaction whose structure can be modified for negotiation of meaning.
7. Learners should engage in L2 tasks designed to maximize opportunities for good interaction.

While the first two of these hypotheses could be said to have found their way into CALL at least to some extent, those that directly or indirectly make feedback on the learner's language production necessary have not been taken into account sufficiently so far, for reasons that I hope will become clear in the following section.

4. The contribution of computational linguistics

As a field, CALL has probably suffered to some extent from exaggerated expectations on the part of naive potential users. Of course, we would all like to have a language machine that makes learning a foreign language an entertaining and expeditious experience, that gives us practice in small talk, corrects our written texts, explains the errors we have made, and then produces a couple of remedial exercises before proceeding to the next stage in our customized, all-purpose language course. But such expectations are well beyond today's technology, and therefore even good programs can be a big disappointment to many people if their expectations are unrealistically high.

The computational techniques used in commercial CALL programs today are relatively simple database algorithms, such as are needed to store multiple-choice questions, check whether the user has chosen the correct answer, and display the pre-programmed feedback on the screen. Programs that allow users to actually type in answers need algorithms that compare the user's input to the stored answer(s) and then produce an appropriate response. Such algorithms work by comparing the user's string to the model answer character-by-character, and – at least in their simplest and therefore most efficient form – are not capable of distinguishing minor variations (such as missing diacritics, superfluous plural endings, or spelling errors) from true errors, let alone of accepting synonyms or alternative syntactic constructions as acceptable alternatives to the model. If a simple CALL program for French thus expects the answer *une école* to be typed in, neither *une ecole*, nor *l'école* or *école* will be counted as correct, as all of these show some variation and do not correspond exactly to the answer expected by the program. As learners' errors often do not correspond to typical typing mistakes, the algorithms used by spell checkers are of relatively little help in this situation. What is needed to detect this type of variation and generate appropriate feedback is an algorithm (coupled with a database) designed to deal specifically with learner language.

In addition to simple string handling technology, CALL packages today use hypertext technology, digital audio, and occasionally video as well, in order to allow the user to read and listen to the target language. Voice recognition software is also increasingly found, though the didactic value of showing spectrograms of their own pronunciation to learners remains to be shown. But the use of this technology allows the producers of CALL material to claim that up-to-date methods are being used in their products and impress any potential buyers. Unfortunately, this is a tendency found rather more often than the use of technology in a pedagogically sound way. As Hewer et al. (1999) rightly point out, CALL producers often seem to prefer to integrate the latest technical features rather than focus on what is useful for language learning:

> As CALL has moved on it appears that certain skills have been lost, e.g. the analysis of free-format input […]. While presentation features such as full-colour graphics, sound and video have improved in leaps and bounds there has been an increasing tendency to neglect features such as discrete error analysis, feedback and branching. The trend today seems to be towards a point-and-click-let's-move-on-quick approach.

If the aim is to deal with learners' language production in a more intelligent and discriminating manner, the next step forward from the common string-handling technology necessarily involves methods developed in computational linguistics and its applied branch, natural language processing (NLP). There have been several interesting and promising projects that incorporate NLP techniques into CALL programs. Holland et al. (1995) and Jager et al. (1998) both contain a number of papers on such projects. None of these projects has made it into the mass market so far, despite the huge amounts of time and effort spent on them by their developers. The main reasons for this failure seem to be the relatively poor reliability of today's error detection techniques and the amount of time needed to scale up small pilot projects. Furthermore, the present state of NLP tools that could be used in CALL differs widely from one linguistic level to another.

On the level of phonology, speech recognition software is often used in CALL packages, but without considerable didactic adaptation this seems of little use to the uninitiated language learner. Dedicated pronunciation programs for learners with specific identifiable pronunciation problems, however, can be very useful to overcome these problems. Menzel et al. (2001) and Tsubota et al. (2002) give examples of such systems.

The latter program, for example, can identify individual phonemes that are problematic for Japanese learners of English. It uses speech recognition techniques coupled with information on the frequency of phonemes mispronounced by this learner group. Users receive easily interpretable feedback on their pronunciation problems (in the form of text and diagrams) and an evaluative score reflecting the comprehensibility of their speech to other English speakers. Brett (2004) describes a similar system for Italian learners of English and gives a good account of the problems program developers are faced with.

For the morphological level of error analysis, a number of systems suitable for large-scale applications such as a CALL program already exist. A morphological analyser is based on an electronic dictionary that does not simply store all full forms, but is capable of recognizing and generating the morphological structure(s) of words. For examples of such systems, see ten Hacken and Tschichold (2001), and L'Haire and Vandeventer Faltin (2003). A morphological component for a CALL system needs a morphological analyser that can deal with erroneous but recognizable forms, e.g. *happyly, *theirselves, *sheeps, *sleeped*, in addition to well-formed input.

Syntax is more difficult to treat. The main challenges on this level concern the scalability from small, experimental projects to full-scale systems, the wide variety of possible grammatical errors learners make, and the interdependence of syntax with other levels of the linguistic system. Most existing projects use computational grammars that have been developed for processing correct language and adapt these grammars by relaxing some of the constraints. Agreement errors and similar learners' mistakes can be caught in this way, but for many other errors, this approach does not seem powerful enough at present. An alternative option is to use algorithms that look for specific types of errors, but the problem with this approach is that it is quite impossible to foresee every type of grammatical error language learners are likely to make. Only the most frequent and clearly identifiable errors can be detected with this method. The systems that exist today provide only partial solutions to this challenge; see for instance Heift (2003), Reuer (2003), Schulze (2003) and Vandeventer (2001). Systems for languages with a richer morphology than English are at an advantage in this respect because firstly such languages are somewhat easier to parse, and secondly because learners tend to have more problems internalizing the morphological details of such languages and consequently produce more errors of agreement and similar types.

Turning finally to semantics (and pragmatics), we reach the linguistic level that is still farthest from any viable NLP system. Existent systems can only treat a small part of any language or a microworld where the amount of vagueness and ambiguity so typical for general language has been drastically reduced. As one of the biggest obstacles for language learners is the foreign language lexicon (Nation 2001), a significant number of their errors arise from lack of appropriate vocabulary (Tschichold 2003). In order to recognize errors arising from the misuse of vocabulary, it is often necessary to take the intended meaning of the sentence into account. In CALL, complete recognition and correction of many learner errors therefore depends at least partly on an NLP component capable of dealing with the semantic and pragmatic levels of language knowledge.

Despite today's incomplete state of NLP tools and the limitations on what CALL programs can offer to users, CALL can be a perfectly reasonable choice for a language learner, especially if the program is used for specific purposes such as listening practice or vocabulary learning outside of classroom teaching. CALL programs are capable of delivering high quality sound and images, in addition to large amounts of text, so if the learner is looking for (extra) exposure to the target language, CALL programs offer an almost ideal solution. Compared to human teachers, CALL programs have the advantage of being very cheap – at least to PC owners, as CALL packages normally use standard multimedia PCs. They are moreover available at any time that suits the learner and never lose their patience, thus allowing as many repetitions of the material as wanted. Some CALL programs have sensible exercises for learning and practising vocabulary, an aspect of language learning often neglected in classrooms, but gaining in importance again. Grammar can also be practised quite adequately with the help of CALL programs that focus on this aspect. According to Nerbonne (2003), CALL still has a large potential for grammar instruction as especially adults seem to make much better progress in the foreign language if they are explicitly taught grammatical rules.

As long as CALL users are aware of the fact that the pragmatic, conversational and cultural adequacy of their language production cannot be evaluated, CALL certainly offers an attractive option to the countless learners willing to spend some time learning a foreign language, but not able or willing to participate in traditional language classes and/or spend time in native speaker communities.

5. Outlook

Looking at the development of CALL over the last few decades, it becomes clear that the field has moved away from delivering text-based exercises and providing immediate feedback and on to the use of the computer as a tool for various kinds of activities. While at the beginning, many CALL practitioners had hoped that CALL would soon be able to teach foreign languages to huge numbers of learners, without major intervention by human teachers, today we find a growing awareness that CALL is highly unlikely to ever replace language teachers fully. What CALL can do – and partly does now – is to offer a valuable alternative to other types of self-directed learning (e.g. books, cassettes, audio CDs) for learners who find themselves without access to a human teacher for a variety of reasons. CALL is also useful for supplementary language practice outside the classroom, and it certainly has the potential for a much more important role if teams of teachers, applied linguists, and NLP specialists are given enough time and resources to develop pedagogically sound CALL.

6. Further reading

Warschauer (1996) and especially the excellent and continuously updated ICT4LT website (which includes the module by Hewer et al.) provide useful introductions to the wider topic of CALL. Levy (1997), one of the few monographs on the topic, attempts to find a theory for CALL. Gamper and Knapp (2002) and Nerbonne (2003) are good, recent overviews of the use of NLP in CALL. The main journals in the field are Computer-Assisted Language Learning, ReCALL, Calico, System, and the electronic journal Language Learning & Technology.

Bibliography

Bax, S. 2003. CALL – past, present and future. *System* 31. 13–28.
Brett, D. 2004. Computer generated feedback on vowel production by learners of English as a second language. *ReCALL* 16 (1) 103–113.
Carter, R. and McCarthy, M. 1988. *Vocabulary and Language Teaching*. London: Longman.
Chapelle, C. 1997. CALL in the year 2000: still in search of research paradigms?. *Language Learning & Technology* 1. 19–43.
Chapelle, C. 1998. Multimedia CALL: lessons to be learned from research on instructed SLA. *Language Learning & Technology* 2. 22–34.
Gamper, J. and Knapp, J. 2002. A review of intelligent CALL systems. *Computer-Assisted Language Learning* 15 (4) 329–342.
ten Hacken, P. and Tschichold, C. 2001. Word manager and CALL: structured access to the lexicon as a tool for enriching learners' vocabulary. *ReCALL* 13. 121–131.
Heift, T. 2003. Multiple learner errors and feedback: a challenge for ICALL systems. *CALICO Journal* 20. 533–548.
Hewer, S., Rendall, H., Walker, R. and Davies, G. 1999. Introduction to computer assisted language learning (CALL). Module 1.4 of *ICT4LT*.
Holland, V. M., Kaplan, J. D. and Sams, M. R. 1995. *Intelligent Language Tutors: Theory Shaping Technology*. New Jersey: Lawrence Erlbaum.
ICT4LT (Information and communications technology for language teachers), available at <www.ICT4LT.org>.
Jager, S., Nerbonne, J. and von Essen, A. 1998. *Language Teaching and Language Technology*. Swets & Zeitlinger.
Larsen-Freeman, D. and Long, M. H. 1991. *An Introduction to Second Language Acquisition Research*. London: Longman.
Levy, M. 1997. *Computer-Assisted Language Learning Concept and Conceptualization*. Oxford: Clarendon Press.
L'Haire, S. and Vandeventer Faltin, A. 2003. Error diagnosis in the free text project. *CALICO Journal* 20. 481–495.
Menzel, W., Herron, D., Morton, R., Pezzotta, D., Bonaventura, P. and Howarth, P. 2001. Interactive pronunciation training. *ReCALL* 13. 67–78.
Nation, I. S. P. 2001. *Learning Vocabulary in Anoher Language*. Cambridge: Cambridge University Press.
Nerbonne, J. 2003. Natural language processing in computer-assisted language learning. In: Mitkov, R. (ed.), *The Oxford Handbook of Computational Linguistics*. Oxford: Oxford University Press. 670–698.
Nesselhauf, N. and Tschichold, C. 2002. Collocations in CALL: an investigation of vocabulary-building software for EFL. *Computer Assisted Language Learning* 15. 251–280.
Reuer, V. 2003. Error recognition and feedback with lexical functional grammar. *CALICO Journal* 20. 497–512.
Schulze, M. 2003. Grammatical errors and feedback: some theoretical insights. *CALICO Journal* 20. 437–450.
Tschichold, C. 1999. Grammar checking for CALL: strategies for improving foreign language grammar checkers. In: Cameron, K. (ed.). *CALL: Media, Design & Applications*. Lisse: Swets & Zeitlinger. 203–222.

Tschichold, C. 2003. Error analysis and lexical errors. In: Tschichold, C. (ed.), *English Core Linguistics*. Bern: Peter Lang. 287–299.
Tsubota, Y., Tatsuya, K. and Dantsuji, M. 2002. CALL system for Japanese students of English using formant structure estimation and pronunciation error prediction. *InSTIL 2002 Advanced Workshop*. Available at <www.ar.media.kyoto-u.ac.jp/lab5/bib-e/instil02-1.pdf>
Vandeventer, A. 2001. Creating a grammar checker for CALL by constraint relaxation: a feasibility study. *ReCALL* 13. 110–120.
Warschauer, M. 1996. Computer-assisted language learning: an introduction. In: Fotos, S. (ed.), *Multimedia Language Teaching*. Tokyo: Logos International. 3–20.

Appendix: Example of a communicative CALL exercise

An Invitation

Click on the answer button to see the correct answers.

A: I'm afraid I ___ your invitation.
    a. can't accept
    b. shouldn't to accept
    c. might not accept

Answer ▼

B: Oh, that's a pity! I'm so sorry.
A: So am I, but Bob ___ me to dinner tonight.
    a. invites
    b. had invited
    c. has invited

Answer ▼

B: Well, I guess you ___ out with Bob than with me.
    a. had rather go
    b. had rather gone
    c. would rather go

Answer ▼

A: No! As a matter of fact, I ___ Bob.
    a. am not really liking
    b. don't really like
    c. shouldn't really like

Answer ▼

B: Really? Then why ___ out with him?
    a. have you gone
    b. are you going
    c. will you to go

Answer ▼

A: Well, you see, Bob is my brother's best friend, and besides ...
B: Oh, it doesn't matter! There's no reason why you ___ polite to me.
    a.   should be
    b.   could be
    c.   ought be

Answer	▼

Copyright © 1998 Vera Mello (vcqm@ruralsp.com.br)
This quiz is part of the HTML-Only Self-Study Quizzes which is part of Activities for ESL Students, a project by The Internet TESL Journal.
<http://a4esl.org/q/h/vm/invitation.html>

Swiss English or simply non-native English? A discussion of two possible features

Yvonne Dröschel, Mercedes Durham and Lukas Rosenberger

Learners of foreign languages invariably encounter difficulties with particular features of the target language. This study discusses two features found in the English of non-native speakers practically all over the world: the pluralization of the non-count noun *information* and the use of temporal adjuncts formed with the prepositions *since* and *for*. These two features are examined within the linguistic context of Switzerland, as it is hypothesized that they are part of a set of features which, in their particular constellation, constitute a specifically Swiss form of English. The motivation for this examination of the Swiss context, despite the fact that these two features are not uniquely Swiss, is that the Swiss national languages share certain structures with each other, but not with English. Furthermore, through language contact between Swiss speakers using English as the contact language we may expect to observe specific accommodation processes not found in other parts of the world. In our analysis we will compare the structural properties of the three major Swiss languages in order to establish the substratal influence each of these languages may have on Swiss English. We will further see whether this selective adoption process results in differences among the linguistic communities or whether the same structure has been adopted by all three language groups.

The study presented here is part of a larger research project[1] which aims at examining the linguistic characteristics of English in Switzerland and at describing and accounting for any focusing which might be taking place. To prepare the ground for the analysis of the two features under discussion, a brief presentation of this SNSF project, as well as a discussion of the role of English as a lingua franca in Switzerland and of new approaches to non-native speaker competence are given first.

1. The SNSF project

Confronted with the increasing popularity of English and its continuing use as a lingua franca in various areas of life within Switzerland (industry, media, sport, youth culture, etc.) the question arises as to what extent this development has had an influence on the forms and functions of English used as a non-native language in Switzerland. Studies

---

1 "Language Contact and Focusing: The Linguistics of English in Switzerland" is a research project funded by the Swiss National Science Foundation (SNSF). Project Coordinators: Prof. Peter Trudgill, University of Fribourg; Prof. Richard J. Watts, University of Bern; Prof. David Allerton, University of Basel; Research Assistants: Yvonne Dröschel, University of Fribourg; Mercedes Durham, University of Fribourg; Lukas Rosenberger, University of Bern.

of multilingual situations have shown that the use of English as a lingua franca has led to the development of distinctive endonormative varieties of English in places such as India and Nigeria. Through processes of "focusing" (LePage and Tabouret-Keller 1985) these varieties have acquired a set of common, non-native norms. Focusing takes place in contexts of speech accommodation and negotiation such as those which typically occur in language-contact situations. Following Whinnom (1971), it is hypothesized that focusing can occur as a result of tertiary hybridization, meaning that the source language is acquired in what he calls a pidginized form by at least two different mother-tongue groups of non-native speakers, who then use it as a lingua franca to communicate with one another. Whereas these processes have already taken place in India and Nigeria, for instance, Switzerland might offer a unique opportunity to observe a similar development in progress. The SNSF research project is based on two main hypotheses, the primary one reading as follows:

> **Hypothesis 1:** There is evidence that the English used by non-native speakers and writers of the language in Switzerland is at present undergoing a process of tertiary hybridization which may result in an endonormative variety of English.

If this proves to be the case, we have a unique opportunity to observe focusing mechanisms, both social and linguistic. This assumption leads to our secondary hypothesis:

> **Hypothesis 2:** Focusing takes place as a result of processes of speech accommodation and negotiation which are observable in both written and oral communication, primarily, however, in oral communication between Swiss non-native speakers of English and secondarily in oral communication between native speakers and Swiss non-native speakers of English.

In line with these two hypotheses, the research involves the detailed observation of English in use as a lingua franca in different social situations to corroborate a set of features assumed to be characteristic of the way in which Swiss English differs from Standard English. Data have been collected in such contexts as business meetings, round-table discussions and e-mail conversations (cf. 2.1) in which English was used as a lingua franca, resulting in a preliminary database for Swiss English. The analysis of these data will focus on morphological, syntactic and phonological structures, since it is precisely these features that can be given as evidence of a process of tertiary hybridization assumed to result in the endonormative variety of English we have classified as Swiss English. In addition, we will be looking for evidence of admixture and reinforcement of regularization processes as the result of similar structures in the native Swiss languages.

2. English as a lingua franca in Switzerland

The use of English in various domains in Switzerland is not unique, since English is continuously gaining in importance for communication between members of different linguistic communities in many places around the world. However, Switzerland is of particular interest in the sense that English is being used to facilitate communication between the different linguistic groups of this multilingual country and thus serves as an intranational lingua franca as well as an international lingua franca. It has been shown (Watts and Murray 2001) that in a wide array of situations, Swiss non-native speakers of English revert to the use of English when faced with linguistic diversity. Considering that Switzerland is a multilingual country with no fewer than four national languages, of which at least German and French could lend themselves readily as possible vehicles of cross-cultural communication, the growing preference for English as a non-indigenous variety may be rather surprising. An explanation for this preference may be the fact that the vast majority of lingua franca interactions world-wide are conducted in English and that the language has consistently gained in importance in areas such as politics, science, culture and business matters, a status that is partly due to the undisputed role of the USA as the leading world power in politics and science (Knapp 1991).

What makes Switzerland a most interesting arena of linguistic research in the development of English as a lingua franca is thus not necessarily its use as a tool for international communication, but the fact that Swiss non-native English speakers choose English rather than French or German to communicate with *each other*.

The phenomenon of internal lingua franca communication can be observed primarily in internal business communication in Switzerland as an international marketplace. More and more globally active companies with headquarters in Switzerland are using English as the lingua franca for internal communication. The adoption of English as the working language of many companies promotes a local need for English and has become almost a prerequisite for professional success. Hence, more and more Swiss people aim either to learn English or improve their ability to speak and write it.

3. New approaches to non-native speaker competence

Since we can expect that slight deficiencies in English competence would not severely impede communicative success, it can be argued that lingua franca communication should not be measured against native speaker competence. Non-native users of a lingua franca can communicate successfully without adhering to native speaker norms, so that the focus on competence in English as a lingua franca should rather be the speaker's flexibility and her/his ability to communicate for as many purposes as are necessary (Widdowson 1997). The focus is therefore on pragmatic and not on cultural competence, so that linguistic and cultural norms have to be flexible and changeable. Speakers of English as a lingua franca are thus able to make use of the enormous negotiability potential of linguistic norms (House 2002). As Seidlhofer (2002: 272) points out:

> While still making use of a code which is recognizably English […], the ELF model should not be exonormatively oriented towards native-speaker usage but *endonormative*. […] the international ELF speech community should no longer be regarded as what Kachru (1995: 16*ff*) has termed 'norm-dependent', but as 'norm-developing' and, ultimately, 'norm-providing'.

Most of the research so far has focused on communication between native and non-native speakers, often regarding non-native users of English as having incomplete communicative competence and conceiving of non-native English as deviant from Standard English and thus in dire need of correction (Widdowson 1997, Seidlhofer 2001). When using English as a lingua franca, non-native speakers naturally deviate from native speaker norms of usage, but to consider these deviations mistakes or communicative failures would be disregarding the communicative success that is regularly achieved in such interactions despite the speakers' so-called imperfect learning.

Despite a growing interest in lingua franca interactions, research has largely been limited to a theoretical level, with only a few empirical studies having been conducted in this field. Some work has recently been carried out into the nature of English as a lingua franca, notably the compilation of the Vienna-Oxford ELF corpus (Seidlhofer 2002). Yet there is still only scarce empirical evidence of how English is actually used as a lingua franca and its differences from native English. As mentioned above, our research project aims at providing such empirical evidence in the form of a database of Swiss English.

4. The data

Our data consist of spoken and written material collected among speakers of at least one Swiss language.[2] The spoken data include interviews as well as recordings of meetings and conferences, while the written data consist predominantly of a corpus of e-mails collected among Swiss medical students. Although the transcripts of the recordings and the e-mails provided the bulk of the data, we have also included anecdotal data from a variety of sources, provided that the author's L1 was known. These anecdotal data include publications in magazines and newspapers, advertisements, and utterances by speakers with whom we have interacted. Even though our corpus is relatively limited in size, we feel that it still allows us to extract representative non-native features of the English used in Switzerland, as the data stem from various contexts in which English is used as a lingua franca.

Part of the analysis of our data involved deciding which features of Swiss English we should focus on. According to Platt et al. (1984: 167), the main criterion for considering a feature to be part of Swiss English would be its systematicity, i.e. it must not be a nonce creation or the idiosyncratic usage of one speaker. Even though we have chosen to consider the frequency of each feature in comparison to Standard English structures, we cannot attempt to provide an extensive quantitative analysis of Swiss English, since this would require a considerably larger corpus of data in order to yield significant results.

---

2 Unfortunately, there are no native speakers of Romansch among our informants. In addition, as speakers of Romansch in most cases have Italian or German as an additional L1, it might have been difficult to establish the influence of Romansch on the English produced by such speakers, and we have therefore abstained from complementing our database with Romansch speaker data.

The following are the individual data sources used for the present study:

- **IFMSA-CH:** The main source of data in this paper, and in fact the only source used to contain pluralized forms of *information/info*, consists of a corpus of e-mails sent by the Swiss members of an international medical students' association, the International Federation of Medical Students' Association (IFMSA).[3] This corpus comprises nearly 1000 e-mails sent over a period of four years by Swiss native speakers of French, German and Italian. It is complemented by transcriptions of recordings made at two of the association's general meetings and two interviews conducted with members of the association. The total number of informants in this group is 43.
- **M4Music:** The M4Music corpus consists of the transcription of a panel discussion held during the M4Music festival in Zurich in April 2002. This discussion focused on the importance and inherent difficulties of exporting Swiss music and was held entirely in English. The six participants were from the French and the German speaking parts of Switzerland.
- **Bank interviews:** Eleven interviews were conducted with employees of an international bank in Zurich. The bank seemed to be an ideal setting to collect data for our research, since its head office is in London and the corporate culture is therefore essentially English. The employees are thus required to conduct all their official exchanges (including e-mails) in English, even though most of its employees are from the Swiss German, French or Italian speaking parts of Switzerland and have learned English only at a later stage in their lives. Three female and seven male employees, all of them Swiss, were interviewed. Seven of the interviewees are native speakers of Swiss German, one of them is a native speaker of French, one of them a native speaker of Italian, and one of them is bilingual Italian and Swiss German. The interviews lasted about thirty minutes each and were based on a set of questions that were adapted to each individual.
- **First Tuesday Group:** Videotaped conferences of the First Tuesday Group in Geneva were made available on the Internet. Since the vast majority of these meetings were either conducted exclusively in French or contained only very short sequences of native speakers of English, we decided to transcribe and use only one two-hour conference that seems to have been held entirely in English because of the presence of several native speakers of English. There were a total of 12 Swiss participants in this conference.

For both features analysed in this paper, all the tokens for the native and non-native variants were extracted from all the data sources and coded for various factors. For the feature *information/informations*, a factor analysis was employed; apart from revealing to what extent the feature is prevalent across the language groups and data sources, this kind of quantitative analysis also allows us to determine the influence of individual factors on the observed variation. In the case of the feature *since/for*, however, the rather small number of tokens does not allow for a detailed factor analysis. While the quantitative analysis is thus more limited, a qualitative analysis in terms of L1 influence is still possible, even though it is necessarily more tentative.

---

3 Cf. Durham (2003) for a more detailed analysis.

5. Quantitative results

5.1 Information/Informations

A preliminary analysis of the data sources of the SNSF project revealed a number of problematic plurals, in particular cases where the plural marker -*s* was used in combination with a few specific non-count nouns, resulting in morphosyntactic forms which are clearly non-standard. Consider the following examples from the IFMSA corpus:

I'm waiting for your *feedbacks*, comments, insults and changes.

Please, send to me the missing *informations* requested in my report.

The most frequent noun in our corpora that is marked in this way is *information*, which is why we have chosen to look at the patterning of this specific noun in the present study. All tokens of *information*, whether in the standard form or a non-native form, in the full or the contracted form (i.e. *information, informations, info, infos*), were extracted from the corpora, providing us with 149 tokens. A majority of these tokens stem from the IFMSA corpus (N = 127), with a further 22 from the three other corpora. The frequency of tokens from the first corpus is possibly due to the nature of the messages sent within the IFMSA, as the exchange of information is an explicit topic in many of these messages. Furthermore, the IFMSA corpus is more extensive than the other three, allowing for more opportunities for the feature to occur.

The factors examined for *information/informations* in this study are native language and preceding structure. In addition, it is worth mentioning that the IFMSA corpus is the only one of the sources considered to contain cases of a pluralized form of *information*. However, this should not be taken to mean that the feature does not appear in other Swiss contexts.[4] A possible explanation could be that the data sources other than IFMSA are either not large enough to contain instances of the non-native variant of this feature or that the English of the speakers from those other sources is different from that of other Swiss speakers, which seems quite likely considering that the three other sources involve groups of people interacting in rather formal settings, where speakers in some cases even make use of notes prepared beforehand. Because of the observed constellation, the quantitative analysis of this feature will focus exclusively on the source which does display variation, i.e. on the IFMSA corpus. In this corpus, a pluralized form is used 42% of the time, as compared to 58% of the standard forms *information/info* (cf. Table 10.1). The total number of tokens is higher for the Italian speakers than for the other groups, despite the fact that Italian speakers constitute the smallest of the three linguistic groups in Switzerland considered in this study. However, as the IFMSA corpus contains a high percentage of e-mails from native Italian

---

4 For example, a Google™ search for *informations* on Swiss web pages in English comes up with about 94,000 hits (as compared to about 200,000 hits for *information* on Swiss web pages in English). Furthermore, our anecdotal data contain a considerable number of pluralizations of *information*, as in the following example:

We finally got all the infos for the rockprize finals,

produced by a male speaker of Swiss German who is highly fluent in English.

speakers, reflecting the fact that at the time of data collection most of the key positions in the association were held by Italian speakers (Durham 2003), this finding is not surprising. The difference in the total number of tokens for the Italian, French and German speakers is not significant (p <0.10) as the overall percentages of Standard versus pluralized form are nevertheless the same for the Italian and French groups, while the German speakers exhibit a slightly less frequent use of *informations/infos*.

Table 10.1 Distribution of standard and pluralized forms of *information* across native languages

Data source: IFMSA	Standard form (%)	Pluralized form (%)	Total (N)
Italian	51	48	64
French	52	48	25
German	73	26	38
Total	58	42	127

The second factor taken into consideration is the preceding determiner, as it seems reasonable to assume that the non-native speakers' choice of form might be influenced by the type of determiner chosen (cf. Table 10.2). For example, for a non-native speaker of English *more information* might seem to carry more of a plural connotation than *this information*. Our results suggest that the preceding determiner does indeed influence the choice of *information* over *informations* and vice versa. For example, with the determiner *more* a pluralized form of *information* is used considerably more often than with the determiner *some*, which would support the hypothesis that a plural connotation of the determiner favours the pluralization of the following noun. The same is true for the determiners *this* versus *these* in that with the plural determiner we find a pluralized form of *information* exclusively, whereas with the singular determiner there is a clear majority of standard uses of *information*. However, the number of tokens is too low to allow us to determine whether the influence of the determiners is statistically significant.

Table 10.2 Distribution of standard and pluralized forms of *information* depending on the determiner

Determiner	Standard form (%)	Pluralized form (%)	Total (N)
the	59	41	27
some	65	35	23
more	33	67	18
all the	56	44	9
this	86	14	7
further	50	50	6

these	0	100	2
our, your	50	50	2
a lot of	0	100	1
no	0	100	1
[blank]	67	33	3
count singular determiner[5]	100	0	2
other forms	69	31	26
Total	**58**	**42**	**127**

Despite the low number of tokens which hinders statistically significant results with respect to the individual factor groups, our data show that the pluralized version of the originally non-count noun information is present in the English used in Switzerland to a considerable degree. Possible reasons for this non-native usage are discussed in section 6.

5.2 For/since

The analysis of our data sources shows that the use of the two temporal prepositions *since* and *for* poses considerable difficulties for Swiss speakers of English. Before presenting non-native uses of *since* and *for* in our data, however, a brief comment on the extraction process is necessary. Not every occurrence of *since* and *for* found its way into the final set of tokens.[6] There are several reasons for this; first of all, all tokens of *since* and *for* functioning in other than temporal adjuncts were obviously excluded from the analysis. Furthermore, as *for* can be used either with a perfect aspect or a simple present/past tense but *since* is only used with a perfect aspect, our analysis focused on those cases when *for* and *since* are being used relatively interchangeably, because we are mainly interested in whether we find a reduction of this marked distinction in our Swiss data. Tokens of *for* that could not be converted in this way were excluded from the initial part of the study, meaning that a majority of instances of *for* within the corpora were excluded, which partly explains why the number of tokens of *for* used for

---

5   As non-native speakers are using *information* as a standard count noun in its plural form, it is not surprising that there are also cases where the singular form has been misinterpreted. This is attested in occurrences of *information* with a count singular determiner, i.e. *one, a, every*, as for example in "This is a short information". However, with only two instances in our data these cases are a lot less frequent than the pluralized form.

6   In addition to the temporal prepositions *since* and *for*, there is also a zero form as in the following example b:

   a) I've lived here for six months.
   b) I've lived here six months.

   However, as according to our data this form seems to be relatively unproblematic for Swiss speakers, i.e., they comply mostly with native speaker usage, we decided to concentrate on the patterning of *since* and *for* only.

analysis is rather small.[7] In addition, there were a few cases of false starts or hesitations, which have all been excluded from the final number of tokens, i.e. both the false start and the consequent correction have been removed.

The extraction provided us with considerably fewer tokens than in the case of *information/informations*, namely with only 28 tokens of *since* and 12 of *for*, rather evenly distributed across the four data sources.[8] This means that the subsequent analysis cannot account for much more than the very basic factors behind the variation. With respect to the choice of variants there are no cases of *for* when it would have seemed more natural to use *since*. However, there are occasional uses of *since* when *for* would have been the norm. Generally, 18 out of the 28 tokens of *since* are used in a clearly native-like manner. Most of the cases of non-native usage of *since* seem to be caused by confusion between *since* and *for*. Consider the following examples:

> it's since three years quite a successful eve – event   (L1: German)
> but since a couple of years, we also have other activities   (L1: Italian)

Furthermore, there are a few isolated cases where *since* is used instead of another preposition:

> for the first time since many years ... (*since* instead of *in* or *for*)
> I would like to take this occasion to deeply thank X, who was the co-president since now. (*since* instead of *until*)

Table 10.3 Distribution of *since* and *for* across native languages

	French	German[9]	Italian	Total
standard use of *since*	6	6	6	18
standard use of *for*	7	3	2	12
since instead of *for*	1	5	2	8
since instead of other	0	1	1	2
standard use of *for* in %	88	38	50	60
overuse of *since* in %	**14**	**50**	**33**	**36**

7 We are aware of the fact that with this small number of tokens it is possible for an individual speaker to influence the results rather heavily. Consequently, special caution is due in the interpretation of the data.
8 Of the 28 tokens of *since*, 14 are found in the IFMSA data, 6 each in M4Music and the bank interviews, and 2 in the First Tuesday Group. Of the 12 tokens of *for*, 4 are found in IFMSA, 2 in M4-Music, and 3 each in the bank interviews and the First Tuesday Group.
9 Among the speakers in our data sources the differences between the individual English language competence levels are considerably greater for the German speakers than for the French and Italian speakers. In particular, there are a few speakers of Swiss German whose competence level in English is rather low as compared to that of the other speakers. This may have contributed to the German speakers' low percentage of standard use of *since* and *for* in this comparison.

Once again, one of the problems with these results is that the total number of tokens is too small to make a statistically significant claim about how exactly the features are patterning.

There seem to be quite a lot of non-native tenses in the data extracted, indicating that the English tense system is difficult for Swiss speakers in general.

6. Explanation and interpretation

6.1 Pluralization of the non-count noun *information*

The count/non-count distinction plays a role in most if not all languages, and certainly does so in all the languages of Switzerland. However, as is pointed out in Quirk et al. (1985: 251), the ways in which particular entities are conceptualized and lexicalized may vary considerably.

> It may be noted that, apart from a tendency for concrete nouns to be count and for abstract nouns to be noncount, there is no necessary connection between the classes of nouns and the entities to which they refer. In some related languages, the nouns corresponding to *information*, *money*, *news*, and *work*, for example are count nouns, but in English they are noncount.

In Standard English count nouns can be either singular or plural, whereas non-count nouns are mostly only singular. This is the case in French, German and Italian as well, yet not the same items are conceptualized according to this dichotomy. The obligatory category of number forces non-native speakers to classify lexical items as either singular or plural and they seem to do so simply by applying the conceptualization prevailing in their mother tongues. Hence, it is not surprising that many Swiss use the non-count noun *information* as a count noun. However, even though this feature is practically universal in non-native varieties of English, it is not the outcome of a process of reducing two grammatical categories to one, but is probably directly related to first language transfer.

In order to evaluate the importance of the mother tongue in the restructuring of English, it is necessary to establish whether the corresponding noun is a count noun in each of the relevant substrate languages. If this is the case, first language transfer can indeed be used to explain the pluralization of *information* (cf. Table 10.4).

Table 10.4 A typological approach to the morphosyntactic structures of *information*

ENGLISH: *information* conceptualized as non-count noun
SINGULAR *Thank you for this important information.*
          This information is not available.
PLURAL   * *Thank you for these important informations.*
          * *More informations are not available.*

FRENCH: *information* **conceptualized as count noun**
S<small>INGULAR</small> *Merci pour cette <u>information</u> importante.*
  Cette <u>information</u> n'est pas disponible.
P<small>LURAL</small> *Merci pour ces <u>informations</u> importantes.*
  D'autres <u>informations</u> ne sont pas disponibles.

GERMAN: *Information* **conceptualized as count noun**
S<small>INGULAR</small> *Danke für diese wichtige <u>Information</u>.*
  Diese <u>Information</u> steht nicht zur Verfügung.
P<small>LURAL</small> *Danke für diese wichtigen <u>Informationen</u>.*
  Weitere <u>Informationen</u> stehen nicht zur Verfügung.

ITALIAN: *informazione* **conceptualized as count noun**
S<small>INGULAR</small> *Grazie per questa <u>informazione</u> importante.*
  Questa <u>informazione</u> non è disponibile.
P<small>LURAL</small> *Grazie per queste <u>informazioni</u> importanti.*
  Altre <u>informazioni</u> non sono disponibili.

As we see in Table 10.4, in French, German and Italian (and Romansch, for that matter) *information* is clearly a count noun, so that the pluralization of *information*, as well as of *info* as a variant of *information*, may be considered a natural reflex for Swiss non-native speakers of English. Hence, in cases where *information* or *info* would be used in their plural form in French, German or Italian respectively, they tend to be used in a pluralized form in English. Since we do not find a general tendency towards a pluralization of non-count nouns in our data, the pluralization of the non-count noun *information* in Swiss English is probably related to first language transfer rather than to simplification processes, as these would lead to an overgeneralization of non-count nouns to a plural morphology. Even though the occurrence of this feature in most second language varieties of English suggests universal tendencies at work, the extensive differences among different speech communities also show that the registers are conventionalized and language-specific.

To summarize, this analysis suggests that the primary source of the pluralization of *information* is transfer from the source languages. Even though many instances of possible substrate transfer may be just as adequately accounted for on the basis of universal processes of simplification (i.e. grammatical reduction or elaboration), *information* is pluralized by being brought into conformity with the morphosyntactic structure of the source languages. The plural morphology of *information* is mapped from the source languages onto the structure of English, a modifying process that does not result in systematic simplification, i.e. the regularization of count and non-count nouns. If this feature could be accounted for by reduction we would expect to find a general tendency towards the pluralization of non-count nouns in Swiss English. However, this is clearly not the case, since we have found instances of pluralization of non-count nouns only in cases where we find morphological plural markers in the source languages (such as *trouble, feedback, effort*). Hence, we would classify the pluralization of *information* as a relatively isolated case of the substitution of a morphosyntactic pattern in the target language by the pattern of the source language.

6.2 The temporal prepositions *since* and *for*

When analysing which processes have contributed to the modification of the use of the temporal prepositions *since* and *for*, we need to consider both their semantic properties as well as the morphosyntactic rules they are subject to, especially since none of the languages spoken in Switzerland make the same semantic and morphosyntactic distinctions as Standard English. Tables 10.5 and 10.6 illustrate the German, French and Italian equivalents of English expressions of temporal location and duration that use the perfect aspect.

Table 10.5 Equivalents of *since* in German, French and Italian

***Since* with a noun phrase denoting a temporal location**

ENGLISH:
Mary has lived in Paris since 1980.
Mary has lived in Paris since she was born.
Mary has lived in Paris since her birth.

GERMAN:
Mary wohnt in Paris seit 1980.
Mary wohnt in Paris seit sie geboren wurde.
Mary wohnt in Paris seit ihrer Geburt.
→ **English *since* = German *seit***

FRENCH:
Mary habite à Paris depuis 1980.
Mary habite à Paris depuis qu'elle est née.
Mary habite à Paris depuis sa naissance.
→ **English *since* = French *depuis***

ITALIAN:
Mary abita a Parigi da 1980.
Mary abita a Parigi da quando è nata.
Mary abita a Parigi dalla sua nascita.
→ **English *since* = Italian *da***

Table 10.6 Equivalents of *for* in German, French and Italian

***For* with a noun phrase denoting a time span**

ENGLISH:
Mary has lived in Paris for 20 years.

GERMAN:
Mary wohnt seit 20 Jahren in Paris.
*Mary lives in Paris since 20 years.
→ **English** *for* = **German** *seit*

FRENCH:
Mary habite à Paris depuis 20 ans.
*Mary lives in Paris since 20 years.
→ **English** *for* = **French** *depuis*

ITALIAN:
Mary abita a Parigi da 20 anni.
*Mary lives in Paris since 20 years.
→ **English** *for* = **Italian** *da*

According to these examples, none of the Swiss languages has a direct equivalent to the English construction *for* + perfect aspect, but the equivalent of *since* is used indiscriminately in these cases. The following examples illustrate some uses of *since* and *for* of Swiss speakers.

And er I never used French since the school.	(L1: German)
[S]ince x er came in THE office it's more natural for me to speak English …	(L1: French)
He is a PhD in law er … and [appearing] court since 1974.	(L1: French)
I am here for five years almost …	(L1: German)
French is a language I didn't use for years …	(L1: Italian)
[W]e are working together about since two months now …	(L1: German)

The examples in our data demonstrate that both the semantic distinction and the morphosyntactic roles of the adjuncts with *since* and *for* are confused or overgeneralized, i.e., *since* is often used instead of *for*, and morphosyntactic constraints are lost. The most likely explanation for the overuse of *since* as a preposition realizing adjuncts of backward span is the fact that all the Swiss languages use one and the same preposition to mark temporal location and duration. English, however, makes a clear semantic distinction between these two functions and uses *since* only in cases where the adjunct has a clear reference to the starting point of the time span.

The prepositional phrases introduced by German *seit*, French *depuis* and Italian *da* differ from their English counterpart *since* + noun phrase in two respects. On a semantic level, English *since* must be followed by a noun phrase denoting a position in time given by a date or another temporal deixis, whereas the respective equivalents in the Swiss languages allow for such complements of temporal location as well as for complements referring to duration, where the complement is the duration of a time span, e.g. 20 years. According to this assessment, in Swiss English, a sentence such as *He lives in Paris since 1980* would say of the time span that its starting point is 1980, whereas a sentence such as *He lives in Paris since 20 years* would say of the time span that it has the length of 20 years. On a morphosyntactic level, the substratum languages differ from English with respect to their tense/aspect system in that there is no perfective aspect in any of the Swiss languages. Instead, all of the Swiss languages use the present tense to mark the relation to the present and extend this usage to English. Hence, the combination of the morphologically distinctive tense/aspect system of English and the prepositions *since* and *for* tends to be reduced to the single preposition *since* and the present tense, although exceptions can still be found.

We can thus conclude that the tendency to confuse or merge *since* and *for* in temporal adjuncts in Swiss English constitutes both a conflation of lexical meaning and a generalization of a complex grammatical rule. According to Mühlhäusler (1974: 230), who defines the term simplification as implying an increase in regularity, such a process could thus be taken as simplifying the target language in a language contact situation. However, this process can be observed in each of the Swiss languages individually and is more likely to be an instance of L1 transfer, i.e. we would argue that it is an effect of substratal influence that is at least initially motivated by the fact that the morphosyntactic patterns of French, German and Italian are closely related and thus tend to substitute for the English one. Simplification and first language transfer tend to be closely related if not interdependent, since our data have shown that the simplification of the target language largely relies on the presence of a relevant matrix in the substratum languages.

7. Focusing

The analysis of L1 influences on the pluralization of the non-count noun *information* has made it clear that accommodation processes do not necessarily have to be involved for this feature to become focused. Since the same structure is found in all three Swiss languages, it may be transferred directly from each substrate language. Nevertheless, it is of course possible that the speakers in each of the three linguistic communities of Switzerland do, in the course of time, accommodate to each other and use *information* in the plural even though they might not have done so if they had not received the non-native input from speakers of one of the other languages. However, in order to support such a hypothesis, a wide-ranging survey based on language in action would be needed; unfortunately, our data base is as yet too small to provide evidence for such a process of accommodation.

Similarly, the overuse of *since* found in Swiss English can be attributed to structural similarities between the Swiss languages just as easily as to accommodation across the different groups, which would be in keeping with what we know of cross-linguistic compromises in other language contact situations. However, accommodation as a compromise between the grammars of the languages in contact is not a necessary cause, but it is certainly a possible, cause of this feature becoming focused in the future. Due to the limited data available so far, our results must remain largely suggestive and illustrative. In order to establish whether the use of *since* and *for* as we have found it in our data is indeed a distinctive characteristic of Swiss English, a larger corpus of data will have to be investigated. In addition, this particular instance of feature selection will have to be compared with other second language varieties of English.

8. Conclusions

We have attempted to trace the sources of the linguistic structures analysed in this study on the basis of empirical documentation. Both of the features examined serve to illustrate ways in which non-native speaker English might be influenced by the speakers' L1. The first feature, the pluralization of the non-count noun *information*, demonstrates how speakers might be compelled by their L1 to create forms which do not exist in English, whereas the second feature, the use of the temporal prepositions *since* and *for*, presents a case where two forms with strictly assigned roles in native speaker English are confused, with a tendency to be reduced to one to match the morphosyntactic patterns of the speakers' respective L1s. Again, the two features considered are not exclusive to Swiss English, but are found in many learner Englishes around the world. However, we may hypothesize that while the English of Switzerland is not unique with respect to the non-native features it displays, it may be of special interest with respect to the focusing mechanisms through which it develops into an endonormative variety. The regular use of English as an intranational lingua franca within Switzerland fosters at least those non-native features where the national languages share certain structures and at the same time differ from English. Among the set of potential features of Swiss English collected so far there are of course features whose equivalents in the national languages differ from each other. In these cases we would expect to observe accommodation processes in language contact situations, which could subsequently result in a focusing process of the relevant features. In order to demonstrate if and to what extent such processes of accommodation between speakers of the different Swiss languages happen, the examination of these features is one of the next steps in the SNSF project. Furthermore, to establish to what extent the non-native features found in the English in Switzerland are present in other contexts, it will obviously be necessary to examine other non-native corpora, such as the *International Corpus of Learner English* (Granger et al., 2002). This component of the analysis is necessary to determine whether it is possible to speak of Swiss English as opposed to, for example, European English (or simply French English, German English and Italian English). A further aspect to be considered in the project is the context of institutionalized English language teaching. An assessment of the amount of attention devoted to, and the importance assigned to potential features of Swiss English in the teaching context may be helpful in speculating about the future development of the English used in Switzerland. Finally, with respect to the two features examined in this study it may be asked why there is still a considerable degree of variation to be found, despite the fact that the influence of French, German and Italian favour the same non-native realization of these features. First of all, the variation found in Swiss English may be argued to be due to the differences in English language competence of the people interacting, and secondly, and more importantly, it is due to the kind of linguistic input available to Swiss speakers of English. In the multilingual setting of Switzerland, speakers are exposed to both native and non-native varieties of English, and consequently, considerable linguistic variation is to be expected even for those features where there is no, or hardly any, variation in native speaker English.

Bibliography

Durham, M. 2003. Language Choice on a Swiss Mailing List. *Journal of Computer Mediated Communication* (JCMC) 9 (1). [Online Journal].
Granger, S., Dagneaux, E. and Meunier, F. 2002. *International Corpus of Learner English*. Louvain: Presses universitaires de Louvain.
House, J. 2002. Developing pragmatic competence in English as a lingua franca. In: Knapp and Meierkord 2002. 245–269.
Kachru, B. B. 1995. *The Other Tongue*. Oxford: Pergamon Press.
Knapp, K. 1991. Zurück zu Babel? Zur Zukunft der Weltsprache Englisch. *Zeitschrift für Literaturwissenschaft und Linguistik* 79. 18–42.
Knapp, K. and Meierkord, C. (eds.), 2002. *Lingua Franca Communication*. Frankfurt am Main: Peter Lang.
LePage, R. and Tabouret Keller, A. 1985. *Acts of Identity*. Cambridge: Cambridge University Press.
Mühlhäusler, P. 1974. *Pidginization and Simplification of Language*. Canberra: Pacific Linguistics.
Platt, J. T., Weber, H. and Ho, M. L. 1984. *The new Englishes*. London: Routledge & Kegan Paul.
Quirk, R., Svartvik, J., Leech, G. and Greenbaum, S. 1985. *A Comprehensive Grammar of the English Language*. London: Longman.
Seidlhofer, B. 2001. Closing a conceptual gap: the case for a description of English as a lingua franca. *International Journal of Applied Linguistics* 11. 133–158.
Seidlhofer, B. 2002. The shape of things to come? Some basic questions about English as a lingua franca. In: Knapp and Meierkord 2002. 269–302.
Watts, R. J. and Murray, H. (eds.). 2001. *Die fünfte Landessprache? Englisch in der Schweiz*. Zürich: Hochschulverlag.
Whinnom, K. 1971. Linguistic hybridisation and the 'special case' of pidgins and creoles. In: Hymes D. (ed.), *Pidginisation and Creolisation of Languages*. Cambridge: Cambridge University Press. 91–115.
Widdowson, H. 1997. EIL, ESL, EFL: global issues and local interests. *World Englishes* 16. 135–146.

English teaching and learning in Hong Kong

R. Shui-Ching Ho

Shortly before Hong Kong (HK) reverted to China as a Specialized Administration Region (SAR) in 1997, millions of tourists rushed to catch a glimpse of the new star of the Far East. It was frequent to hear even those of non-native English origin complain about the unexpectedly low standard of English spoken by people in this metropolis, despite its international outlook and 150 years' colonial administration. Visitors were often astonished to find that most bus-drivers did not speak English at all. The sales personnel in fashionable boutiques had very limited competence in English (Platt 1982). Even the kind of 'good' English spoken by the minority group of people engaged in the business or academic sector was a "learner's language, a developmental continuum rather than a lectal and developmental continuum as in the case of Singapore English", and speakers did "not 'drop down the continuum' for stylistic purposes" (Platt 1982: 409). The aim of the present essay is to focus on various aspects of the formative stages of this kind of English.

1. Introduction

1.1 Socio-economical background

Under British sovereignty from 1842 to 1997, Hong Kong was transformed from a humble fishing harbour to one of the world's biggest trading ports. Its population increased from less than half a million in 1911 to about 6.5 million towards the eve of the handover. The dynamic change undergone by Hong Kong, however, was far from uniform. The major momentum of explosion, gathered in the second half of the century after the Second World War and the civil war in China, when the Communists Party came to power, bringing an influx of refugees from mainland China to a safe haven. Most of the present population has its origin in the waves of new immigrants in the post-war period and reflects their high birth rate. The 2001 census showed that two fifths of the Chinese population were born in China. The newly arrived immigrants, essentially illiterate and poorly educated, triggered off half a century's economic growth. Fuelled by the manufacturing industry, enhanced by the colonial government's laissez-faire, low tax and free trade policy, and accelerated by China's open door policy in the 1980s, the new economy experienced an unprecedented and persistent growth, shifting gradually to service industries towards the turn of the last century and leading to the emergence of Hong Kong as one of the most envied financial centres in the world.

1.2 Educational expansion

Like all other sectors, education experienced a huge and steady expansion in the post-war era. By the late 70s, the population had expanded several fold. Over three fifths of the population were under 20 and over a quarter were under 15. There was an urgent need to provide basic education for the young population (HKG 1965 & 1974). Tens of thousands of primary school places were created per year. By 1970, universal free education was achieved for primary levels (Grades 1 to 6), followed by an extension to the junior secondary level (Grades 7 to 9) in 1978. Major expansion efforts in the remaining decades were made for the senior secondary up to the tertiary level. The number of universities grew from one in the post-war decade to nine in the 90s. There are at present approximately 500 secondary schools and 850 primary schools in an area of slightly over 1000 square kilometres.

1.3 English-speaking development

In the course of one and a half centuries, Hong Kong has evolved from a non-English speaking to an English-dependent and English-learning community. In the pre-war era, it was not in the interest of the colonial government to over-educate the community. Only a rich and elitist minority was given the opportunity to learn good English. As a result of post-war mass education, access to English learning became general. But the people who were supposed to speak 'good' English were still relatively rare. The label "learner's language", applied by Platt (1982) to the English used by these fluent speakers, is more appropriate for the kind of English learnt and taught at school, spoken by primary school teachers, secondary school teachers and, to a large extent, by locally trained university lecturers.

In the past, spoken English was used mainly for colonial or international affairs. Now it is only used for international purposes. While most people need to speak English only in an artificial teaching/learning setting, those who need to speak it in a natural setting belong to two minority groups with contrasting language competence and social status. At a fairly high level of complexity, English is used by a small group of high-ranking administrative and managerial personnel for the purpose of communication with their rulers in government bodies and multinational corporations. At a more rudimentary level, English is spoken by another group of workers predominantly engaged in the service sector. However, there are as yet large numbers in the latter group who do not speak English at all.

2. Peculiarities of English teaching and learning in Hong Kong

The way that English has been learnt in this ex-colonial metropolis is possibly unique. In contrast with many other former British colonies, where English came to be a neutral language, there is no place for English in intra-national communication in Hong Kong, as the population is overwhelmingly ethnic Chinese (98%) and predominantly Cantonese-speaking, to such an extent that it is more homogeneous than the population of most

British cities (Gibbons 1982). By contrast with non-colonial monolingual communities where English is introduced as a foreign language at a much later stage of education, children in Hong Kong start acquiring English as a core subject as early as in kindergarten. Of course, they do so mostly within a monolingual school environment and the medium of instruction is mainly Cantonese. Most of them will not have any opportunity for using English until ten to fifteen years later, others never.

A second educational peculiarity experienced by a Hong Kong child occurred, and for some children still occurs, at the notorious primary-secondary interface. Equipped "with no more than the most rudimentary competence in English, and many even without this" (Tongue and Gibbons 1982: 61), a primary school leaver at 11 or 12 proceeding to an English-medium secondary school was paralysed by the abrupt and drastic change from learning English as only one subject to learning everything in English except for one or two subjects. Thus lessons in any subject turned into English lessons. Learning became the tedious routine of wading through dictionaries. In examinations pupils invariably regurgitated prescribed passages learnt by heart but not understood. Examinations became a test of memorization power. The enforcement of universal junior secondary education in the late 70s rendered the English medium "unusable" (Gibbons 1982: 123) for most pupils, producing large numbers of early losers, a large group of taciturn, apathetic and minimalist learners and speakers. Indeed, Hong Kong can be said to be a city which is bilingual in print but monolingual Cantonese in speech.

The colonial government had been aware of the educational and psychological undesirability of English as a medium of instruction for junior secondary education but had not followed proposals to impose Chinese-medium instruction because of parental wishes and economic need (see Hong Kong Government reports and white papers listed in the bibliography). As parents and students continued to favour English-medium schools for pragmatic reasons and English-medium schools were not willing to take the initiative to change the medium of instruction for fear of a decline in intake quality, the number of English-medium secondary schools had increased to an all-time high of 90% by the eve of colonization.

In the past decades, the medium of instruction has been a main theme dominating writings by a new generation of local researchers on English learning and teaching in Hong Kong, whether focusing on the pedagogical problem (Cheng 1973, 1979; Cheung 1974; Poon 1978; Siu et al. 1979; Tam 1980), responding critically to new policies (e.g. ECHK 1990), or speculating on the future juxtaposition of Cantonese, English and Mandarin in the shadow of the handover (Boyle 1998). Instead of joining the current of sociolinguistic debates, it is timely to pause and to reflect on some much neglected core aspects of English teaching and learning, which have been evolving at a very slow pace amidst the torrents of socio-economic change.

It was not atypical for colonial scholars, under the patronage of colonial institutions, to hold the simplistic view that learners' English in Hong Kong was modelled on the norm of native speakers. However, it is probably justified to say that there is no "social motivation for the indigenization of English in Hong Kong" (Tay 1991: 327), as far as lexis and syntax are concerned. As in any country where English is learnt and spoken as a foreign language, learners, especially the less fluent, normally talk with a local accent. And history has shown that the characteristic accent of a newly decolonized community usually takes shape long before its formal linguistic features are granted due academic recognition. The present essay will set out to give a participant-observer, a first-hand account of some typical scenarios of English teaching and learning in the formative period of primary education up to 1997. The way that English was learnt and taught at this period laid a solid foundation for the formation of what can be regarded as the Hong Kong English accent and is worth a closer look.

3. Primary education in Hong Kong

3.1 Teaching force

Before 9-year free education was implemented, only a small fraction of pupils, mostly from established households in the urban areas, could proceed to senior secondary education, which was sufficient to qualify them for many relatively well-paid white-collar jobs. During the period of massive expansion of basic education, many local secondary school leavers and mainland tertiary leavers were recruited and minimally trained to meet the great demand for teachers. I call those who started their teaching careers before 1970 the "first-generation teachers". Those holding important decision-making positions in schools nowadays were recruited and trained locally in the 70s, and will be referred to as the "core teaching force". They have played a central role in shaping a conservative teaching scenario in schools in the past decades. Despite their minimal training and the rapid development of HK society, both groups of teachers enjoyed a golden period up to the 90s, helped by constant economic growth, when the salary increments, fringe benefits and retirement schemes were at their most attractive while the teaching load was relatively undemanding and they were never asked to undergo additional training.

3.2 Traditional approach to teaching and learning

The Chinese tradition of pedagogy is embodied in the semantics of the words for 'teaching' and 'learning'. While *teaching* in Chinese, translated morpheme-by-morpheme, means literally 'teach books', the Chinese expression for 'learning/going to school/studying' means 'reading books'. This probably explains why most teachers simply follow textbooks strictly and leave little room for curiosity, initiative and active participation on the part of students. This obsession with books is fully reflected in the way Chinese is taught. Pupils are required to learn by rote and recite passages regularly. To be able to read books, one needs to be able to read words. The role words play in the Chinese language differs considerably from that in a language with an alphabetically based script in the relationship between the spoken and written forms of a language. Probably due to the logographic nature of the Chinese orthography, children need to spend a much longer time acquiring the sophisticated script.

The traditional approach to achieving and consolidating an accurate reproduction of the strokes of Chinese characters is extensive and repetitive copying, popularly implemented as "vocabulary-copying" at primary schools, in all but the few practical subjects. Thus, "health education", for instance, is not simply health education but becomes to a large extent learning to write the Chinese vocabulary used in health education. An exercise book is devoted to vocabulary-copying for each such subject. Teachers usually prescribe a dozen or two new and difficult glosses for practice. Depending on the schools and teachers, the quantity of vocabulary-copying can be disproportionate. Undoubtedly, it is the least stimulating kind of homework for pupils but the least demanding kind for teachers. The performance of pupils is constantly monitored and evaluated through excessive dictation sessions, tests and examinations, with their brothers and sisters, parents or private tutors coaching them at home.

Although international trends of pedagogical ideology led to certain recommendations and curriculum innovations, such as the Activity Approach (AA) in 1972, the School-based Curriculum Project Scheme (Skilbeck 1984) in 1988 and the Target-Oriented Curriculum (TOC) in the 90s, nothing much was achieved. Publishers, school heads and teachers in fact put much energy into giving some old practices a new appearance, while keeping most others unchanged. As a result, the recommendations did not bring much change to the everyday reality of teaching but simply popularized a new kind of jargon.

4. The teaching and learning of English in primary schools

4.1 Teachers

A group of first-generation and core-generation primary teachers, when interviewed by the writer, unanimously lamented the fact that they had never had any native-English input during their own education. Audio materials were not available in those days. Another problem was that they learnt English only because the system required it of them, just as many pupils in Europe had to learn Latin. The stereotype of a pupil who was good at English was one who had a large vocabulary, was accurate in using grammar and spelling words, but not one who could speak good English. When they became teachers, they passed on their limited skills. They were aware that their spoken English was very different from that of native-speakers. However, it was beyond their ability to train pupils to speak native-like English; nor did the syllabus require it of them. Until recently they were never expected to improve their own English.

4.2 Methodology

The entire methodology of English teaching and learning, from the organization of lessons to the nature of homework and examinations, was taken over from that used for other subjects in general, and from that used for Chinese in particular. Whichever English-language textbook was used, the concept of learning by dictation was not new.

"Penmanship" or "new word" exercises, invented to add to the variety of homework, were essentially new names for vocabulary copying. Homework assigned for the long holidays was by no means symbolic in quantity and was quite enough to occupy students for more than half of their days off. To foster the growth of pupils' vocabulary, new words, phrases and passages were picked out for copying, spelling drills and quizzes, and regular dictation. In the higher forms, a comprehensive grammar drill was common in earlier decades. Teachers often had difficulties themselves with the exercises and relied heavily on the teachers' key to solve them. When ambiguities and questions arose, they would appeal to the model answers without giving adequate explanations to pupils.

4.3 Spoken English input

As Gibbons (1982: 122) commented, "the English of many Hong Kong secondary school teachers is not of native speaker standard", but what can we expect of the English standard of primary school English teachers in Hong Kong, in view of their rudimentary educational background and minimal English training? Until recently, teachers conducted English classes predominantly in Cantonese, the language shared by all pupils. A typical teaching method was to pick out words and write them on the blackboard. Pupils were asked to read them several times, repeating after the teacher. As the text got longer at higher levels of primary school, an English teacher would ask pupils to read it once or twice after him. Explanations were given in Cantonese anyway. Pupils were not required to involve themselves actively in class. They were picked out perhaps to give a one-word answer or asked to write down an answer on the blackboard. For the rest of the lesson, they wrote in their workbooks or practised penmanship. The main function of the spoken input was to enable pupils to match the teacher's pronunciation with a word during dictation. The only real conversational exchange in English occurred at the beginning and end of classes, as in the following scenes:

> CLASS-PREFECT, *raising his/her voice upon seeing the teacher enter the classroom.* Stand up.
> TEACHER. Good morning class.
> ALL PUPILS TOGETHER. Good morning. Mr. Wong. *(syllable-timed, lengthened to 4 or 5 seconds)*
> TEACHER. Sit down.
> *Then the teacher starts conducting his lesson in Cantonese.*
>
> *At the end of the lesson, the bell rings*
> TEACHER. Goodbye, class.
> ALL PUPILS TOGETHER. Goodbye, Mr. Wong.

Because pupils had to say "Good morning, Mr. Wong" in chorus, they would lengthen the initial syllable until everybody had got the beat and then slowly utter out the whole phrase syllable by syllable in equal timing, taking four or five seconds. No one educated in Hong Kong will have escaped this much ridiculed, typical scenario.

Younger teachers have begun to experiment with the use of more spoken English in English lessons. However, this is restricted to the higher primary classes, with teachers relying on a limited and invariant repertoire of commands like:

Who's on duty today? / Clean the blackboard. / Pass up your homework. / Take out your dictation. / Take out your penmanship. / Turn to page 30. / Stop talking. / Shut up. / Please read together.

Since most teaching is still in Cantonese, this is the only spoken English experienced by most pupils between the age of 6 and 12.

4.4 Spoken output

Juggling with large classes and tight teaching schedules, teachers could hardly attend to the pronunciation problems of individual pupils. While old-fashioned teachers tended to pick out one of the few bright pupils to practise reciting, teachers of the newer generation who tried to be fair to each pupil would divide a text up into sentences so that all pupils would have a chance to read at least once. On the whole, emphasis was given to the relatively passive skills of reading and grammar rather than listening and speaking. In the higher forms, teachers were busy helping pupils achieve a better grade. English was not tested in the Academic Aptitude Test after 1978 and was relatively neglected. This led to a decline in the standard of English. Oral skills were not introduced until the late 80s and early 90s. But their weighting was at best marginal and at worst symbolic. In short, pronunciation has always been a neglected area in schools and in teacher training. Teachers themselves would frankly admit their own limitations.

4.5 Native English input

Although education television (ETV) had already been introduced in the 70s, it did not bring any new stimulus, either to pupils or teachers. Both local broadcasting companies ran an English channel devoted to the small group of foreigners living somewhere out there in an inaccessible and insulated environment that ordinary citizens did not need to have any contact with. Owing to the existence of English channels, local citizens were aware that native speakers spoke English in a way so alien to the way people learnt it at school that they would scarcely think it was possible to overcome such a difference. People turned to the English channels only from time to time for a special programme, like a famous film with subtitles, a sports event or a live broadcast like World Cup Soccer or Miss Universe, if it was not available on the Chinese channel. However, due to the congested living environment, limited TV channels, collective Cantonese cultures, pressure from peer groups and other social factors, switching to an English channel was not simply an individual's decision. For most families, who were living in a highly homogeneous Cantonese-speaking environment, there was hardly any room for an appreciation of native English.

Under these circumstances, ETV became an additional routine rather than a useful teaching tool. After all, a new programme came out only every two weeks and lasted merely ten minutes. Many teachers played it to pupils as a routine or as a pastime if they were ahead of schedule and left it for the enjoyment of pupils without much guidance and explanation, and continued their homework marking. Others would skip it because of lack of time for teaching. Hardly any teacher would bother to get pupils to imitate a native pronunciation with reference to ETV, as they did not have the relevant training, and their own pronunciation was too deviant. As far as the first two generations of primary teachers were concerned, it was questionable if they had understood everything in the programmes in view of the exoticness of the native accent, although the content was usually quite simple. Their own weakness would be concealed from pupils thanks to teachers' guides where all the answers to the exercises were provided. ETV has continued even up to the present but its role has always been marginal. In the 90s, listening was added to the English curriculum, but its importance, like that of oral skills in general, was minimal. On the whole, spoken English input received by primary pupils has been marginal.

5. Cantonese English nativization

5.1 Vowels and consonants

Kindergarten and primary teachers have played a significant role in shaping what I call the classic accent of Hong Kong English. Over the decades, the strong influence of the source language has proved highly resistant to any move towards the adoption of native speaker features of L2. While some features have been eliminated, many others have been retained. Before the 80s, it was almost universal in kindergarten teachers and typical of primary teachers to say

[ɛlou] instead of /el/ for the name of the letter *l*,
[ɛsi:] instead of /es/ for the name of the letter *s*,
[alou] instead of /ɑ: (r)/ for the name of the letter *r*,
[jisɛt̚] instead of /zed/ for the name of the letter *z*,
[ɡœlou] instead of /gɜ:l/ for *girl*.

Such examples belong to a classic repertoire stemming from the pre-war period and are typical of primary school leavers or lower of the 50s and 60s. Most such classic forms can be explained by accommodation to the L1 phonology as revealed by a contrastive analysis (see James, this volume). In the course of evolution across different generations of learners at the formative stage of primary education, pupils and students have gradually realized or been told that the pronunciation of their kindergarten or primary teachers was wrong. So they try to replace the [lou] in *l* [ɛlou], *r* [alou] and *girl* [ɡœlou] by [lou] with various degrees of reduction of [o], by [ou] with reduced [o], or by [u]. While there are a considerable number of teachers who manage to cut away the extra syllable of the letter *l* by saying [ɛu] or [ɛl], many others are still struggling with *z* producing a pronunciation approximating to [jisɛt], using various degrees of reduction of the vowel [i]. It has become common for people to make fun of such a classic style of pronunciation by attributing its origin to primary schools teachers, with primary teachers attributing it to kindergarten teachers. Despite a growing consensus that such a classic pronunciation is manifestly erroneous, there is no established substitute. Primary school English teachers in general have no idea of the concept of 'dark *l*'. Many primary school pupils are still using the classic pronunciation, partly because they fail to reproduce the better approximation transmitted by teachers and partly because some teachers either unconsciously or intentionally go back to classic pronunciation as a tentative solution. Numerous kindergarten teachers still adhere to it out of ignorance or lack of training. As a result, although such classic forms are slowly disappearing, it is a very slow process. Along the continuum of pronunciation of a certain phoneme or syllable, such as [lou], a well-defined classic norm has diverged into a narrow spectrum of different realizations. But in people's minds, the classic form is still vivid. Though people are well aware that it is manifestly inappropriate, especially in the presence of a native speaker, they will nevertheless fall back on it from time to time depending on the degree of formality. In a code-switching environment particularly, the use of the classic form is unanimous.

Many primary teachers of the core generation managed to break through some of the L1 phonological constraints and did not find it difficult to produce some sounds like final fricatives, though it was not uncommon for them to leave out the final *–s* of a verb in the case of the third person singular present tense or the final *–s* of a plural noun, out of carelessness. However, a significant proportion of pronunciation inherited from the classic repertoire of the 50s was preserved, e.g.

[d̥œ] instead of /ðə/ for the weak form of *the*,
[fand̥] instead of /faʊnd/ for *found*.

Most teachers could produce consonant clusters occurring in common words of the primary school vocabulary, for example in *desk*, but could not manage most of the others. Thus, it is possible to work out a detailed list of features that constitute the classic English pronunciation shared by the overwhelming majority of average Hong Kong speakers. Features like the omission of consonants following nasals in a consonant cluster, the reduction of nasals, the devoicing of voiced consonants, the simplification of diphthongs, the merging of strong and weak forms, the clipping of plosives, etc., can be traced back to the first generation teachers and most core generation teachers.

Although there has been recognizable progress over time, this has occurred very slowly and has been restricted to certain segmental features, and a classic Hong Kong English accent can be defined at the segmental level. It is a common observation in monolingual countries where English is learnt as a foreign language that the way English is spoken by an average learner exhibits many features attributable to his or her first language phonology. The case of Hong Kong can be seen as particularly extreme in view of the prevalence and consistency of the collective transfer. This is hardly surprising as all the socio-pedagogical conditions contributing to the phenomenon are themselves extremes – highly centralized education system, mass education environment, highly homogeneous linguistic and ethnic L1 community, lack of exposure to native English for both pupils and teachers and lack of training in English pronunciation on the part of teachers, and a great typological difference between the source and target language. Probably no place on earth can demonstrate the collective effect of L1 phonology on L2 acquisition as effectively and thoroughly as Hong Kong.

5.2 Tones

Turning to supra-segmental phonology, we should note at the outset that Cantonese is a so-called "tone language", in the sense that it has lexical tone: in other words, tone (alongside consonantal and vocalic features) is one of the features by which individual words are recognized. In Cantonese there are six such tones (by contrast with the four of Mandarin), and every syllable is characterized by one of them. The Cantonese tones are conventionally numbered as follows:

1. high-to-mid falling / high level
2. mid-to-rising
3. mid level
4. low-to-bottom falling / bottom level
5. low-to-mid rising
6. low level

The writer has discovered, over decades of participant observation in the learning-teaching arena and during many interviews, a prevalent linguistic feature which is more uniquely and uniformly characteristic of Hong Kong learners' English than the segmental ones. A first observation is that for an overwhelming majority of primary school teachers, and of course their pupils, the supra-segmental level is almost perfectly tonalized – every syllable of an English word is assigned a Cantonese lexical tone. The tones carried by the typical classroom language mentioned above can be transcribed as follows:

Stand up.	[sdɛnt⁻¹ ʔɐp⁻¹]
Good morning class.	[g̊ut⁻⁶ mɔ¹ nɪŋ¹ klaːs¹]
Good morning. Mr. Wong.	[g̊uːt⁻⁶ mɔː¹ nɪŋː¹ mi¹ staː¹ wɔŋ¹]
Sit down.	[sit⁻¹ d̥an⁻¹]
Goodbye class.	[g̊ut⁻⁶ bai¹ klaːs¹]
Goodbye Miss Wong.	[g̊uːt⁻⁶ baːi¹ miːs⁶ wɔŋ¹]
Who's on duty today?	[hus¹ ʔɔn⁶ d̥iu¹ ti¹ tu⁶ d̥ei⁻¹]
Clean the blackboard, please.	[kiːn¹ d̥œ⁶ blɛk⁻¹ bɔt⁻¹ piːs¹]
Pass up your homework.	[pas¹ ʔɐp⁻¹ jɔː⁶ hʊm⁻¹ wœk⁻¹]
Take out your 'dictation'.	[tɪk⁻¹ ʔɐʊt¹ jɔː⁶ d̥ɪk⁻⁶ tei⁻¹ ʃœn⁴]
Take out your 'penmanship'.	[tɪk⁻¹ ʔɐʊt¹ jɔː⁶ pen⁻¹ mɐn⁻⁴ ʃip⁻⁴]
Turn to page 30.	[tœn⁻¹ tu⁶ peid̥ʒ¹ fœ¹ ti⁴]
Stop talking.	[sd̥ɔp⁻¹ tɔk⁻¹ kɪŋ⁴]
Shut up.	[ʃɐt⁻¹ ʔɐp⁻¹]
Please read together.	[piːs¹ wiːt⁻¹ tu⁶ g̊e¹ d̥ɐ⁴]

Far from being a random process, the assignment of Cantonese tones to English words follows a set of strict rules (Ho 1996). Close observation allows one to correlate the inputted English stress system and grammatical function of words with the selective employment of the six Cantonese lexical tones.

6. English learning at secondary schools

Upon entering the so-called English-medium secondary schools, which are, however, "grossly inadequate for receiving instruction in that language" (Gibbons 1982: 123), students are bombarded with hundreds and thousands of new English terms. Collective learning and self-study in secondary school merely reinforce the typically Cantonese-flavoured 'English' taught in primary school, with the phonology of the expanded English lexicon conforming to the tonalization constraints governing the existing lexicon. In all schools, even the most English-oriented privileged ones, it is common to hear students recite in chorus or individually in a typical Cantonese tonalized English accent, e.g. (Ho 1996).

Our father in heaven,	[ʔau⁶ fa¹ d̥ɐ¹ ʔin⁶ he¹ fɐn¹]
Holy be your name,	[hou¹ li¹ b̥i⁶ jɔ⁶ neim¹]
Your kingdom come,	[jɔ⁶ kɪŋ¹ d̥ɐm¹ kɐm¹]
Your will be done on earth,	[jɔ⁶ wiu¹ b̥i⁶ d̥ɐn¹ ʔon⁶ ʔœf¹]
As it is in heaven.	[ʔɛs⁶ ʔit¹ tis⁶ ʔin⁶ he¹ fɐn⁴]

In the more senior grades of secondary education, the teaching and learning of native-like English is actually hindered by an inappropriate and overloaded syllabus, an excess of homework and internal assessment, internal examinations that are designed to weed out students and highly centralized and competitive external examinations. The established accent remains entrenched until the end of secondary education.

7. Post-colonial prospect

The post-colonial secondary education scenario has been marked by a shift to Chinese (Cantonese) as the medium of instruction for the junior forms of the secondary schools for all subjects except the English language. However, the yoke has been too costly to cast off completely in view of the established status of English as the international language of business and tertiary education. While the colonial government held off the recommended enforcement of mother-tongue education for decades, the HKSAR government adopted the much criticized streaming proposal (ECHK 1990). Instead of all secondary schools implementing a gradual change or delaying the change from Chinese-medium to English-medium teaching, about one quarter of the 400 odd government or subsidized secondary schools has from September 1998 onwards had the right to continue as before.

The natural process of decolonization is complemented by a wave of unprecedented efforts to maintain the English standard of both teachers and students. The most radical one is the introduction of an English benchmark test to assess the English competence of English teachers. Those who do not meet the requirements will not be permitted to teach English. As a result, teachers even took to the streets. Moreover, most primary school teachers, who are not degree holders, are required to upgrade their qualifications in due course. Never before have so many core-generation teachers found themselves in such an embarrassing situation after enjoying a stable teaching career for decades. Many have turned to early retirement to escape the humiliation. Together with a large-scale education reform programme, the main characteristics of which are summarized in Cheng and Townsend (2000), under the motif of life-long learning (ECHK 2000), the workload is constantly increasing and becoming unbearable. Weekends and summer holidays are reserved for further training and doing assignments. The demands made on teachers have never been so great before, to the extent that there are regular reports of teachers taking their own lives due to insurmountable pressure. It is doubtful whether increasing the pressure on teachers and students will lead to an ever higher level. It seems that we will have to wait at least another generation to see the effects of teaching reforms on this English-learning community.

Teachers reveal that in spite of reforms of the curriculum and teaching methodology, most first-generation and core-generation heads and teachers have been slow to change. While new teaching tasks and methods are added to meet the requirements of the authorities, old methods have been preserved. Vocabulary copying, passage recitation and dictation, which have become the hallmark of homework of Hong Kong primary schools, have survived, although the quantity is smaller. Although a communicative approach has been encouraged and grammar drills have been officially discouraged, they may still be done unofficially to help students survive better. Ironically, pre-dictation sessions to prepare for dictation have become common. As regards the phonological evolution of the learner's English, the symbolic increase of exposure to native-English input through the introduction of the Foreign Teachers Scheme, like that of ETV in the 70s and listening exercises in the late 80s, is only symbolic and not enough to counteract established tonalization. Like an old star which enters another phase of burning, it is more likely that its evolution will continue at a slower rate.

Bibliography

Boyle, J. 1998. What hope for a trilingual Hong Kong? *English Today*. 14 (4). 34–39.
Cheng, N.-L. 1973. *At What Cost? Instruction through the English Medium in Hong Kong Schools*. Hong Kong: Shum Shing Printing Co.
Cheng, N-L. (ed.) 1979. *Issues in Language of Instruction in Hong Kong*. Hong Kong: Comos.
Cheng, Y. C. and Townsend, T. 2000. Educational change and development in the Asia-Pacific Region: Trends and Issues. In: Townsend, T. and Cheng, Y. C. (eds.), *Educational Change and Development in the Asia-Pacific Region: Challenges for the Future*. The Netherlands: Swets and Zeitlinger. 317–344.
Cheung, M. W. 1974. *A Comparison of Comprehension for Hong Kong Secondary School Students Taught in Cantonese and English*. M.A. Thesis. Chinese University of Hong Kong. [In Chinese].
Gibbons, J. 1982. The issue of the language of instruction in the lower forms of Hong Kong secondary schools. *Journal of Multilingual & Multicultural Development*. 3. 117–128.
Ho, S.-C. 1996. *Analysis of the intonation pattern of Hong Kong Cantonese English*. Unpublished M. Phil Proposal. University of Hong Kong.
Johnson, R. K. and Lee, P. L. M. 1987. Modes of Instruction: teaching strategies and student responses. In: Lord, R. and Cheng, H. N.-L. (eds.), *Language Education in Hong Kong*. Hong Kong: The Chinese University Press. 99–121.

Lado, R. 1957. *Linguistics Across Cultures: Applied Linguistics for Language Teachers*. Ann Arbor: University of Michigan Press.
Lau, S. 1977. *A Practical Cantonese-English Dictionary*. Hong Kong: The Government Printer.
Llewellyn, J. et al. 1982. *A Perspective on Education in Hong Kong: Report by a Visiting Panel*. Hong Kong: Government Printer.
Lord, R. (ed.) 1979. *Hong Kong Language Papers.* Hong Kong: Hong Kong University Press.
Poon, S.-K. 1978. *An Investigation of the Language Difficulties Experienced by Hong Kong Primary School Leavers in Learning Mathematics through the Medium of English*. Unpublished M. Phil. Thesis. University of Hong Kong.
Platt, J. T. 1982. English in Singapore, Malaysia and Hong Kong. In: Bailey, R. and Görlach, M. (eds.), *English as a World Language*. Ann Arbor: University of Michigan Press. 384–414.
Siu, P.-K., Cheng, S.-C., Hinton, A., Cheng, Y.-N., Lo, L.-F., Luk, H.-K., Chung, Y.-P. and Hsia, Y.-S. 1979. *The Final Report on the Effects of the Medium of Instruction on Student Cognitive Development and Academic Achievement*. School of Education. Chinese University of Hong Kong.
Skilbeck, M. 1984. *School-Based Curriculum Development*. London: Harper & Row Ltd.
Tam, P. T.-K. 1980. A survey of the language mode used in teaching junior forms in Anglo-Chinese secondary schools in Hong Kong. *RELC Journal*. 11. 43–60.
Tay, M. W. J. 1991. Southeast Asia and Hong Kong. In: Cheshire, J. (ed.), *English around the World: Sociolinguistic Perspectives*. Cambridge. Cambridge University Press. 319–332.
Tongue, R. and Gibbons, J. 1982. Structural syllabuses and the young beginner. *Applied Linguistics*. 3. 60–69.

White papers and other Hong Kong government documents

Education Commission Hong Kong 1984. *Education Commission Report No. 1: Educational policy and planning for Hong Kong*. http://www.emb.gov.hk/EDNEWHP/resource/edu_doc/English/download/ecr1_e.doc
Education Commission Hong Kong. 1986. *Education Commission Report No. 2*.
Education Commission Hong Kong. 1990. *Education Commission Report No. 4: Curriculum and students' behavioral problems in schools*.
Education Commission Hong Kong. 2000. *Learning for Life – Learning through Life. Reform Proposals for the Education System in Hong Kong*. http://www.e-c.edu.hk/eng/reform/index_e.html
Hong Kong Government. 1935. *Burney Report*.
Hong Kong Government. 1963. *Report of the (Marsh-Sampson) Education Commission*.
Hong Kong Government. 1965. *White Paper: Education policy*.
Hong Kong Government. 1973. *Green Paper: Report on the proposed expansion of secondary school education over the next decade*.
Hong Kong Government. 1974. *White Paper: Secondary education in Hong Kong over the next decade*.

Universal Grammar and Second Language Acquisition

Pius ten Hacken

In the field of theoretical linguistics, Universal Grammar (UG) is an important concept. Although not generally accepted, it serves as an anchor point for the characterization of individual approaches. In this contribution, the interaction of the study of UG and L2 acquisition will be explored. Before embarking on this exploration, the nature and function of UG will be clarified. As will become clear from the discussion, UG is primarily meant as a basis for the explanation of acquisition of the L1. However, this orientation does not make it irrelevant for the acquisition and teaching of an L2.

1. The nature of Universal Grammar

Technically, Universal Grammar (UG), as it is considered here, is a theoretical construct in Chomskyan linguistics. As a theoretical construct, UG has a status in linguistics comparable to an atomic model in physics. An atomic model describes the internal structure of an atom. A number of atomic models have been proposed and worked with in the course of the 20th century. Early models assumed that an atom consists of a nucleus with electrons moving around it in a circular orbit. Later models analysed the nucleus into various smaller particles.

Two important properties shared by UG and atomic models are, first, that they are supposed to describe real entities although these entities cannot be observed directly and, second, that they are meant to explain observable phenomena. Nobody has ever seen an electron circling around a nucleus, because they are too small. The example of atomic models shows that there is nothing unscientific about adopting a model of an aspect of the real world which is not directly observable but can be used to explain observable phenomena. As will be shown in the next section, in this sense UG functions in much the same way as atomic models.

A concept still to be explained is Chomskyan linguistics. A common misunderstanding is that Chomskyan linguistics is whatever Chomsky does in the study of language. As explained in more detail by Botha (1989: 1–11), there is a crucial difference between *Chomsky's linguistics* and *Chomskyan linguistics*. The former includes all linguistic assumptions made by Noam Chomsky at a particular point in time. They encompass specific theoretical assumptions, e.g. on the status of deep structure or barriers, which have evolved considerably over time. Chomskyan linguistics, by contrast, is a framework for approaching linguistics. It makes no assumptions on theory-internal concepts such as deep structure and barriers, but specifies what linguistics is about. It has remained stable since at least the early 1960s. Whereas Chomskyan linguistics provides a framework for discussing theories about UG, Chomsky's linguistics incorporates, at any point in time at least from the 1970s onwards, a particular theory of what UG is like.

2. The function of Universal Grammar

In order to understand the role of UG in Chomskyan linguistics, we have to start from the notion of competence, the linguistic knowledge of the individual speaker. In Chomskyan linguistics the goal of the study of language is to describe and explain language. Language is seen first of all as the competence of an individual speaker, which is contrasted on the one hand with a corpus of linguistic utterances, and on the other hand with a set of sentences deemed grammatical in the language.

The first contrast is a special case of the opposition between competence and performance discussed, for instance, by Chomsky (1980). Performance is the result of using competence. A collection of utterances or texts in a corpus is an example of performance, but also a collection of grammaticality judgements or the results of psycholinguistic tests asking you to press a button as soon as you recognize a word. All of these have in common that they do not reflect competence in isolation, but in interaction with various other factors. Which other factors are involved and what role these factors have varies with the type of performance data. As discussed in more detail by ten Hacken (2002), the study of performance in order to identify and explain its regularities is by no means incompatible with the study of competence. A theory of competence is essential in an account of language use. Conversely, performance is an important source of data about competence, provided one is aware of the fact that other factors than competence are involved as well.

The second contrast is the opposition between what Chomsky (1986) calls I-language and E-language. In these expressions, "I" stands for "Internalized" and "E" for "Externalized". I-language is a different name for competence, a knowledge component in the speaker's mind. An E-language is a language perceived as a set of grammatical sentences. An example is the norm as stipulated by an authoritative grammar and dictionary. An E-language differs from a corpus of utterances because the E-language is independent of anyone using or even knowing the grammatical sentences. While competence and performance are both real, natural phenomena, E-language is the result of artificial, conscious decisions.

A final contrast to be mentioned here is the one between competence and grammar. Although it is not always rigidly maintained in the literature, it is convenient to have different names for the real-life entity described, an I-language or competence, and its description, a grammar.

Of the four concepts introduced so far, competence, performance, E-language, and grammar, UG is most closely related to the last one. This is not to say that UG is simply a set of universals found in the grammars of all languages. Instead, it is the description of another real entity, the language faculty.

In Chomskyan linguistics, the role of the language faculty is twofold. First it is part of the solution to the empirical problem of language acquisition. At the same time, it provides a solution to the epistemological problem of determining which of the possible grammars which account for a given set of data is the actual one. The epistemological problem arises because at any time the set of performance data taken into account in the characterization of an I-language is finite. It is a purely mathematical point that for any finite set of data, there is an infinite set of possible grammars compatible with these data. The choice between these grammars can never be based solely on more data of the same type, but must take into account independent, external evidence. A characteristic of the research programme of Chomskyan linguistics is the choice of language acquisition as a source of independent data.

There are two reasons why language acquisition is an attractive choice for the source of external evidence to narrow down the choice of a grammar as the description of an individual speaker's competence. First, language acquisition takes place for every natural language. Whatever the language of a community, a child growing up in this community will acquire its language. Second, the knowledge acquired by the child is so complex that its full, explicit formulation by linguists is a hard and as yet not entirely solved problem. Together with the lack of effort on the part of the child and the inevitability of the acquisition (the child cannot choose not to learn any language at all), this suggests that a genetic component is involved in the acquisition process. This component is called the language faculty.

It is interesting to note the consequences of considering language as both a genetically determined, universal language faculty, to be described by UG, and as the individual speaker's competence, to be described by an individual grammar. The requirement to come up with a UG as well as with a range of individual grammars constrains the possibilities considerably. Given the wide variety of languages in the world, i.e. different I-languages, we must not make UG more specific than necessary. Every specification in UG reduces the range of grammars we have at our disposal, thus complicating the task of describing all I-languages. On the other hand, we must not make UG less specific than possible because everything which is not in UG has to be learned by the child on the basis of a highly restricted set of data. For everything a child has to learn in language acquisition, it has to be shown that it is in fact learnable in principle.

The model of UG which has emerged in Chomskyan linguistics and stabilized since the late 1970s is the Principles & Parameters (P&P) model. UG describes the language faculty in terms of a number of innate, genetically determined principles. These principles are assumed to be valid for all I-languages. Differences between I-languages are accounted for in terms of parameters associated with the principles. The nature of the parameters and the range of their values are taken to be innate and invariable, but individual I-languages differ in the choice of the values from the range specified for the parameters. Language acquisition consists in setting the parameters by choosing one of the available values. In the P&P model, parameter setting is usually modelled as setting switches.

The role of visualization in the P&P model in linguistics is not unlike its role in an atomic model in physics. In both cases, the model represents the underlying system of the observable reality. These systems are not directly observable themselves, but they constitute the basis for an explanation of a wide range of observations. The visualization facilitates the understanding of the abstract model.

3. Universal Grammar and L1 acquisition

Given the prominent position of language acquisition in Chomskyan linguistics, one might be tempted to consider UG as a theory of how children acquire their first language. Some critical assessments of Chomskyan theories are based on this misapprehension. Pinker (1982), for instance, criticizes theories formulated in Chomskyan linguistics for failing to account for the order of acquisition of linguistic phenomena by the child. In such a context it is difficult to make sense of Chomsky and Halle's (1968: 331) idealization of language acquisition as an instantaneous process, i.e. a process whose duration is zero. Clearly, language acquisition is not instantaneous.

As explained by Hornstein and Lightfoot (1981), the solution to this problem is to distinguish the logical problem of language acquisition from the empirical problem of language acquisition. UG is first of all meant to solve the logical problem of how it is possible for children to acquire an I-language which is much richer than can be deduced from the input data they have at their disposal. In particular, how is it possible that the I-languages of many people converge when it comes to complex constructions that are so rare that they are unlikely to have been in the input data at all? The logical problem is concerned with the transition from the initial state of the language faculty to the stable state corresponding to full competence. The theory explaining the transition does not appeal to events happening in the course of the transition process, but only to the initial state, formulated as UG. In this sense, instantaneous acquisition is an appropriate idealization.

The fact that the logical problem of language acquisition has this central role in Chomskyan linguistics does not remove the need to account for the empirical problem of language acquisition. Indeed, whereas Hornstein and Lightfoot (1981) only refer to future work in this respect, since then an increasing number of studies in the framework of Chomskyan linguistics have addressed this empirical problem. There are at least two reasons to do this. First, Chomskyan linguistics is meant to provide a basis for explaining all phenomena involving language. This means that UG should be compatible with the data, and what it cannot explain should be plausibly attributed to the domain of another theory. In the case of L1 acquisition, theories of cognitive development of children are an obvious candidate. Another reason for the interest is that observations in the domain of language acquisition may provide invaluable external evidence for choosing between two theoretical options when performance data (including grammaticality judgements) are not sufficient to make a choice.

Currently, there are two main hypotheses in Chomskyan linguistics about the interaction of the language faculty, as described by UG, and L1 acquisition: the Maturation Hypothesis, expounded by Wexler (1999), and the Strong Continuity Hypothesis, presented by Lust (1999). It is worth looking at the opposition between them here, because they have strong implications for L2 acquisition.

According to the version of the Maturation Hypothesis presented by Wexler (1999), the full complexity of the language faculty gradually develops in the child. While adult competence corresponds to UG with parameters set according to the requirements of the I-language, different stages of the child's competence do not necessarily correspond to the full UG with some parameters still to be set. Rather, the growth of the language faculty and the setting of parameters are overlapping processes. This means that at intermediate stages of this development, the language faculty corresponds to a different grammar than that of adult competence. Child language data diverging from adult L1 data, such as the one-word stage and the two-word stage, are thus accounted for by a grammar of the intermediate stage which need not correspond to a fully developed adult UG with some of the parameters not set. Since the maturation of the language faculty occurs together with the development of L1 competence, at the end of the L1 acquisition process, there is only one knowledge component, which can be described as UG with parameters set according to L1.

The Maturation Hypothesis is compatible with the hypothesis of a critical period for language acquisition. According to this hypothesis, after a certain age it is no longer possible to start L1 acquisition, because the language faculty is no longer available for this task. The most extensive evidence for this hypothesis stems from the domain of the non-hearing community. When non-hearing children grow up in an environment with non-hearing adults, they develop a fully fledged natural language expressed by visual instead of acoustic means. As described by Neidle et al. (2000: 7–25), the study of these sign languages is seriously complicated by the fact that only 5–10% of non-hearing children grow up in this type of environment. The others have a more or less defective L1 competence, because the essential input was not available to them at the required time, i.e. before the end of the critical period.

According to the Strong Continuity Hypothesis (SCH) as presented by Lust (1999), the language faculty is in place when the L1 acquisition process starts and does not change after that. In the process of L1 acquisition, the child uses input data to map from the language faculty to L1 competence. At any point during the acquisition process, there are two components, the language faculty and the L1 competence. Divergence from the adult L1 competence can still be accounted for by a different grammar, but UG remains the same throughout the process. According to the SCH, if there is a critical period for L1 acquisition, it cannot be explained in terms of changes in the language faculty, but must be the result of other factors, for instance the cognitive development of the child.

An empirical difference between Maturation and the SCH is that the former but not the latter predicts that the order of initial presentation of the data affects the final outcome of acquisition. Maturation of the language faculty implies that at a particular stage the child is looking for a particular type of data, for instance evidence for setting a particular parameter. If for whatever reason this evidence is not available at this point in time, there is a problem, because the time slot for setting this parameter is restricted. The SCH, by contrast, predicts that no such time slots exist and that the child simply proceeds with the setting of any parameters for which data are available, because the full language faculty can be accessed at any time of the L1 acquisition process.

The status of UG is different in the Maturation Hypothesis and the SCH. In the SCH, UG describes the language faculty as it exists throughout. In a model adopting the Maturation Hypothesis, there are two possibilities. One option is to have UG describe the maturation process. This means that the time factor is incorporated into UG. The other option is to take these two components apart. UG is then an idealization which can be described in the P&P model, while a separate maturation theory interacts with UG to explain what is available to the child at a particular point in the acquisition process.

The most prominent difference between the two hypotheses in view of their application to L2 acquisition is the status of UG at the end of the L1 acquisition process. In the SCH, the language faculty is not affected by L1 acquisition. At the end of the process, there are two components of knowledge, described by UG and by the grammar of the adult L1 competence. According to the Maturation Hypothesis, by contrast, the language faculty develops during and under the influence of the L1 acquisition process. The result is a knowledge component to be described by an L1 grammar which is in accordance with UG. It is obvious, therefore, that these hypotheses result in rather different starting points for L2 acquisition.

4. From L1 to L2

Given the status of UG as a theoretical construct whose main functions are to explain L1 acquisition and to select a grammar from among the many possible ones for a particular I-language, it is not immediately obvious why Chomskyan linguistics should have more than a passing interest in L2 acquisition. Conversely, the universalist implications of UG seem likely to arouse considerable interest within the second language teaching community. In fact, the pattern observed at present is rather the inverse of this picture. While there is an active research community working on L2 acquisition from a Chomskyan perspective, in language teaching UG is often dismissed rather cursorily.

The most likely cause of the lack of interest in the language teaching community is disappointment with the potential for applying UG in teaching practice. The clash involved here is the familiar one between pure and applied science. It seems reasonable to assume that scientific knowledge can be used to solve practical problems. The purpose of (pure) science, however, is understanding the world rather than solving practical problems. The latter is a desirable side effect, but never a criterion for the evaluation of theories.

The analogy with atomic models is useful to understand the issue. The purpose of an atomic model is to explain reality. Whether it can also be used to produce instruments or techniques that can be applied in a more general context is immaterial to the researcher, at least in principle. In practice, of course, the resources needed to pursue research depend on the ability to convince potential funding bodies that there will be such spin-off applications.

Similarly, UG is embedded in a framework geared towards the explanation of language. A lack of applicability to language-related problems cannot be considered as an indication of scientific deficiency. It is therefore in a sense unreasonable to expect UG to contribute to the solution of L2 teaching problems. Moreover, much of the disappointment in the SLA community seems to be caused by an interpretation of concepts such as universalism and deep structure which are not in line with the technical meaning of these terms in the framework of Chomskyan linguistics. As Joseph (2002: 181*ff*) shows in some detail, the interpretation of "deep structure" Chomsky became famous for was not the one he intended.

The interest in L2 acquisition from within Chomskyan linguistics is a consequence of the same attitude we encountered in the discussion of the process of L1 acquisition. L2 acquisition is an empirical phenomenon about language. A full theory of language has to account for it. To the extent that UG can explain it, the UG hypothesis is strengthened, and data from L2 acquisition can be brought to bear on the formulation of UG. For whatever cannot be explained by UG, a plausible alternative explanation has to be found which is compatible with UG.

5. The scope of a UG-based theory of Second Language Acquisition

The reason why we consider L1 acquisition and L2 acquisition to be different fields, whereas L3 or L4 acquisition is rarely considered as such, is that there are a number of significant differences between the acquisition of L1 and of any other language. First of all, there is a considerable epistemological difference. L1 acquisition is necessary for the existence of language, but L2 acquisition is not. Therefore, it makes sense to assume a special facility for L1 acquisition, but the possibility of L2 acquisition should not require specific further assumptions.

If we concentrate on the most extreme (but by no means rare) case of L2 acquisition by adults living in an L1 speaking environment, we also find a number of significant empirical differences compared with L1 acquisition. Since some of these differences are somewhat blurred when we consider L2 acquisition by children, we will concentrate here on the most extreme case. Taking the case with the properties furthest removed from L1 acquisition as a basis provides the best point of departure for an eventual extension to the full range of language acquisition phenomena, including child L2 acquisition and simultaneous acquisition of two native languages.

A learner's knowledge of a second language is often called their INTERLANGUAGE (cf. James, this volume). A first point to be made in the context of Chomskyan linguistics is that this interlanguage constitutes an I-language in the mind of the speaker. Although it is an empirical issue to determine the properties of the interlanguage, it is a knowledge component of the same basic type as L1 competence. Empirical phenomena related to L2 acquisition can then be divided into properties of the interlanguage, properties of the acquisition process, and properties of L2 performance.

At the level of the I-language, one of the major differences between L1 competence and L2 interlanguage is that the latter shows a much larger degree of interpersonal variation. Although the language norm, as stated above, is rather an E-language than an I-language, we can observe a high degree of convergence between I-languages of different speakers with the same L1. Taking native-like competence as the target of L2 acquisition, the interlanguage competence acquired constitutes only a partial success at the individual level, and there is much less convergence at interpersonal level among different L2 learners.

Turning to the acquisition process, the most important differences are found in the influence of motivation and teaching. In L1 acquisition, the child has no choice but to acquire the language, whereas the degree of success in L2 acquisition depends to a considerable extent on whether and how much the learner wants to learn the L2. As for teaching, numerous anecdotes illustrate the fact that the child learning a first language is not dependent on and often even unresponsive to explicit teaching, which is obviously not the case to the same extent in L2 acquisition. A phenomenon related to the L2 acquisition process is fossilization, the persistence of certain errors in a learner's interlanguage. In a UG-based approach, fossilization means that a steady state of the L2 competence is reached which diverges significantly from the target.

Without reference to a precise theoretical framework, it is not possible to answer the question as to whether particular phenomena in interlanguage performance should be explained as properties of interlanguage competence, of the L2 acquisition process, or as the influence of other factors. The answer depends on the analysis of the roles attributed to UG, interlanguage competence and other factors in L2 performance. This can be illustrated with the well-known phenomenon of TRANSFER, i.e. the assignment of lexical, morphological or syntactic properties of L1 elements to the corresponding L2 elements. One way of looking at transfer is to consider it a property of the interlanguage. In that case the interlanguage competence has features corresponding to the L1 competence rather than to the target L2 competence. Another way of accounting for transfer is to see it as a performance phenomenon, resulting from the interaction of the interlanguage competence and the L1 competence, perhaps influenced by other factors such as stress and the organization of memory. In this case, L2 data showing transfer are interpreted not as showing properties of the L2 competence, but only of the way this competence is used. Another empirical phenomenon which is not so easy to assign to a particular cause is the perception of some languages as more difficult than others.

Hence, UG does not by itself explain L2 acquisition. UG is designed to explain that L1 acquisition is possible. At the same time, the central position UG assigns to the logical problem of language acquisition implies that in a UG-based approach, each empirical phenomenon concerning L2 acquisition and L2 competence should be accounted for in a way compatible with UG, whether it is explained by UG, by other factors, or by their interaction.

6. The nature of a UG-based explanation of Second Language Acquisition

By definition, adult L2 acquisition differs in its point of departure from L1 acquisition in at least two respects. First, during L2 acquisition L1 is in place, which in Chomskyan linguistics means that L1 competence has reached a steady state. Second, cognitive development has been completed. This removes an important source of ambiguity in the interpretation of data gathered from the language learner which complicates the use of early child performance data. In L1 acquisition studies, it is difficult to tell whether, for instance, one-word and two-word stages reflect incomplete language acquisition or incomplete cognitive development. In a Chomskyan framework, the former means that non-mature performance reflects non-mature competence, while the latter means that other factors than competence explain the non-mature performance of the child. Although one might favour the hypothesis that children do not have more competence than reflected in their performance out of epistemological parsimony, the fact that children understand more than they express rather points to other factors, such as incomplete cognitive development, which constrain the full use of available competence. In L2 acquisition, performance data may be distorted by the consciousness that one is learning towards a certain target, but not by incomplete cognitive development.

The main issue in SLA studies in the framework of Chomskyan linguistics is the role of the language faculty. There are at least four hypotheses as to its role which have been entertained by proponents of a theory of L1 acquisition based on UG. On the basis of their assumptions as to the L2 learner's access to UG, they are called the No Access, Full Access, Indirect Access, and Partial Access hypotheses. They imply different types of interaction between UG, L1 competence, and general cognitive abilities in the L2 acquisition process.

The No Access Hypothesis (NAH) assumes that L2 acquisition can only draw on L1 competence and general cognitive abilities. Access to UG is phased out after the critical period (cf. section 3). Johnson and Newport (1989) find support for the NAH in an experiment with Chinese and Korean L1 speakers who learned L2 English after moving to the United States. They observe a clear correlation between the age of arrival in the US and the score in a test of grammaticality judgements for English sentences. The decline in ultimate attainment sets in from arrival after age 8 and gradually increases until adulthood. As the sentences in the test focus on grammatical intricacies supposed to invoke the language faculty, they conclude that the latter is not available to adult L2 learners. As this example shows, the NAH emphasizes the differences between L1 and L2 acquisition. It presupposes the Maturation Hypothesis for L1 acquisition with a strong interpretation of the critical period.

A second hypothesis compatible with the Maturation Hypothesis for L1 acquisition is the Indirect Access Hypothesis (IAH) presented by Schachter (1996). According to this hypothesis, the language faculty is available in L2 acquisition only to the extent that it is represented in L1. The difference compared with the NAH resides in the interpretation of the critical period for language acquisition. The NAH claims that after the critical period access to UG is blocked for any purpose. The IAH claims that after the critical period only parts of language faculty represented in L1 are available for L2 acquisition.

An example of the line of argument for the IAH is Schachter's discussion of the acquisition of question formation. Languages such as English, German, and Italian mark interrogative sentences by movement of the question word to the beginning of the sentence. This movement is subject to intricate constraints, as illustrated in (1–2):

(1) What$_i$ do you think John told me Mary had bought t_i ?
(2) *What$_i$ do you believe the claim that Mary had bought t_i ?

While it is possible for the object of *bought* in (1) to be questioned, as indicated by the coindexation of *what* with the trace *t*, in (2) such a question is ungrammatical. In English L1 acquisition, the principles governing the difference between such sentences are provided by the language faculty. Parameters account for the differences with German and Italian. An English L2 learner with German or Italian L1 can use the relevant principles of UG in the acquisition of question formation. Other languages, however, lack movement of the type illustrated in (1) completely. One example is Korean. According to the IAH, Korean L1 learners of English L2 cannot use the language faculty to learn the difference in grammaticality between (1) and (2). Schachter (1996: 174–179) describes an experiment which supports the IAH on this basis.

It should be noted that the data from Johnson and Newport's (1989) experiment, described above as an example of support for the NAH, can be analysed equally as compatible with the IAH. The compatibility depends on the interaction of a number of factors, such as the results of L2 learners with different L1, the analysis of the phenomena in the test sentences, and the structure of UG assumed. This shows that the choice between these two hypotheses about access to UG in SLA cannot be derived straightforwardly from experiments, but depends in part on the specific version of the theory of UG adopted.

At the other end of the spectrum compared to the NAH, we find the Full Access Hypothesis (FAH), presented by Flynn (1996). It assumes that the language faculty as described by UG is fully available to the L2 learner. This does not exclude, of course, that L1 competence and general cognitive abilities are also active in L2 acquisition. Thus, although the FAH stresses the similarities between L1 and L2 acquisition, it does not have to claim that they are the same. The differences can be explained as a consequence of the different point of departure as explained in section 5, i.e. the existence of L1 competence and the completion of cognitive development. The FAH presupposes the Strong Continuity Hypothesis for L1 acquisition, because UG has to exist as a separate component after L1 acquisition.

In support of the FAH, Flynn (1996) points to several empirical studies showing that parameters can be reset. Some of these studies concern Japanese L1 speakers, learning English as an L2. One of the differences between Japanese and English is that the complementizer (e.g. *that*, *whether*) precedes the subordinate clause in English, but follows it in Japanese. In the theory of UG, this difference is expressed as a different parameter setting, which has consequences for a wide range of phenomena. The L2 acquisition studies referred to by Flynn (1996: 134–142) suggest that the Japanese learners reset this parameter in the course of their English L2 acquisition. They not only adopt the correct order of complementizers in subordinate clauses, but when they reach a certain level of fluency they also correctly apply the new parameter value in other contexts. This includes contexts not explicitly learned. Therefore, Flynn concludes that it is possible to set a parameter to a different value in L2 from the one it has in L1.

In the FAH, data such as the acquisition of English L2 question formation illustrated in (1) and (2) have to be reinterpreted. The difference between German and Italian L1 learners on the one hand and Korean L1 learners on the other is not attributed to the inherent impossibility of Korean learners acquiring the relevant principles. In the acquisition of constraints on the movement of question words, German and Italian L1 learners have the advantage that their L1 also has such movement, with similar though not quite identical constraints. Therefore both L1 competence and UG can be used to acquire the English rules. For Korean learners the acquisition of these rules is more difficult, because they only have the language faculty as a relevant resource. Given the implausibility of learning such intricate principles by general cognitive mechanisms, successful acquisition of English constraints on questions by at least some Korean L1 learners is taken to indicate that UG is indeed available in L2 acquisition.

As opposed to the three other main hypotheses, the label Partial Access Hypothesis (PAH) refers to a class of hypotheses rather than to a single, specific one. A PAH claims that some parts of UG are available in L2 acquisition, but not all of it. It is a more complex hypothesis than the FAH, because for each part of UG the argument arises whether it is available or not. Flynn (1996: 133) calls the IAH as defended by Schachter (1996) an example of a PAH. Mitchell and Myles (1998: 68), however, distinguish the two and reserve the label PAH for a hypothesis which constrains the available parts in terms of UG rather than L1.

A PAH may be the best compromise to account for the partial success of L2 acquisition if the partial nature of the success can be expressed in terms of UG. If, for instance, certain principles of UG are available to all L2 learners, independent of their L1 and of the L2 involved, all interlanguage competence should reflect these principles. Otherwise, the availability of the principle depends on its activation in L1. A similar hypothesis can be proposed for parameters. If a parameter is available to L2 learners as a property of UG, it can be set to a different value from the one in L1. Otherwise, only the value in L1 is available for the L2 interlanguage. Accessible parts of the language faculty must exist independently of the L1 competence. Therefore, a PAH is not compatible with maturation resulting in a single component of the language faculty with parameters set according to L1. At the same time it does not require the Strong Continuity Hypothesis, because the non-available parts need not exist independently at the end of L1 acquisition. This suggests a Partial Continuity Hypothesis for L1 acquisition, which distinguishes continuous and non-continuous parts of the language faculty.

One thing the discussion of the different possible hypotheses as to the involvement of UG in L2 acquisition has shown is that it is difficult to collect pertinent experimental data for the choice between them. Many of the results obtained can be interpreted according to more than one of the hypotheses. A further point emerging from the discussion is that L1 and L2 acquisition theories cannot be combined freely. The two most influential clusters at present are, on the one hand, the Maturation Hypothesis combined with Indirect Access and, on the other, the Strict Continuity Hypothesis combined with Full Access. The No Access Hypothesis is less attractive because there is now quite considerable evidence that at least some elements of UG do play a role in L2 acquisition. Partial Access is less attractive because it has serious epistemological drawbacks. As mentioned above, it is not a single hypothesis but a set of related hypotheses. Adopting a PAH would therefore immediately raise the question of why particular elements of UG do and others do not play a role in L2 acquisition. Moreover, PAHs are not compatible with an independently motivated L1 acquisition theory. The convergence of independently developed hypotheses for L1 and L2 acquisition strengthens the plausibility of the two clusters mentioned before.

7. From L2 acquisition to L2 teaching

Questions about how to evaluate a teaching method, how to improve it, or indeed how to arrive at the optimal methodology for L2 teaching are of a very different nature from the question of how to explain L2 acquisition. As highlighted in section 4 above, the former questions pertain to applied science as opposed to 'pure' empirical science. It is almost as unreasonable to expect a theory of UG to improve classroom teaching as it is to expect particle physics to lead to reduced fuel consumption for the next car you are going to buy.

A more reasonable expectation of UG in L2 teaching seems to be then that it will explain the success or otherwise of a teaching method. If we understand why a particular teaching method works to a given degree, we can also hope to improve it. There are a number of reasons, however, why this expectation is also beyond the power of a theory of UG.

One important restriction is that UG interacts with a number of other factors in the explanation of L2 acquisition. Nobody has ever made the claim that UG should explain differences in motivation, although it is obvious that such factors as whether the society the learner lives in speaks the L2 or not, or whether the L2 teacher is perceived as a nice person, do of course play a role in the success of teaching. A complicating factor is that the interaction of UG with other sources of knowledge in L2 acquisition is actually at the centre of the debate outlined in section 6.

A further reason why UG cannot provide a full explanation of the success of L2 teaching is that UG is concerned with syntax and the syntactic properties of lexical items, but not with other domains in L2 teaching. Successful L2 acquisition also covers pronunciation, vocabulary, pragmatic knowledge of communicative expectations in the L2 language community, etc. The relative contribution of these areas to the evaluation of success determines to a large extent how important UG is perceived to be.

In the debate on the involvement of UG in L2 acquisition, opposing the IAH and the FAH, the results of different teaching methods might supply important evidence for one side or the other. One practical problem, however, remains: it is often possible to interpret the same data in different ways according to either hypothesis. For a conclusive experiment we would need an unambiguous link from one of the hypotheses to a teaching method.

8. Conclusion

UG is a theoretical construct in Chomskyan linguistics, introduced in order to explain the logical problem of L1 acquisition and thus choose the actual ('psychologically real') grammar to describe a particular I-language. There are different hypotheses on how UG relates to the processes of L1 acquisition and L2 acquisition. The main opposition is between the Maturation Hypothesis for L1 and Indirect Access for L2, on the one hand, and the Strong Continuity Hypothesis for L1 and Full Access for L2, on the other. In the former, UG is more of an abstraction, viz. the knowledge presupposed for language acquisition, which develops into the L1 competence and is subsequently accessible through the L1. In the latter, UG describes an independent module of knowledge in the mind, which is used to develop the competence for L1 as well as for subsequent languages.

Bibliography

Botha, R. P. 1989. *Challenging Chomsky: The Generative Garden Game*. Oxford: Blackwell.
Chomsky, N. and Halle, M. 1968. *The Sound Pattern of English*. New York: Harper and Row.
Chomsky, N. 1980. *Rules and Representations*. New York: Columbia University Press.
Chomsky, N. 1986. *Knowledge of Language: Its Nature, Origin, and Use*. Westport (Conn.): Praeger.
Flynn, S. 1996. A parameter-setting approach to second language acquisition. In: Ritchie and Bhatia 1996. 121–158.
ten Hacken, P. 2002. Chomskyan linguistics and the sciences of communication. *Studies in Communication Sciences* 2. 109–134.
Hornstein, N. and Lightfoot, D. 1981. Introduction. In: Hornstein, N. and Lightfoot, D. (eds.), *Explanation in Linguistics: The Logical Problem of Language Acquisition*. London and New York: Longman. 9–31.
Johnson, J. S. and Newport, E. L. 1989. Critical period effects in second language learning: the influence of maturational state on the acquisition of English as a second language. *Cognitive Psychology* 21. 60–99.
Joseph, J. 2002. *From Whitney to Chomsky: Essays in the History of American Linguistics*. Amsterdam: Benjamins.
Lust, B. 1999. Universal Grammar: the strong continuity hypothesis in first language acquisition. In: Ritchie and Bhatia 1999. 111–155.
Mitchell, R. and Myles, F. 1998. *Second Language Learning Theories*. London: Arnold.
Neidle, C., Kegl, J., MacLaughlin, D., Bahan, B. and Lee, R. G. 2000. *The Syntax of American Sign Language: Functional Categories and Hierarchical Structure*. Cambridge (Mass.): MIT Press.
Pinker, S. 1982. A theory of the acquisition of lexical interpretive grammars. In: Bresnan, J. (ed.), *The Mental Representation of Grammatical Relations*. Cambridge (Mass.): MIT Press. 655–726.
Ritchie, W. C. and Bhatia, T. K. 1996. *Handbook of Second Language Acquisition*. San Diego: Academic Press.
Ritchie, W. C. and Bhatia, T. K. 1999. *Handbook of Child Language Acquisition*. San Diego: Academic Press.
Schachter, J. 1996. Maturation and the issue of Universal Grammar in second language acquisition. In: Ritchie and Bhatia 1996. 159–193.
Wexler, K. 1999. Maturation and growth of grammar. In: Ritchie and Bhatia 1999. 55–109.

Index

Academic 5, 17, 28, 32, 36, 37, 41–56, 89, 131, 149, 177, 180, 183
  discourse 43, 44, 46, 48, 50, 51, 53, 55
  exchange 41–42
  lingua franca 52
  paper/text 43, 45, 46, 47, 48, 51, 52, 53, 54, 55
  publishing, publication(s) 42, 44, 46, 55
Accent 94, 180, 184, 185, 187
  phraseological 94
Acceptability 55, 121
  "Acceptability thresholds" 55
Accessibility hierarchy (-ies) 2
Acquisition, second language 5, 34, 112, 119, 120, 123, 130, 131, 151, 152, 193–203
Adjunct(s) 85, 86–88, 88–90, 91, 92–97, 97–99, 161, 168, 173, 174
  circumstantial 96–97
  clause-level 86
  conjunctive 87, 89, 95–96
  frequentatives 87, 88
  modal comment 90, 92, 93, 95, 103
  modal mood 92, 93–95, 103
  obligatory 98
  of usuality 93
  placement 85–104
  post-verbal 88, 92, 95, 97, 98, 99
  prepositional 94
  VP-level 86
Adverb(s) 85, 86, 87, 88, 89, 90, 91, 94, 96, 99, 128
  grammatical 85, 86, 89, 90
  lexical/functional 89
  variable scope 87
Age 9, 33, 37, 52, 69, 78, 97, 111, 121, 124, 139, 151, 183, 195, 199
Analysability 135, 136
  semantic *see* semantic transparency
Analysis 1–20, 21, 33, 42, 44, 51, 52, 53, 85, 88, 90, 98, 99, 102, 105, 106, 108, 109, 111, 112, 113, 114, 116, 119–130, 134, 135, 136, 137, 138, 139, 144, 145, 153, 154, 161, 162, 164, 165, 166, 168, 169, 171, 174, 175, 184, 198, 200
  computer-aided 119–123, 124–125
  contrastive 1–20, 21, 120, 144, 184
  error 5, 10, 21, 85, 102, 111, 119–130, 153, 154
Analytic scope 50

Applied linguistics 5, 10, 18, 119, 122, 131, 147, 150–152
Appropriateness 121
Assimilation 57
Associative connection(s) 137
Avoid (-ance) 1, 15, 16, 18, 36, 61, 69, 73, 75, 76, 79, 89, 107, 117, 120, 122, 130, 148
Awareness 6, 12, 13, 28, 34, 45, 92, 143, 145, 155
  L1 6, 12

Behaviourist /-ism 1, 4, 120, 147, 150
Bilingualism 7, 16
Boundary (-ies) 27, 28, 31, 42, 87, 88, 149
  Bounding effect(s) 87
  Mood-Residue 87
  Theme-Rheme 87

CALL programs 108, 113, 147–159
  corpus-based 108
Chunk(s) / chunking 85, 132, 136–138, 139, 142, 143, 144, 145
  lexical 132, 136–138, 139
  pedagogical 142, 143, 145
Clefting 86
Cognate(s) 58, 59, 61, 65, 73
Cognitive linguistics 132, 135, 144
  see also metaphor
Cognitive revolution 120
Co-hyponymy 63, 64, 65, 68, 79
Collocation 85, 89, 95, 96, 107, 121, 137, 138, 140
  collocational pattern 90
  collocational restriction(s) 99
  lexical 89, 95
Complementation 86, 115, 116, 140
  of adjective(s) 115
  of noun(s) 115
  of verb(s) 115
Comprehension 42, 47, 92, 111, 131–146
  of metaphor *see* metaphor
Concordance 89, 107, 108, 109, 115, 116, 117, 128, 129
  concordance lines 89, 107, 108, 109, 115, 117
  parallel concordancer 109
  see also corpus

Connectionist model / research 138
Contrastive Analysis (CA) 1–20, 21, 120, 144, 184
  diachronic CA 3
  pedagogic CA 4
Contrastive error analysis 85
Contrastive linguistics 1, 21–39
Contrastive rhetoric (C-Rh) 1, 2, 4–6, 18, 41–56
Conventionality, of meaning 134, 143, 145
Co-occurrence 116, 137, 145
  restriction 137
Corder, Pit 120, 122
Corpus (-ora) 21, 50, 52, 53, 71, 85–104, 105–118, 119–130, 132, 136, 137, 164, 165, 166, 168, 175, 192
  corpus analysis 108, 111, 112, 113, 114
  ELF (English as a Lingua Franca) corpora 106, 163, 164
  ICE-corpus 106
  ICLE corpus (International Corpus of Learner English) 110, 115, 116, 123, 124, 175
  learner corpus 99, 105–118, 119–130
  linguistics 107, 108, 132, 136, 137
  multilingual corpus 108, 109
  native speaker control corpora 110, 111
  native speaker corpus 105, 106, 108, 109, 110, 111, 114, 115, 117, 123, 129
  parallel corpus 108, 109
  subcorpora 52, 108, 110, 115, 116, 124, 126, 128, 129
  textbook corpus 106, 108, 109
Cultural 1, 4, 5, 6, 11, 29, 30, 31, 32, 33, 41, 42, 43, 46, 47, 48, 49, 51, 52, 53, 55, 88, 143, 155, 163
  difference 5, 32, 47, 48, 51, 53, 143
  relativity (of academic discourse) 46

Data 8, 44, 49, 50, 51, 53, 69, 91, 97, 99, 105, 106, 107, 111, 114, 121, 122, 123, 124, 127, 148, 151, 162, 164–165, 166, 167, 168, 169, 170, 171, 173, 174, 175, 192, 193, 194, 195, 196, 197, 198, 199, 200, 201, 203
  collection(s) 121, 122, 123, 167
  selection(s) 50
Data-driven learning 32, 105, 107, 108, 109, 114, 116, 117, 149
Determinism, linguistic 6
Dictionary 106, 107, 112, 126, 141, 148, 154, 179, 192
  learner 112
  monolingual 106
Directionality, of learning 4

Discipline, sub-discipline 1, 11, 42, 43, 44, 45, 50, 51, 52, 53, 55, 147
Discourse strategy (-ies) 53
Distinction(s) 21, 33, 57, 70, 86, 91, 135, 137, 144, 168, 170, 172, 173
  phonemic 57
  phonetic 57

Elicitation, elicited 8, 109, 111, 121
Elision 57
ELT (English language teaching) 105, 176
Embedding 96
Empirical 3, 21, 43, 48, 49, 51, 52, 59, 69–79, 80, 134, 135, 144, 164, 175, 193, 194, 195, 197, 198, 200, 202
  basis 49, 51
  research 42, 80, 134
English as an international (post-national) language 54
Error(s) 1, 2, 4, 5, 6, 9, 10, 13, 14, 21, 47, 61, 69, 70, 71, 72, 73, 74, 75, 79, 85, 92, 93, 94, 95, 96, 97, 99, 102, 103, 104, 111, 112, 113, 114, 117, 119–130, 152, 153, 154, 164, 198
  analysis 5, 10, 21, 85, 102, 111, 119–130, 153, 154
  collection(s) 111
  collocational 94
  frequency (-ies) 113, 126–127
  grammar 127
  grammatical 47, 122, 154
  learner / student errors 93, 94, 95, 97, 99, 119, 120, 122, 152, 153, 154, 198
  lexical 127–129
  lexico-grammatical 97
  misuse 112, 115, 155
  morphology 92, 102, 121, 125, 126, 127
  phraseological 92
  taxonomy (-ies) 121, 122, 124, 125
  typology 92
"Essay rules" 5
Etymological relatedness/relationship 58, 59
Expletive 3
Extralinguistic factor(s) 111

Fakes, academic 42, 43
False friend(s) 57–83
  lexico-semantic 58, 59
  one-directional (asymmetrical) 62, 63, 66
  pair 58, 59, 62, 63, 64, 70, 72, 73, 74, 75, 76, 78, 79, 81
  partial 58, 59, 65, 69, 70, 71, 73, 79

total 58, 59, 69, 70, 71, 75, 78, 79
type 57, 59, 60, 62, 65, 68, 69, 70, 71, 72, 73
Familiarity 8, 46, 73, 134, 140
Feature(s) 2, 3, 4, 5, 6, 9, 13, 14, 26, 27, 28, 46, 48, 50, 53, 54, 60, 61, 78, 85, 86–88, 92, 98, 107, 111, 114, 115, 117, 120, 124, 130, 132, 140, 150, 152, 153, 161–176, 180, 184, 185, 186, 198
  grammatical 26, 53, 86–88, 107, 115
  inappropriate feature(s) 114
  overuse and underuse 73, 76, 77, 79, 111, 115, 130, 139, 169, 173, 175
  selection of features for teaching 114
  see also teaching
Fluency 17, 114, 137, 138, 139, 142, 145, 201
Foreign language teaching /-er 27, 34, 48, 50, 51, 106, 150
Formula / formulaic 90–92, 93, 114, 136, 137, 138, 139
  routine formula 137
  sequence 136, 137, 138, 139
Frequency (of words / vocabulary) 71, 72, 73, 74, 75, 77, 78, 79, 80, 106, 107, 108, 111, 140, 141, 142, 166
  frequent/infrequent word(s) 89, 93, 95, 107, 108, 116, 131, 132, 134, 135, 136, 137, 138, 141, 144, 166
  high-frequency 141
  low-frequency 131
Frozenness, syntactic 138
Functional linguistics (Halliday) 87

Gender 12, 52, 53, 121, 125, 140
Generative grammar / theory 26, 85, 87, 93, 97, 98, 99, 136
Generativist 52, 136
Generic structure(s) 5
Genre 5, 6, 29, 32, 49, 107
German *passim, espec.* 119–130
Goal 31, 91, 92, 94, 98, 104, 144, 148, 192
  mental 91
Grammar 2, 5, 6, 12, 22, 26, 27, 31, 32, 85, 88, 102, 107, 109, 112, 113, 121, 126, 127, 131, 137, 148, 149, 150, 154, 155, 175, 181, 182, 183, 188, 191–203
  reference grammar(s) 107, 109, 112
Grammaticality 24, 121, 192, 194, 199, 200
Grounds *see* metaphor, cognitive linguistics

Head-first, -last *see* parameter(s)
Hedging 50, 53, 89

Homonym 60, 62, 63, 133
  interlingual homonym 60
Homonymous 59, 61, 62, 63, 72
Homonymy, cross-language 57–83
Hong Kong 110, 113, 177–189

Idiom(s) 85, 88, 132, 133, 134, 135, 136, 137, 138, 139, 140, 141, 142, 143, 144, 145
  idiomaticity (i.e. native-like production) 138, 139, 145
  key 135, 136
  opaque idioms 135, 136, 138, 142, 145
  phrases 131–146
Idiom principle 85, 137
Implicational scales 2
Inference(s) 117
Interference 1, 8, 13, 16, 17, 57, 58, 60, 141
International Corpus of Learner English (ICLE) 110, 115, 116, 123, 124, 175
Internationalism 63, 65
Intertextuality 53
Intonation 57, 87

Language user, professional 52
Learner(s) 1–20, 21, 22, 27, 29, 30, 32, 34, 49, 52, 57, 58, 59, 60, 61, 62, 63, 64, 65, 66, 67, 68, 69, 71, 73, 75, 76, 77, 79, 80, 85–104, 105–118, 119–130, 131, 132, 136, 139, 140, 141, 142, 143, 144, 145, 150, 151, 152, 153, 154, 155, 161, 175, 177, 179, 180, 184, 185, 186, 188, 197, 198, 199, 200, 201, 202
  autonomy 117, 143
  characteristics 112
  corpus 21, 99, 105–118, 119–130
  intermediate / advanced learner 6, 17, 27, 29, 30, 32, 34, 86, 102, 110, 113, 117, 123, 130, 132, 139, 141, 142, 152
  language 1–20, 49, 60, 105, 108, 119, 123, 131, 139, 148, 153, 154, 155, 180, 199
  of English 13, 14, 16, 32, 33, 57, 59, 61, 62, 63, 65, 67, 69, 71, 79, 85, 86, 92, 102, 107, 113, 114, 130, 154, 181, 200
  of German 61, 62
  varieties 110
Lexical 5, 9, 45, 57, 58, 59, 62, 70, 71, 78, 79, 85, 86, 88, 89, 90, 92, 93, 95, 96, 97, 99, 102, 108, 122, 123, 127–129, 130, 132, 134, 135, 136–138, 139, 140, 141, 142, 143, 144, 145, 150, 151, 170, 174, 186, 198, 202
  ambiguity 59
  fixed lexical expression 90
  formulae 90, 93

item 57, 58, 59, 62, 71, 108, 138, 140, 141, 151, 170, 202
  phrase 92, 93, 99, 137, 144
  predicator 96
  system 58, 59
  unit(s) 132, 136, 137, 138, 141, 142, 145
Lexicalized sentence stems 88, 89
Lexicogrammatical information 107
Lexicon 71, 131, 134, 135, 136, 138, 143, 144, 154, 187
  (de)lexicalization 7
  lexeme 57, 58, 59, 61, 62, 63, 64, 66, 71, 76, 140, 141, 144
  multiple storage 138
Literal-first hypothesis 134

Macrostructural vs. microstructural level 43
Markedness 2, 4–6, 18, 94, 98, 141, 166
Meaning 7, 9, 12, 17, 18, 26, 28, 58, 59, 60, 61, 64, 65, 66, 67, 68, 69, 72, 73, 75, 76, 77, 78, 79, 83, 87, 88, 89, 90, 107, 129, 131, 132, 133, 134, 135, 136, 137, 138, 139, 140, 141, 142, 143, 144, 145, 152, 154, 162, 168, 174, 197
Mentalese 7
Meta-communication 53
Metaphor / metaphoricity 53, 90, 131–146
  awareness 143
  comprehension 131–146
  ground 132, 133
  metaphorical concept 135, 144
  nominal metaphor(s) 132
  source/target domain 132, 133, 143
  topic 132, 133, 136
  type(s) 133, 134, 136, 138, 140
  vehicle 132, 133, 136
Method(s) 5, 119, 120, 123, 129, 140, 147, 153, 154, 182, 188, 202, 203
Methodology 50, 51, 53, 99, 119, 122, 181–182, 188, 202
Mistake(s) *see* error(s)
Misunderstanding(s) 29, 45–48, 191
Modality 88, 93
  mental 93
  quantificational 93
  temporal 93
  verbal 93
Mood-Residue boundary 87
Morphology 6, 92, 102, 121, 126, 127, 154, 171
  derivational suffix 65
  morpheme 59, 65, 137, 180
  morphological relation/morphologically related 22, 59, 65, 74, 75
Move(s) 5, 27, 28, 89, 152, 184

Multilingualism 7, 15, 131, 162, 163, 176
Multiple storage *see* lexicon
Multi-word unit(s) 134, 137, 139, 142, 145

Native speaker 6, 9, 10, 11, 13, 15, 17, 43, 45, 48, 49, 53, 54, 55, 57, 105, 106, 108, 109, 110, 111, 114, 115, 117, 121, 123, 129, 130, 131, 136, 139, 141, 145, 148, 151, 155, 162, 163, 164, 165, 168, 175, 176, 179, 181, 182, 183, 184, 185
  judgement(s) 48, 54, 136, 139
  norm(s) 6, 54, 163, 164, 179
Non-native speaker 41–56, 85, 94, 115, 161, 162, 163–164, 167, 168, 170, 171, 175
Norm(s) 3, 6, 8, 10, 11, 43, 48, 53, 54, 55, 121, 162, 163, 164, 169, 179, 185, 192, 198
Noticing 13–15, 17, 141

Opaque, semantically 131, 133, 134, 135, 136, 138, 142, 144, 145
Open choice principle *see* idiom principle
Overdifferentiation /-ate 57
Overgeneralization 73, 171, 173
Overuse 73, 76, 77, 79, 111, 130, 169, 173, 175

Parameter(s) 2, 3, 4, 18, 98, 193, 195, 196, 200, 201
  head-first 2
  head-last 2
  PRO-drop 3
  settings 2, 18, 193, 200
  transfer 2
Phenomenon 6, 17, 50, 53, 57, 58, 87, 91, 111, 113, 115, 122, 130, 132, 133, 139, 144, 163, 185, 191, 192, 194, 197, 198, 200
Phonology 6, 57, 153, 184, 185, 186, 187
  phonolexical connection 58
  phonological system 57
Phraseology 85, 88, 92, 96, 102
  phraseological accent 94
  phraseological unit 67, 89, 92, 99
Polysemy 57–83, 133, 135
  cross-language 57–83
  internal 62, 64, 65, 66, 69, 73, 77, 79
  polysemous reading 64, 66
  polysemous submeaning 65
Preconstructed clauses *see* formulaic sequence(s)
Principles and parameters 4, 193, 194, 196
Processing 17, 26, 80, 123, 131, 132, 134, 135, 136, 138, 139, 141, 144, 145, 147, 152, 153, 154

analytic vs. holistic 138, 139
bottom up vs. top down 138
lexical 135, 136
parallel 134, 135
speed 138, 145
Production 13, 15, 16, 53, 63, 79, 108, 110, 111, 115, 123, 124, 132, 140, 142, 144, 145, 151, 152, 153, 155
Proficiency 15, 17, 111, 121, 123, 124, 126, 131, 139, 141, 150, 151
see also learner(s)
Pronunciation 11, 57, 85, 103, 104, 153, 154, 182, 183, 184, 185, 202
Propositional network(s) 50, 53
Prosodic detachment 85, 88, 99
Psychotypology 4, 8
Publishing 42, 43, 45, 47, 110, 112

Range 32, 37, 53, 91, 92, 94, 95, 96, 97, 98, 123, 142, 149, 193, 194, 197, 200
entity range 95, 96
process range 96, 97
Relativity 6, 46
Research language (English) 50
Resemblance/similarity
formal 58, 60, 61, 62, 64, 65, 68, 71, 72, 76, 77, 78, 79
graphemic resemblance, graphemically similar 58, 59, 60, 63, 68, 72, 73
morphologically similar 65, 75
phonological/phonetic resemblance, phonetically/phonologically similar 58, 59, 60, 61, 62, 63, 64, 65, 68, 72, 73, 76, 78
Restriction 33, 86, 93, 95, 97, 98, 99, 202
categorically unrestricted 86
collocational 99
lexical 97
Review(s) 1, 46, 47, 48, 52, 150
Rhetorical figure(s) 48

Salient, saliency 13, 14, 18, 134, 136, 144, 152
Scope 50, 85, 86, 87, 88, 91, 94, 96, 99, 119, 121, 122, 197–198
semantic 85, 99
variable scope adverbs 87
Second Language Acquisition (SLA) 5, 6, 17, 112, 119, 120, 123, 130, 131, 132, 139, 151, 152, 191–203
Selection, native-like 139
Semantic 9, 23, 25, 57–83, 85, 86, 90, 93, 99, 107, 131, 133, 134, 135, 138, 140, 141, 144, 152, 154, 172, 173, 174, 180

feature 60, 61
prosody 107
reinforcement 90
relatedness, relation/connection, semantically related/unrelated 59, 60, 61, 62, 63, 64, 65, 68, 71, 72, 75, 76, 78, 79, 80
Sense of word(s) 46, 61, 62, 90, 107, 134
Similarity *see* resemblance
Size 5, 50, 52, 67, 78, 110, 112, 124, 164
corpus 50, 110, 112, 124, 164
sample 50, 52, 89, 92, 123
SLA research 6, 120, 132, 139
"Smallwords" 114
Specifier(s) 85, 89
Spelling 70, 72, 73, 75, 76, 77, 78, 102, 103, 111, 122, 140, 153, 181, 182
Step(s) 5, 12, 14, 18, 30, 32, 60, 79, 120, 150, 153, 175
Structure 1, 2, 5, 11, 17, 27, 28, 42, 46, 49, 51, 52, 53, 54, 55, 59, 76, 85, 86, 88, 97, 98, 99, 108, 121, 122, 125, 136, 137, 140, 143, 150, 151, 152, 154, 161, 162, 164, 166, 170, 171, 174, 175, 191, 197, 200
text/discourse structure 42, 46, 51, 52, 55
Style, of communication 6, 29, 34, 46, 47
Substitution 57, 58, 172
Syllabus 108, 114, 117, 129, 181, 187

Target language (TL) 2, 10, 11, 12, 14, 16, 17, 43, 57, 148, 151, 152, 153, 155, 161, 172, 174, 185
Teaching 10–11, 13, 16, 18, 21, 28, 32, 33, 34, 36, 43, 41–56, 93, 105–118, 131, 139, 140, 141–144, 147, 148, 149, 150, 151, 155, 176, 177–189, 191, 196, 197, 198, 202–203
English Language Teaching (ELT) 105, 176, 177–189
pedagogic material 112–114, 117, 150, 151, 152, 153, 155
Tertium comparationis 5
Testing 17, 69, 70, 77, 86, 88, 108, 111, 114, 120, 126, 179, 181, 183, 187, 192, 199, 200
Text(s) 4, 5, 6, 9, 22, 27–29, 30, 32, 42, 43, 45, 46, 47, 48, 50, 51, 52, 53, 54, 55, 85, 87, 89, 97, 102, 105, 106, 107, 108, 109, 110, 111, 112, 113, 114, 115, 124, 125, 131, 141, 142, 147, 150, 152, 154, 155, 182, 183, 192
comprehension 47
naturally occurring 105, 109
structure 42, 46, 51, 52, 55
text-commenting devices 47
type(s) 32, 42, 50, 51, 52, 106, 108, 110, 111, 112, 115, 124

Textbook(s)   71, 73, 78, 80, 106, 107, 108, 109, 180, 181
  corpus-based   107
Thematic structure   85, 86, 88, 99
Theme, position (Theme-Rheme boundary)   87, 88, 93
"Thinking for speaking"   7
Topic *see* metaphor
Transfer   1, 2, 4, 6, 7, 8, 10, 11, 12, 13, 18, 70, 78, 97, 132, 133, 141, 144, 170, 171, 174, 185, 198
Transitivity role(s)   98
Translation   12, 22, 27, 28, 46, 58, 59, 60, 61, 64, 65, 69, 70, 71, 72, 73, 75, 78, 79, 80, 81, 144, 147, 148
  equivalent   58, 59, 60, 61, 64, 65, 70, 71, 72, 73, 75, 78, 79, 80
  task   69, 70, 147
Transparent, semantically   133, 134, 135, 143, 145
True friend(s)   58, 59, 61, 62, 63, 65, 67, 70, 71, 79, 81
Typology   2–4, 18, 21–39, 90, 92, 140, 144
  of errors   92
  PRO-drop language   3, 4
  satellite-framed language   7
  studies   98
  verb-framed language   7

Underdifferentiation /-ate   57, 62, 66, 69, 74
Unrandomness   137

Variety (-ies)   52, 53, 98, 106, 109, 110, 121, 130, 143, 149, 154, 155, 162, 163, 164, 170, 171, 175, 176, 182, 193
Vehicle *see* metaphor
Verb   2, 3, 7, 9, 22, 23, 24, 26, 50, 73, 78, 85, 86, 88, 89, 90, 91, 92, 93, 94, 95, 96, 97, 98, 99, 106, 113, 115, 128, 129, 133, 136, 148, 185
  complex verb group   90, 96, 99
  material process verb(s)   91, 94, 96
  phrasal verb(s)   22, 90
  relational process verb(s)   91, 94
  semantically light verb(s)   90
  stretched verb(s)   90, 95, 99
Vocabulary   38, 80, 107, 121, 122, 131, 132, 137, 139–141, 142, 150, 154, 155, 181, 182, 185, 188, 202
  acquisition   80, 131, 132, 139–141
  frequency   132, 141
  learning   137, 140, 150, 155
  size   131
  teaching   131, 139, 140
VP-shell   97

Word family   64, 65, 68, 75, 131

ICSELL · International Cooper Series in English Language and Literature

---

Series Editors: D. J. Allerton, Willy Elmer, Balz Engler, Hartwig Isernhagen

The International Cooper Series in English Language and Literature (which appeared from 1956 to 1990 under the title "Cooper Monographs"), usually known as ICSELL, has since 2001 been published by Schwabe. The series is international both in the range of scholars represented in it and in the prominence given to comparative topics from linguistics and literary studies. It encompasses the English language in all its forms and aspects and all genres of literature throughout the English-speaking world. This gives due recognition to the international status of English, something that is particularly evident in Switzerland, and, most appropriately, it was the international nature of the English language that provided the topic for the first volume to appear at the new publishers (*Perspectives on English as a World Language,* ICSELL 6). The editors of ICSELL are the professors of English at the University of the city variously known as Basle, Basel and Bâle and internationally situated on the Rhine at the junction of Switzerland, Germany and France.

ICSELL 1 Hugo Caviola. *In the Zone. Perception and Presentation of Space in German and American Postmodernism.* 1991. viii, 215 pages.
ISBN 3-7965-1827-3.

ICSELL 2 Itsuki Koya. *Subjecthood and Related Notions. A Contrastive Study of English, German and Japanese.* 1992. viii, 226 pages.
ISBN 3-7965-1828-1.

ICSELL 3 Thomas Pughe. *Comic Sense. Reading Robert Coover, Stanley Elkin, Philip Roth.* 1994. xiv, 195 pages.
ISBN 3-7965-1829-X.

ICSELL 4 Gert Buelens and Ernst Rudin. *Deferring a Dream. Literary Sub-Versions of the American Columbiad.* 1994. xvi, 144 pages.
ISBN 3-7965-1830-3.

ICSELL 5 Mark Kyburz. *"Voi Altri Pochi": Ezra Pound and his Audience, 1908–1925.* 1996. x, 181 pages.
ISBN 3-7965-1831-1.

ICSELL 6 D. J. Allerton, Paul Skandera and Cornelia Tschichold, editors. *Perspectives on English as a World Language.* 2002. xiv, 175 pages.
ISBN 3-7965-1740-4.

ICSELL 7 Lyndon Higgs. *A Description of Grammatical Features and their Variation in the Black Country Dialect.* 2004. xvi, 296 pages.
ISBN 3-7965-1948-2.

ICSELL 8 D. J. Allerton, Nadja Nesselhauf and Paul Skandera, editors. *Phraseological Units: basic concepts and their application.* 2004. xii, 188 pages.
ISBN 3-7965-1949-0.

ICSELL 9   Otto Heim and Caroline Wiedmer, editors. *Inventing the Past: Memory Work in Culture and History.* 2005. x, 235 pages. ISBN 3-7965-2047-2.
ICSELL 10 D. J. Allerton, Cornelia Tschichold and Judith Wieser, editors. *Linguistics, Language Learning and Language Teaching.* 2005. xiv, 210 pages. ISBN 3-7965-2065-0.

The mark of the printing and publishing house Schwabe, founded in 1488, dates back to the very beginnings of the art of printing and derives from the circle of artists around Hans Holbein. It is the printer's mark of the Petris, and illustrates Jeremiah 23:29: "Is not my word like as a fire? saith the LORD; and like a hammer that breaketh the rock in pieces?"